The Victorian Experience:
The Prose Writers

THE VICTORIAN EXPERIENCE:
The Prose Writers

Edited by
RICHARD A. LEVINE

**OHIO UNIVERSITY PRESS
ATHENS, OHIO**

Library of Congress Cataloging in Publication Data
Main entry under title:

The Victorian experience.

    Includes bibliographical references.
    1. English prose literature—19th century—
History and criticism.   I. Levine, Richard A.
PR781.V5   828'.808'09   81–22493
ISBN 0–8214–0446–6   AACR2
ISBN 0-8214-0707-4 pbk.

Contents

INTRODUCTION

RICHARD A. LEVINE

This book and one on the poets are companion volumes to *The Victorian Experience: The Novelists*. As with the *Novelists*, the charge to the critics was to discuss their writer from the vantage point of their familiarity with the author's work and times, and in the process to comment on a number of basic questions such as why they teach the writer, their involvement with the writer, and their response to the writer after years of study. These are important concerns in an age of increasingly specialized studies where we run the danger of sometimes losing sight of the whole writer and of our chosen mission of teaching. Once again, happily, the essays are more than personal testaments and qualitatively very different from critical introductions to major authors. I gave the critics only the most broad and general guidelines and urged them to develop their essays as their imaginations and interests dictated.

As I wrote in the opening chapter of the novelists volume, the thesis of *The Victorian Experience* grows out of a Victorian critic's concern with the artistic engagement and the sometimes confused, often precarious state of literary studies in our own time. It was Walter Pater who said, "Not the fruit of experience, but experience itself, is the end." Pater was distinguishing between one's direct engagement with the artistic work (experience) and the intellectual process by which one attempts to recapture and make some rational sense of that engagement (the fruit of experience). If one might quarrel with Pater's sense of the "end," one cannot argue with Pater's chronology here: the experience clearly must precede the fruit of the experience. That some readers, for example, try to interpose the intellectualizing process between themselves and the literary work is a violation not merely of Pater's notion, but—more importantly—of the integrity of the engagement itself. Upon reflection, most of us would acknowledge that our initial responses to works which moved or touched or excited us (and not only in positive or favorable ways) were not, properly speaking, intellectual. Certainly a portion of that initial response might well be intellectual, but the totality of our response comes much closer to Pater's sense of the fundamentally dynamic and individual quality of perception:

> the whole scope of observation is dwarfed into the narrow chamber of the individual mind. Experience, already reduced to a group of impressions, is ringed round for each of us by that thick wall of personality through which no real voice has ever pierced on its way to us, or from us to that which we can only conjecture to be without. Every one of those impressions is the impression of the individual in his isolation, each mind keeping as a solitary prisoner its own dream of a world. Analysis goes a step farther still, and assures us that those impressions of the individual mind to which, for each one of us, experience dwindles down, are in perpetual flight; that each of them is limited by time, and that as time is infinitely divisible, each of them is infinitely divisible also; all that is actual in it being a single moment, gone while we try to apprehend it, of which it may ever be more truly said that it has ceased to be than that it is.

And when Pater says that "he who experiences these impressions strongly, and drives directly at the discrimination and analysis of them," he is still articulating the same ordering of critical activity: experience followed by the fruit of experience; experience followed by discrimination and analysis of the experience.

For some teachers of literature, especially in our age of the rhetorician, Pater's priorities can be unnerving, although they should not be. Indeed, Pater might well be offering a necessary corrective to much that has gone wrong in the academy. Too often the intensity of textual analysis—especially when elevated almost to an end in itself—has blunted the reader's sense of experiencing the artistic work rather than having complemented and augmented it. Certainly if we have learned something in the last quarter-century of academic criticism, it is precisely that explication of the text can enrich the reader's experience of the work. It is the quality of the engagement of the reader and the literary work which is at the heart of all criticism and scholarship. It is this wedding of experience and the fruit of experience which gives new meaning to Carlyle's statement in *The Hero as Poet*: "We are all poets when we read a poem well."

The premise of this book is that we can go a step beyond Pater's concept of experience and the fruit of experience by adding as a third possibility a new kind of experience which grows out of the first two. This is not intuitive or impressionistic criticism, because the critic's response is predicated on a considerable amount of learning and thought. Even though I believe that Pater is right when he talks of the fruit of experience being secondary to the experience itself, I see the essays in this book combining the experience and the fruit of experience and in the process producing a different kind of experience as the critic attempts to isolate and develop his experience of a writer. Put in another way, we assume that the critic has spent a great deal of time in learning and study, in close analysis, in scholarship and criticism. Now, in a crucially important moment, the critic embraces the subject and tries to capture the distillation of all those factors having been forced to run together—the critic attempts to describe his experience of the writer: not a new kind of criticism, but perhaps one of the logical ends of criticism and scholarship.

I rehearse all of this for two reasons. First, of course, I wish to offer a context for the essays which follow. Second, however, there were objections to the approach of *The Victorian Experience* which are important enough to require comment. Those few objections are symptomatic of an illness within the academic world of letters which threatens to become more serious if untreated—and if untreated, to become epidemic. Because the movement from epidemic to normative to endemic is not unknown to us, I believe there is reasonable cause for alarm. My quarrel with particular critics is not the result of conventional thrusts and parries of academic dueling, but rather the result of the critics' basic lack of sympathy for the kind of criticism which *The Victorian Experience* strives to demonstrate. It is precisely that lack of sympathy which speaks to a major problem facing literary studies in our time. I do not refer only to the French critical orbit. As with any new intellectual or ideological movement, literary or otherwise, there will be excesses. Nevertheless, in the hands of talented readers the continental mode of inquiry has produced illuminating commentary. However, the failing I refer to may have been enlarged by the rush to embrace the "new" criticism, for in that rush too many understood too little of the method and aims of the new approaches.

While one realizes that some modes of discourse are admittedly difficult because a new language is being developed or because the ideas they convey are particularly dense, one must at the same time insist upon a style as close as possible to the lucid and fluent of the best writers among us and upon a subject matter and approach which ultimately broaden rather than narrow the literary experience. To applaud the opaque and the insignificant is to limit dangerously the audience and force of literary commentary. It is, in Gerald Graff's term, to turn literature against itself. Therefore, I worry about those who questioned the validity of critics' caring about their own involvement with writers and the wider consideration of the relationship between literature and life. In a paradoxical turn, such a position seems to frown not only on the clarity of critical prose, but upon the humanity of literary studies—perhaps, even, upon the humanity of literature itself. It is particularly ironic that such positions have found their way into the study of Victorian life and letters, into a time which witnessed the growth of realism and an acute relationship between belles-lettres and life.

It is toward the broadening and liberating possibilities of literature that the approach of *The Victorian Experience* is directed. In accepting the Nobel Prize in 1962, John Steinbeck said: "Literature was not promulgated by a pale and emasculated critical priesthood singing their litanies in empty churches—nor is it a game for the cloistered elect." Steinbeck concluded his speech with the following: "Having taken God-like power, we must seek in ourselves for the responsibility and the wisdom we once prayed some deity might have. Man himself has become our greatest hazard and our only hope. So that today, Saint John the Apostle may well be paraphrased: In the end is the *word*, and the word is *man*, and the word is *with* man." And if the future of literature is immense, it is so because the word is with men and women who will share it with others.

CARLYLE: BEGINNING WITH THE WORD

G. B. TENNYSON

The late Geoffrey Tillotson labored for many years on what was to be a two-volume contribution, covering the years 1832–1880, to the "Oxford History of English Literature." At his death he left a "substantial manuscript," but one which for various reasons could not be made to fit into the Oxford series. Nevertheless, the greater part of it has been published separately as *A View of Victorian Literature* (London, 1978). As such it represents the mature thinking of one of the distinguished scholars of Victorian literature in our time, which in itself makes it interesting. But what is arresting about the book from the point of view of the present undertaking is that the author whose name appears most frequently in the text, as evidenced by the entries in the index, is—Thomas Carlyle. What is more, the index contains a note to the effect that only selected references to Carlyle's works have been listed, which is to say that his name appears even more often than the index shows. Although Carlyle has always loomed large in the study of Victorian letters, this degree of prominence, prominence exceeding even that of Dickens in Tillotson's index, would almost certainly not have been vouchsafed Carlyle in any view of Victorian literature published in the first thirty, perhaps even in the first fifty, years of this century. Thus, although it was surely not his intention to do so, by the abundance of his references to Carlyle, Tillotson has confirmed the claim I made a few years earlier in an essay titled "Carlyle Today" (in *Carlyle Past and Present*, 1976), namely, that the distinguishing feature of

1

modern studies of Carlyle from the 1930s onward has been a scholarly-critical approach to Carlyle as an influence.

As I put it in that earlier essay, the study of Carlyle can be divided into three main periods—the first during his lifetime, the second from his death in 1881 until about 1930, and the third from 1930 to the present. I called these three periods the Popular, the Reactionary, and the Scholarly-Critical, and I offered the following characterization of each:

> The Popular period was dominated by the image of Carlyle as Teacher; the Reactionary period was dominated by the image of Carlyle as Denouncer, often as not turned back upon the Sage himself as Carlyle the Denounced. The Scholarly or Scholarly-Critical period is dominated by the image of Carlyle as Influence.

Later I noted that the Scholarly-Critical period was directed toward "seeing the man the Victorians venerated as a Professor-of-Things-in-General and the late Victorians and Edwardians alternately venerated and deplored as a Denouncer-of-Things-in-General, rather more as an Influence-on-Things-in-General."

It is, of course, gratifying to see one's judgments confirmed, not so much by stated agreement as by the unmistakable evidence of practice, as I find mine confirmed by Tillotson's richness of reference to Carlyle in a general study of the literature of the Victorian age. At the same time one has to allow that I, in turn, was doing little more than confirming the judgment reached as early as 1855 by the penetrating mind of George Eliot, who has left for us what is still the most aptly expressed assessment of Carlyle as influence. Although George Eliot's remarks have been cited by more than one student of Carlyle, including the present one, they deserve to be cited again:

> It is an idle question to ask whether [Carlyle's] books will be read a century hence: if they were all burnt as the grandest of Sutees on his funeral pile, it would be only like cutting down an oak after its acorns have sown a forest. For there is hardly a superior or active mind of this generation that has not been modified by Carlyle's writings; there has hardly been an English book written for the last ten or twelve years that would not have been different if Carlyle had not lived.

The George Eliot image of oak and acorns is itself a Carlylean image, for he never tired of talking about influence and intellectual development in metaphors of plant growth: "Cast forth thy Act, thy Word, into the ever-living, ever-working Universe: it is a seed-grain that cannot die, unnoticed today (says one), it will be found flourishing as a Banyan-grove (perhaps, alas, as a Hemlock-forest) after a thousand years" (*Sartor Resartus*). Even closer to George Eliot's image (was it perhaps her source?) is this typical Carlyle utterance: "Every mortal can and shall himself be a true man: it is a great thing, and the parent of great things; as from a single acorn the whole earth might in the end be peopled with oaks!" (*Chartism*). All of these organic metaphors remind one of the lines from Goethe that Carlyle adopted as the epigraph for *Sartor Resartus*:

> My inheritance, how wide and fair!
> Time is my fair seed-field, of Time I'm heir.

Thus George Eliot's Carlylean image still has a rightness, for in the intervening century and more we have had yet greater opportunity to see Carlyle as an influence extending through generations not yet born when George Eliot was writing.

All of this is, as I say, very gratifying to one who has devoted more than passing attention to Carlyle and his works for more than twenty years. There is something respectable and comforting about an influence, even more about an Influence, as we must now take Carlyle to be. As I wrote in that earlier essay:

> The influence approach is both safer and more in keeping with the supposed objectivity of scholarship than either of the previous approaches [i.e., Carlyle as Teacher, Carlyle as Denouncer and Denounced]. One can, for instance, explore an influence without having to support it. One can for that matter lament it while still chronicling carefully how it was manifested. Thus it has been possible in the scholarly period of Carlyle studies to write about Carlyle without necessarily appearing as either his sycophant or his grim-eyed detractor.

In other words, Carlyle as Influence has been a logical and necessary avenue for scholarly-critical travel and one we very much needed to journey on to gain perspective on a figure whose capacity to rouse passions can hardly be overestimated. Carlyle as Influence justifies any number of scholarly enterprises about him that are underway in our time—the superb Duke-Edinburgh edition of the letters of the two Carlyles under the editorship of C. R. Sanders and K. J. Fielding, the various bibliographies of Carlyle's writings,

3

and writings about him published or in process by Rodger Tarr, a new re-issue of the Centenary Edition of his *Works* in thirty volumes with an introduction from my own hand, and the various scholarly observances of the one-hundredth anniversary of Carlyle's death in 1881. These and many other scholarly activities related to Carlyle can be sufficiently justified on the grounds of his undeniable importance as an influence on nineteenth-century life and letters.

And yet, if one really likes Carlyle, all of this sound and necessary scholarly respectability from George Eliot to Geoffrey Tillotson to the current work in Carlyle studies is not quite enough. It would not have been quite enough for Carlyle himself. He was after all the man who held respectability up to scorn by his repeated retelling of the story of the man with a gig, a story that he had first come upon in an account of a trial:

> In Thurtell's trial (says the *Quarterly Review*) occurred the following colloquy: 'Q. What sort of person was Mr. Weare? A. He was always a respectable person. Q. What do you mean by respectable? A. He kept a gig.' ("Jean Paul Friedrich Richter")

Carlyle eventually developed a shorthand notation for such a condition and such an attitude towards it, as he did for so many others; in this case it was "Gigmanity," which we could define as that portion of humanity that is taken to be respectable because it drives a gig, that is, because it has a certain level of financial means. Gigmanity was closely connected with the concept of the *philistine* which Carlyle introduced into Victorian discourse in our modern secular sense and Matthew Arnold later made his own. Carlyle's scorn for philistine concepts of respectability and for those who held them knew no bounds. I rather suspect that his scorn for any today who countenance his works solely on the grounds that they are after all respectable because of having been influential would be almost as intense. Carlyle would be anything but satisfied to see himself part of scholarly gigmanity.

In a sense Carlyle had a foretaste of what such a status was like, and he did not altogether care for it. For the three stages of Carlyle studies that I outlined earlier as extending from his lifetime up to about the present were themselves anticipated within the first stage, the so-called Popular stage, and were thus themselves experienced

4

by Carlyle in his own lifetime. It is worth reviewing the sequence because of what it tells us about the Victorian experience of Carlyle and about the modern one. It runs something like this: once Carlyle made an impact on the public (and he was admittedly one of the latest blooming authors in all English literature), he was enthusiastically received. The work that did the trick was that extraordinary amalgam of history and prophecy known as *The French Revolution*. The year was 1837, the year of Queen Victoria's accession, hence the official dawn of the Victorian age. Because of the *The French Revolution* Carlyle's earlier works were lifted from the coterie audience they had been reaching since the late 1820s and were made part of the general intellectual equipment of the Victorian mind. Among these none had a greater impact than his *Sartor Resartus*, to which we shall return later. By the 1840s Carlyle himself enjoyed the adulation of the multitude. That was the decade of his greatest and most visible contemporary influence. In addition to *Sartor* and *The French Revolution*, by 1845 Carlyle had to his credit four volumes of essays, *Chartism, On Heroes and Hero-Worship, Past and Present*, and *Cromwell*. It was that body of work that George Eliot had most in mind when she wrote of Carlyle as a great oak from which so many acorns had been sown. It was in that period when even from Oxford Matthew Arnold heard Carlyle's "puissant voice" alongside of and equal in power to the "religious music" of John Henry Newman. That was the high point of Carlyle's own Popular period.

But by the 1850s a reaction set in, an anticipation of the period following Carlyle's death up to the nineteen-thirties. The Reactionary Period in Carlyle's lifetime was primarily occasioned by the *Latter-Day Pamphlets* (1850), a series of writings that even today causes pain to less uncompromising sensibilities than Carlyle's own, which is to say to most. Even the much gentler *Life of John Sterling* (1851) did not still the resentment, and the reaction (which was, of course, never total and did not include such staunch admirers as John Ruskin, or, for that matter, Dickens and Tennyson) lasted until the mid 1860s and the completion of *Frederick the Great*, considered by many at the time to be Carlyle's masterwork, though few would so describe it today. There was then for the rest of Carlyle's life, until 1881, a general restoration of Carlyle in public esteem, a kind of anticipation of the mid-twentieth-century

5

period I have called the Scholarly-Critical. His output slackened during this time (he was by now in his seventies and eighties), but he did issue various essays and shorter works and he wrote for posthumous publication the moving *Reminiscences*, now recognized as among his most affecting pieces. During these later years Carlyle was revered as a kind of grand old man who had wrought much in his time and could now be safely enshrined as an essentially harmless ikon.

While there was much honor in the role of living ikon, and no doubt a certain satisfaction that he had prevailed despite all odds, Carlyle certainly felt dissatisfaction as well. Surely much of the woebegone utterances of the later Carlyle can be attributed to the sense of frustration that he experienced in being everywhere honored and nowhere heeded. I think he would feel something of the same sort today in the scholarly-critical phase of the public study of his life and works, a sense that being respectable is by itself not quite enough.

Put another way, it is a question of what being respectable really is. Carlyle once wrote:

> The Real, if you will stand by it, is respectable. The coarsest hobnailed pair of shoes, if honestly made according to the laws of fact and leather, are not ugly, they are honest and fit for their object: the highest eye may look on them without displeasure, nay with a kind of satisfaction. This rude packing case, it is faithfully made: square to the rule, and formed with rough-and-ready strength against injury—fit for its use; not a pretentious hypocrisy, but a modest, serviceable fact; whoever pleases to look upon it will find the image of humble manfulness in it, and will pass on with some infinitesimal impulse to thank the gods. ("Hudson's Statue," *Latter-Day Pamphlets*)

In Carlyle's view, then, being respectable is a consequence of a correspondence between form and use, wherein the former suits the latter and the latter implies the former. It is not merely in being *thought* respectable because of outward appearance, but being in fact (that is, in Carlyle's sense of fact, *in truth*) a harmony. And the inescapable result of recognizing this kind of respectability was "to thank the gods," to give vent to a natural piety that Carlyle thought lay slumbering in all hearts. Quite a different thing from gigmanity, even scholarly gigmanity.

So, if respectability in the conventional sense was not to Carlyle's taste, we cannot be content with it as the final resting place for his work. We must ask again, what is the experience of Carlyle over and above the scholarly respectability of being an Influence, over and above being raw material for what Carlyle was fond of ridiculing as the labor of Dryasdust? To answer such a question means looking both before and after, approximating Carlyle's own method in *Past and Present*:

> Out of old Books, new Writings, and much Meditation not of yesterday, [the author] will endeavour to select a thing or two; and from the Past, in a circuitous way, illustrate the Present and the Future. The Past is a dim indubitable fact: the Future too is one, only dimmer; nay properly it is the *same* fact in new dress and development. For the Present holds in it both the whole Past and the whole Future;—as the LIFE-TREE IGDRASIL, wide-waving, many-toned, has its roots down deep in the Death-kingdoms, among the oldest dead dust of men, and with its boughs reaches beyond the stars; and in all times and places is one and the same Life-tree!

Carlyle had in himself more than a little of the impulse of Dryasdust the Scholar. In *"Sartor" Called "Resartus"* (1965) I argued that the editorial and commentary role was fundamental to Carlyle's creative methods, not only in *Sartor* but throughout his writing career; that he developed this approach through his ten-year apprenticeship in the 1820s in the writing of essays, especially those on German literature for an uninformed English audience. In writing now of the experience of Carlyle I am taking a leaf from his book by considering his works in something of the same light as he considered the Chronicle of Jocelin of Brakelond—as a quarry, but in the present case a quarry for building an understanding of the Victorian and the modern encounter with Carlyle.

Despite all the changes from the Victorian age to our own, the experience of reading Carlyle today is not so very different from what appears to have been the Victorian experience. Nor should it be, with Carlyle or with any other author, for if there is a common thread in human nature through all ages, it must disclose itself in a common response to great works of literature: the first lord and the first groundling who listened to Hamlet's soliloquies or Lear's ravings on the heath or Prospero's incantations must have had a response that has more likenesses to yours and mine than it has differences from them. Such a response in the case of Shakespeare or Carlyle has nothing to do with perceiving influence. It is a response to the language itself, an imaginative response to the power of the author's words that enables the reader (or auditor) to share the author's vision, to participate in the same reality the author perceived, which, to be Romantic and Coleridgean about it, is part of a universal reality that is the mind of God, "a repetition in the finite mind of the eternal act of creation in the infinite I AM." Such, I believe, must be the initial point of departure in the response to any great work of literature.

In the case of the Victorians, in my own case, and in the cases of those who come today for the first time upon the writings of Carlyle, the matter of Carlyle's language is paramount. The sheer exhilaration of it is at once its initial and its enduring appeal. The place to begin is the same place where the Victorians began, once they had been properly alerted by *The French Revolution*—with *Sartor Resartus* at the dawn of Carlyle's popular period. With *Sartor* we are with the essential Carlyle, with a book that looks both before and after, irradiating his previous work and making it worth the reading and anticipating all that is to come over the next half-century. The appeal, the impact, of *Sartor* is as potent now as it was then, for those that have ears to hear, for it makes its appeal through language. It is language that is at once majestic and mournful, playful and profound. The range of language in so relatively slender a book is nothing short of spectacular and can be matched only in the greatest works in our literature. I cannot help thinking of it in quasi-Carlylean terms; hence the designations for the instances that follow:

The serio-satiric

Man's whole life and environment have been laid open and elucidated; scarcely a fragment or fibre of his Soul, Body, and Possession, but has been probed, dissected, distilled, desiccated, and scientifically decomposed: our spiritual Faculties, of which it appears there are not a few, have their Stewarts, Cousins, Royer Collards: every cellular, vascular, muscular Tissue glories in its Lawrences, Majendies, Bichâts.

The eloquent-evocative

That living flood, pouring through these streets, of all qualities and ages, knowest thou whence it is coming, whither it is going? *Aus der Ewigkeit, zu der Ewigkeit hin.* From Eternity, onwards to Eternity!

8

The serious-playful

'As Montesquieu wrote a *Spirit of Laws*,' observes our Professor, 'so could I write a *Spirit of Clothes*; thus, with an *Esprit des Lois*, properly an *Esprit de Coutumes*, we should have an *Esprit de Costumes*.'

The seraphic-diabolical

'Reader, the heaven-inspired melodious Singer; loftiest Serene Highness; nay thy own amber-locked, snow-and-rosebloom Maiden, worthy to glide sylphlike, almost on air, whom thou lovest, worshippest as a divine Presence, which, indeed, symbolically taken, she is,—has descended, like thyself, from that same hair-mantled, flint-hurling Aboriginal Anthropophagus!

The exaggerated-ridiculous

Lives the man that can figure a naked Duke of Windlestraw addressing a naked House of Lords? Imagination, choked as in mephitic air, recoils on itself, and will not forward with the picture. The Woolsack, the Ministerial, the Opposition Benches—*infandum, infandum!* And yet why is the thing impossible? Was not every soul, or rather every body, of these Guardians of our Liberties, naked, or nearly so, last night; 'a forked radish with a head fantastically carved'?

The elevating-mystical

To the eye of Pure Reason what is [man]? A Soul, a Spirit, and divine Apparition. Round his mysterious ME, there lies, under all those woolrags, a Garment of Flesh (or of Senses), contextured in the Loom of Heaven; whereby he is revealed to his like, and dwells with them in UNION and DIVISION; and sees and fashions for himself a Universe, with azure Starry Spaces, and long Thousands of Years.

All of the above examples are from Book I of *Sartor*; none is from those now justly celebrated set pieces, the "Everlasting Yea" at the close of Book II, or "Symbols" or "Natural Supernaturalism" of Book III, where Carlyle's verbal organ-rolls pour forth with overwhelming power. These are examples of Carlyle in first or, at most, second gear.

What can be the responses to this sort of writing? One still encountered today among undergraduates of limited literary background is like that of many of the first readers of *Sartor* in *Fraser's Magazine*, namely, that the whole business is a farrago of nonsense and should be stopped at once. But these are the sorts of people who would find the *Alice* books childish and who think Shakespeare is too windy. To those with a sense of the possibilities of language —and among early readers this included John Stuart Mill as well as, less surprisingly, Emerson—the language of *Sartor* is like the language of poetry at its best. It stimulates and soothes at the same time; it takes the reader outside himself by making him feel himself more intensely; it seems to bring the reader into the presence of a reality more powerful, more real than the everyday reality he knows.

Of course not even Carlyle's language is divorced from thought and ideas, for there is no such thing as "pure poetry," if by that we mean that will-o'-the-wisp pursued later in Carlyle's same century by continental and subsequently English aesthetes; that is, poetry or writing that has no referential content, that not only aspires to but attains the condition of music. Carlyle, that earnest Victorian, would be the last to subscribe to such a proposition or consciously aim to realize such a condition in his writing. Thus, I am not trying to suggest that Carlyle's language casts a reader into some kind of contentless reverie. The content is indisputably there and must be considered. The point at the moment, however, is that, to the extent that form and content are ever separable in literature, Carlyle's writing (even the later more offensive pieces) has a power and a vitality that are in themselves aesthetically pleasing. Without that as starting point, we will never understand the Victorian or the modern experience of Carlyle.

If the initial experience of Carlyle is the experience of an intensely felt verbal presence, as I have argued, so all subsequent experience of Carlyle is colored by that same verbal power. Not only the still popular works, *Past and Present*, say, or *Heroes*; but even the least of Carlyle's writings, early and late, exhibit his characteristic power. Carlyle's *Cromwell* is little read today, despite the fact that Carlyle labored mightily on it, whereas *Past and Present*, which he virtually dashed off during an interruption on his Cromwell researches, holds its own as a Carlyle and Victorian classic. Yet *Cromwell*, no less than *Past and Present* has passages of such extraordinary power and pathos that one can read them for their own sake, apart from any aid and encouragement they may give in their setting to Carlyle's (to my mind) perverse defense of the seventeenth-century despot. Such is the following luminous Carlyle account from Scandinavian mythology of the death of Balder:

Here is another Mythus. Balder the white Sungod, say our Norse Skalds, Balder, beautiful as the summer-dawn, loved of Gods and men, was dead. His brother Hermoder, urged by his Mother's tears and the tears of the Universe, went forth to seek him. He rode through gloomy winding valleys, of a dismal leaden colour, full of howling winds and subterranean torrents; nine days; ever deeper, down towards Hela's Deathrealm: at Lonesome Bridge, which, with its gold gate, spans the River of Moaning, he found the Portress, an ancient woman, called Modgudr, 'the Vexer of Minds,' keeping watch as usual: Modgudr answered him, 'Yes, Balder passed this way; but he is not here; he is down yonder,—far, still far to the North, within Hela's Gates yonder.' Hermoder rode on, still dauntless, on his horse, named 'Swiftness' or 'Mane of Gold'; reached Hela's Gates; leapt sheer over them, mounted as he was; *saw* Balder, the very Balder, with his eyes;—but could not bring him back! Balder beckoned him mournfully a still adieu; Nanna, Balder's Wife, sent 'a thimble' to her mother as a memorial: Balder never could return!—Is not this an emblem?

And Carlyle never lost his power. Hear this denunciation of the eighteenth century from his *Frederick the Great*:

For there was need once more of a Divine Revelation to the torpid frivolous children of men, if they were not to sink altogether into the ape condition, and in that whirlwind of the Universe,—lights obliterated, and the torn wrecks of Earth and Hell hurled aloft into the Empyrean; black whirlwind, which made even apes serious, and drove most of them mad,—there was, to men, a voice audible; voice from the heart of things once more, as if to say: 'Lying is not permitted in this Universe. The wages of lying, you behold, are death. Lying means damnation in this Universe; and Beelzebub, never so elaborately decked in crowns and mitres, is *not* God!' This was a revelation truly to be named of the Eternal, in our poor Eighteenth Century; and has greatly altered the complexion of said Century to the Historian ever since.

Nor is it a matter of lightning and thunder alone, but often the power of feeling, of sympathy, as in this passage from his reminiscence of the sad life of his closest friend, Edward Irving:

What a falling of the curtain; upon what a Drama! Rustic Annandale begins it, with its homely honesties, rough vernacularities, safe, innocently kind, ruggedly motherlike, cheery, wholesome, like its airy hills and clear-rushing streams; prurient London is the middle part, with its volcanic stupidities and bottomless confusions;—and the end is terrible, mysterious, godlike and awful; what Patmos could be more so? It is as if the vials of Heaven's wrath were pouring down upon a man; yet not wrath alone, for his heart is filled with trust in Heaven's goodness withal. It must be said, Irving nobly expiates whatever errors he has fallen into; like an Antique Evangelist he walks his stony course, the fixed thought of his heart, at all times, 'Though He slay me, yet will I trust in Him;' and these final deluges of sorrow are but washing the faithful soul of him clean. ("Edward Irving," *Reminiscences*)

Turn where you will in Carlyle, from now forgotten pieces like *Chartism* to the classics of his pen like *Sartor* or *Past and Present*, everywhere you will find this verbal power, this capacity to quicken the sensibility. Sometimes it has much to do with the choice of subject, as in the account of Balder; for one remembers how C. S. Lewis claimed that hearing as a youth the words "Balder is dead," he was moved almost to tears, knowing not why, knowing not who Baldur was. That, Lewis would say, was the power of the myth itself, regardless of the rendition. But how much more moving in Carlyle's treatment: "Balder the white Sungod . . . Balder, beautiful as the summer-dawn, loved of Gods and men, was dead." Moreover, Carlyle can do the same with lesser material. In the account of Edward Irving we have a subject now all but unknown; yet the mythic quality is there as well: ". . . like an Antique Evangelist he walks his stony course, the fixed thought of his heart, at all times, 'Though he slay me, yet will I trust in Him;' and these final deluges of sorrow are but washing the faithful soul of him clean."

There is a temptation to which all lovers of Carlyle, Victorian and modern, are tempted to succumb, namely, to stop with the language itself. Nor would such be the worst possible response. There must be many who can read with delight Ulysses' speech on degree in Shakespeare's *Troilus* without sharing the worldview that lies behind it, and many more who can thrill to Shakespearean laudations of kingship while holding themselves to be staunch democrats. Carlyle is perhaps still too close to us to allow for as much of this sort of response as will eventually come to be his. But it is a response that Ruskin has already in large measure attained. It would be no easy task to find persons who actually agree with all of Ruskin's sentiments (Ruskin himself, of course, does not agree with all his sentiments); but it is a simple task to find unabashed lovers of Ruskin the writer. Increasingly this is true of Carlyle, as it was early in Carlyle's career. There is more than a little of this response in George Eliot herself, who conceded that Carlyle's chief virtue lay in quickening the imagination:

He does not teach men how to use sword and musket, but he inspires their souls with courage and sends a strong will into their muscles. He does not, perhaps, enrich your stock of data, but he clears away the film from your eyes that you may search for data to some purpose. He does not, perhaps, convince you, but he strikes you, undeceives you, animates you. You are not directly fed by his books, but you are braced as by a walk up to an alpine summit, and yet subdued to calm and reverence as by the sublime things to be seen from that summit.

For lovers of the word, then, Carlyle's verbal brilliance is almost enough in itself. Dryasdust, including, be it noted, the present author, has devoted no little attention to cataloguing Carlyle's style and mannerisms—his inversions, exhortations, word coinages, Germanisms, biblicalisms—in short, examining "Carlylese" and "Carlylisms," to use the words that came into currency even in Carlyle's lifetime. Such a procedure is but the scholarly version of the more exuberant response that has moved so many to mock and parody Carlyle's style. In a study I made of the numerous parodies of Carlyle from his age to our own (in *Carlyle and His Contemporaries*, 1976), I found that, beginning in the eighteen-twenties with Jane Welsh and continuing into the nineteen-seventies in an address I gave to the Carlyle Society in Edinburgh, those who have come under Carlyle's spell have been almost irresistibly drawn to dabbling a bit in Carlylese themselves. In so doing we are in the company, not only of *Punch* (as might be expected), but of readers as various as James Russell Lowell, Meredith, Trollope, and James Joyce. Is that not the blessed company of all faithful readers?

Thus, I repeat, it is my conviction that the experience of Carlyle begins today where it began for the Victorians—with the word, with Carlyle's language. I believe Lytton Strachey was off the mark in attempting to dispose of Carlyle on the grounds that he is, after all, just language. Strachey likened him to the Northern Lights, brilliant but emitting no heat; and to a hurricane hurling itself upon "tremulous reeds," which, though "they bend down low, to the very earth, as the gale passes," nevertheless "immediately . . . spring up again and are seen to be precisely as they were before." Anyone who has endured a hurricane does not soon forget it; nor is he precisely as he was before, though he may seem to be seen to be.

By beginning with the word in Carlyle I have in large measure recapitulated the Victorian experience, especially in the initial phases of Carlyle's Popular period. It is my contention that this experience is also enduring, that it is not merely a hurricane among the reeds. As long as Carlyle is read, as opposed to being read about, the experience of the reader will be that of an encounter with a titanic verbal presence. As long as there are readers who can respond to that, Carlyle will retain his relevance. At the same time it is idle to pretend that the word can long exist apart from what it signifies, or, to put it in Victorian terms, that one can rest solely in Carlyle's manner without reference to his "message." For many in the Victorian age and for more today, that means the ushering in of a Reactionary period. No experience of Carlyle would be complete without it.

The reaction to Carlyle, when that reaction comes, is likely to be stronger and somehow more resentful than the reaction to most authors. I believe the fundamental cause lies in the very power of the language that swept the reader up in the first place. One has farther to fall. Arthur Hugh Clough, that casualty of the Victorian crisis of faith, put it well enough when he complained that Carlyle had led us out into the wilderness—and left us there. The marching orders were rousing enough, Clough seems to be saying, the commands stirringly given, but what is one to do after one reaches the battlefield and finds, not the enemy, but a darkling plain full of confused alarms of struggle and flight? Perhaps Clough had too little appreciation of George Eliot's sense of the necessity of simply being stirred in the first place, but his dissatisfaction does raise the issue of what Carlyle himself thought he was stirring people to do and what any reader, then or now, can take away from Carlyle after the battle-cry has been issued.

My own experience in studying Carlyle leads me to believe that the wrong sort of attention has often been paid to Carlyle's "message," or to parts of it. Readers have been led to look for a systematic philosophy and for specific answers to specific social ills. When they find that there is no systematic philosophy and that some of Carlyle's prescriptions for specific ills are uncongenial, they react against the teacher, feeling somehow betrayed, as Clough did. Nor is Carlyle wholly guiltless in this matter. Despite the fact that he consistently derided system and denied that he offered one, at the same time he just as consistently came before his readers as a mentor, as a "spiritual guide in matters of faith," to use the subtitle a late Victorian gave to a book treating, among others, Carlyle. Further, Carlyle compounded the problem by working in a mode normally associated with fact, not fiction; that is, he wrote nonfiction, or what is generally classified as nonfiction. *Sartor Resartus* is, after all, a fiction, despite the unwillingness of commentators so to denominate it. And all the rest of Carlyle's nonfiction is so highly unconventional in mode—was there ever a *history* like *The French Revolution*?—that it is a nice question whether it should be classified as nonfiction at all. But all of Carlyle's writing is normally so classified.

Now this issue of nonfiction is not just a mere quibble. Readers regularly suspend disbelief with authors of admitted fictions. The same reader can entertain alternately the world views of Virgil or Chaucer or Pope or Hardy without the slightest difficulty and is unlikely to hold any one of them responsible if his own experience fails to confirm their views. Perhaps there is too much suspension of disbelief in the reading of poetry and fiction, leading to the unfortunate modern condition of never asking whether *anything* earlier authors said is really true. That, of course, is another and interesting question to which we cannot address ourselves here. But certainly Carlyle shows that there is not *enough* suspension of disbelief in the reading of nonfiction, even such unconventional nonfiction as that written by Carlyle.

If an author comes before you writing what is purportedly fact, is it any wonder that the reader submits those "facts," (whether empirical facts or philosophic facts) to the kind of judgment he would apply to any other factual assertion? Thus it comes that Carlyle's philosophy is subjected to a scrutiny and testing that readers would hardly dream of applying to, say, Dickens, even on those occasions when Dickens is presenting in his fictions the same philosophy, openly appropriated from Carlyle. Perhaps Carlyle brought it on himself by his chosen mode of writing. A comparison with other nonfiction prose writers would seem to confirm it: Dr. Johnson not only comes before the reader uttering truths, but he wants the reader to subject those truths to whatever philosophic test is relevant. And by and large Dr. Johnson comes off very well. Why not, then, do the same with Carlyle? The answer is that Carlyle, though writing nonfiction, was not writing conventional eighteenth-century nonfiction or the nonfiction of textbooks. Carlyle was pioneering a new mode in writing, one that sometimes demands *the* traditional tests, one that at other times is best judged as we judge fiction—as an imaginative construct. Today, with such forms as the nonfiction novel and various kinds of interpretive and investigative reporting, we should be more at home with Carlyle's methods than we are. What is *Past and Present* but a kind of nonfiction novel in which Carlyle creates out of factual raw material an imagined, a brilliantly imagined, twelfth century in order to use it as a stick with which to beat the nineteenth? The method here is almost impossible to disentangle from the message. And this kind of imaginative creation is the rule rather than the exception in Carlyle.

Lest all this appear to be some kind of dodge, let me explain that I believe Carlyle should be held as responsible as any other author for the truth or falsity, wisdom or unwisdom, of his utterances. *As* responsible but not more so. Dickens' "philosophy of Christmas" is in my judgment pretty thin philosophic gruel. But it is not grounds to throw all Dickens out with the bathwater. Likewise Carlyle sometimes says foolish or pernicious things. They should be so identified. Chances are they were foolish when uttered and contributed to the inevitable Victorian reaction against him. But Carlyle is above all an imaginative writer, someone who enlarges our awareness, who takes us outside ourselves, who lets us see the world from a different perspective, who in short works upon the reader as imaginative writers always do. If this seems to be an undermining of Carlyle's own sense of himself and of his own sense of mission, I can only say that it is not intended as such. Carlyle's sense of mission was less immediately political than we generally suppose. To be sure, he hoped to affect his world; he sought constantly, and in vain, for the right leader; and he frequently pictured himself as an unheeded prophet. All of this suggests that kind of immediate political program that, especially in our time, we take to be the natural aim of all who address the public. But far more than an immediate political program Carlyle had a long range vision. He spoke to the age, certainly, but he spoke with an eye to after-times as well. Had his aims been immediately political, he would surely not have invested so much effort in the study of history, so much effort in trying to understand the past, from the distant mythological past to the closer eighteenth-century past. Carlyle saw his message as working itself out over long millenia, not by the end of the next decade or before the next election. (He was in any event notably indifferent to elections and saw little hope for solution of problems from that source.) It was Carlyle after all, speaking of the world-phoenix, who saw the process of social change and renewal extending over centuries:

> 'For the rest, in what year of grace such Phoenix-cremation will be complete, you need not ask. The law of Perseverance is among the deepest in man: by nature he hates change; seldom will he quit his old house till it has actually fallen about his ears. Thus have I seen Solemnities linger as Ceremonies, sacred Symbols as idle Pageants, to the extent of three-hundred years and more after all life and sacredness had evaporated out of them. And then, finally, what time the Phoenix Death-Birth itself will require, depends on unseen contingencies.—Meanwhile, would Destiny offer Mankind, that after, say two centuries of convulsion and conflagration, more or less vivid, the fire-creation should be accomplished, and we find ourselves again in a Living Society, and no longer fighting but working,—were it not perhaps prudent in Mankind to strike the bargain?'

So much by way of caveat on Carlyle and his message. The question remains, what was that message? John Holloway in *The Victorian Sage* comes close to the mark in insisting that everything that Carlyle thought stems from a single overriding conviction. "In a word," says Holloway, "it is anti-mechanism." Close, but not exactly on the mark. In an introduction I wrote to an anthology of Carlyle's writings, I, too, found a single fundamental conviction animating all. I prefer my formulation because it is couched in positive terms and because it seems to me to dovetail with the methods Carlyle used to proclaim it. I wrote that the foremost of Carlyle's fundamental ideas is his "conviction of the transcendent reality of God." It is from this conviction that all else flows, including ineluctably anti-mechanism and much else besides.

Carlyle was a God-intoxicated man. This was his glory. His tragedy was that he was never able to reconcile his awesome awareness of God with any actual existing system or form for its expression. Society no longer appeared to him as operating in harmony with the divine. Even less did the organized churches so appear. He dismissed Newman as having the intellect of only a moderate-sized rabbit, he spoke with contempt of "spectral Puseyisms," he called Methodism navel-gazing, and he put down as pathetic, or as Dupe and Quackery, the strivings of earnest Calvinists like Edward Irving.

But all this should not obscure the fact that Carlyle himself was obsessed with the idea of God.

Look where you will in Carlyle you will find his text shot through with his awareness of the reality of the transcendent. It is more than just the explicit exhortations to the reader to become aware of the Almighty, pervasive though such exhortations are. It is also the biblical language, the characteristic imagery, tone, manner—everything that makes the texture of a Carlyle passage so unmistakably Carlyle's. That sense of wonder about the variety of the physical world—is that not an element making the reader aware of the supreme creator? That sense of doom and foreboding—is that not a prefigurement of the last days? Those eternities, those cosmoses, those immeasurable vast aeons of time—are they not part of God's superintendence of the universe? Is it finally possible to read any length in Carlyle without becoming aware of the presence of God? Instances abound, but among the best are the following two passages from *Past and Present*. They can stand for many. The real difference between the twelfth century and the nineteenth lies precisely in the different attitudes towards God of the two ages. Of the twelfth century Carlyle wrote:

> Imperfect as we may be, we are here, with our litanies, shaven crowns, vows of poverty, to testify incessantly and indisputably to every heart, That this Earthly Life, and *its* riches and possessions, and good and evil hap, are not intrinsically a reality at all, but *are* a shadow of realities eternal, infinite; that this Time-world, as an air-image, fearfully *emblematic*, plays and flickers in the grand still mirror of Eternity; and man's little Life has Duties that are great, that are alone great, and go up to Heaven and down to Hell. This, with our poor litanies, we testify and struggle to testify.

Of the nineteenth century, however:

> There is no longer any God for us! God's Laws are become a Greatest-Happiness Principle, a Parliamentary Expedience: the Heavens overarch us only as an Astronomical Time-keeper; a butt for Herschel-telescopes to shoot science at, to shoot sentimentalities at:—in our and old Jonson's dialect, man has lost the *soul* out of him; and now, after the due period,—begins to find the want of it! This is verily the plague-spot; centre of the universal Social Gangrene, threatening all modern things with frightful death. To him that will consider it, here is the stem, with its roots and taproot, with its world-wide upas-boughs and accursed poison-exudations, under which the world lies writhing in atrophy and

agony. You touch the focal-centre of all our disease, of our frightful nosology of diseases, when you lay your hand on this. There is no religion; there is no God; man has lost his soul, and vainly seeks antiseptic salt. Vainly: in killing Kings, in passing Reform Bills, in French Revolutions, Manchester Insurrections, is found no remedy. The foul elephantine leprosy, alleviated for an hour, reappears in new force and desperateness next hour.

All of Carlyle's specific positions and attitudes, the ones we agree with and the ones we do not, stem from his perception of the nature of the universe and the relation of society to it: the universe as God-created and sustained—society past or present as seen in terms of its relation to the truth of the universe. The celebrated social positions that Carlyle takes are finally corollaries, of greater or less accuracy as may be, to his principal axiom. Likewise much of the criticism and interpretation of Carlyle can be oriented in terms of *its* relation to his fundamental conviction. The school of Carlyle as a Calvinist *manqué* is a good example, as is the school of Carlyle as herald of German romantic idealism. We should not forget that even T. H. Huxley, the founder as it were of agnosticism, was as a young man much affected by reading *Sartor Resartus* because it seemed to him to give him Christianity without the theology.

Therein lies the rub in Carlyle's position and the cause of much reaction for and against him. A religion without theology is, if not quite a contradiction in terms, at least very difficult to sustain and easily lends itself to distortion, both by the spokesman for it like Carlyle and by those who react to that spokesman. Thus Nietzsche virtually founded a school of post-Popular Carlyle studies of the reactionary sort by declaring that Carlyle was an "atheist who makes it a point of honor not to be so." This has led, even in our own times, to a body of criticism that seeks to turn Carlyle inside out, to find that at bottom he truly did despair and hence his prescriptions for the world are to be, as it were, secularized. From that it is easy to move on to Carlyle as Fascist or Marxist or both (the two are finally not very different in any case). In fairness to such critics one has to allow that Carlyle's position lends itself to such varied interpretations. That is perhaps part of its interest, even if it is also part of its danger. But to press the corollaries and overlook the axiom is to misread Carlyle and to fall back into the errors of the Reactionary Period. Returning to the word is the necessary corrective.

For some time, as I have argued, the safest way to avoid the excesses of both the Popular and the Reactionary periods in the experience of Carlyle has been to concern oneself with the scholarly-critical study of Carlyle as Influence. But this phase, too, will have its close. The encounter with Carlyle's own words will see to that. Readers and students of Carlyle will be led to ask whether Carlyle's writings fit Carlyle's own definition of the Respectable; that is, whether they are in Carlyle's sense "real." As I interpreted Carlyle's concept of the real and the respectable, it was that of a correspondence between form and use. As Carlyle insisted, such a correspondence impels the observer to "pass on with some infinitesimal impulse to thank the gods." Do Carlyle's writings do that? I think the answer must be yes.

This is not to say that there are no coarse and rough edges, as with Carlyle's example of the hobnailed boots. The coarse and rough edges are exactly what Carlyle would find imparting a certain "manfulness" to the product. But the coarse and rough edges are not finally the whole product or even the greater part of it. Carlyle's Victorian contemporaries saw that and responded to the dominant element in Carlyle, to the recalling of society to an awareness of God. That widespread Victorian response is the grounds for the current study of Carlyle as Influence, as symbolized by Geoffrey Tillotson's repeated references to Carlyle in the work I cited at the beginning. This kind of attention cannot help having the effect of bringing us back to an encounter with Carlyle's words, and there the advantage will be very largely on Carlyle's side.

More than any other nonfiction prose writer in the age, arguably more than any other in other ages, Carlyle created his own world out of the power of his words. That world contains a vast gallery of characters and creatures, human and animal, demonic and divine. It spans uncountable ages, from the dawn of history to future times. It contains depictions of a great variety of societies and ways of life. In the nonfiction of Carlyle's contemporaries, whether Macaulay or Mill, Ruskin or Arnold, we find nothing like this. The comparisons that come to mind are invariably with great novelists and dramatists, with those who appeal through the word to our imaginative faculty even more than to our purely rational one.

The fact that Carlyle dwelt in the imaginative word did not escape the attention of his Victorian readers. Nor were certain ironies of the situation lost on them. Carlyle's glorification of doing over thinking ("The end of man is an action, not a thought"), his elevation of silence over speech ("Speech is silver, silence is golden") were even then occasion for a certain risibility: "The doctrine of silence in thirty volumes" is the best known. Like us, Victorians were aware that Carlyle found no contemporary doer satisfactory and most of contemporary life a babble of not even silver speech. No social or religious institution came close to embodying his vision of the right relation of man and society to the power and majesty of the divine. Thus, though they quickened to Carlyle's message, they also often came to react against it, and we their successors are wont to find it safest to approach from a purely historical perspective.

But it is in the word that all of Carlyle's contradictions can be reconciled. The word was truly Carlyle's action, his way of doing. Through the word he created doers (Odin, Cromwell, Frederick, and all the rest) who satisfied his vision of what a great leader should be. Through the word he led readers to a condition of wonder and reverence that induced, at least in them, the golden silence Carlyle sought. Finally, through the word, Carlyle created his own religion that had an external form appropriate to its inner passion. The word was Carlyle's Everlasting Yea wherein all contradiction was solved, wherein so long as he walked and worked, it was well with him. And well for us, too.

T. B. MACAULAY:
THE ACTIVE AND CONTEMPLATIVE LIVES

BERNARD SEMMEL

Thomas Babington Macaulay, the Victorian historian and statesman, wished to unite the fruits of the contemplative and active lives, and to join theory and pragmatic experience, in his writings as well as in his political life: this was, as I hope to show, at once his most characteristic quality and his most useful legacy. For the most part, the masters of philosophy and of rhetoric in the ancient and medieval worlds had insisted on the separation of the members of antinomies. There were defenders of matter and those of the spirit, partisans of liberty and those of order, proponents of free will and advocates of determinism. Such philosophical conflicts were seen in purely speculative terms, the formulation of an intellectual ideal unsullied by its opposite. Where such ideals had to be applied in practice, however, the philosophers understood that a proper balance of the contradictions was to be preferred, for life could not be forced into extremes without unhappy results. They consequently recognized that antinomies in some way expressing this distinction, as for example the classic one of the *vita activa* and the *vita contemplativa*, constituted special cases, requiring a careful mix of both members. Macaulay represented this balanced view of the ancients, at a time when systems drawn from theory, from contemplation alone, were becoming the intellectual and political fashion.

Since the Renaissance, a number of thinkers of a logical bent,

22

and persuaded of the absolute truth of their designs, have condescendingly dismissed this moderation of the ancients, and have tried to impose the principles of one or another ideal conception upon the every-day life of society. These enthusiasts and zealots, who have unfortunately dominated recent political discourse, have tried to construct societies upon visions derived from a philosophical or a divine purpose which they saw as immanent in the moral or physical universe. In this way, Savonarola attempted to realize the imaginings of his monastic contemplation by transforming the life of fifteenth-century Florence, and Calvin to incorporate his understanding of God's intent in the Genevan theocracy he established some decades later. Similarly, though his devotion was not to a divine plan but to a moral ideal, Robespierre inflicted his conception of Virtue on revolutionary France. In our own time, adherents of quasi-religious, secular faiths, following both Hegel and Marx, have moved to create a synthesis of theory and practice, or, in their term, *praxis* (which they see as practice thoroughly permeated by theory), and this from the standpoint of believers in a transcendent purpose embodied in an inevitable course of History.

Macaulay was convinced that those whose vision had been formed by either action or contemplation alone were the makers of catastrophe—inept politicians whose apparent practicality fomented revolution or rigid ideologues who became enemies of liberty. The religious and metaphysical impulses of a Calvin or a Marx would have been foreign, indeed abhorrent, to him. Although his field of contemplation was History, as was that of the adherents of Hegelian *praxis*, he saw not divine or providential patterns but merely human and circumstantial ones, which he tried to interpret according to the facts of a particular case. His was a more commonsensical effort to bring abstractions into line with real circumstances, an ambition that helped to define his views in both politics and history.

When I began my graduate work, a number of writers, disparagingly and I think mistakenly, described the Whig historians, whose patron was Macaulay, as envisioning a history in which the protagonists were motivated exclusively by such lofty sentiments as a concern for the Anglican Church and the divine right of kings, on the one hand, or for the liberty of the individual and the rights of parliament, on the other.[1] The rival history, they wished us to understand, was a more sophisticated, more realistic product. Its master, Sir Lewis Namier, saw politics not as motivated by principles or ideas, which he thought mere trimmings, but rather in terms of economic interests, or as struggles for power or status. Namier's perspective—his interest in economic and psychological motives—was akin to the crude Marxism and Freudianism which by the 1930s and 1940s were well on their way to becoming the academy's Establishment. Namierite history was widely praised, particularly in contrast to what was decried as the merely belletristic interests of Macaulay and his successors.

But even a cursory reading of the Whigs, I discovered, cleared them of the charge of neglecting the material or psychological motives in active politics. They viewed them, indeed, as of the highest importance. This did not, however, prevent their seeing ideas as frequently decisive. The Namierites, in their deliberate effort to describe merely the impulses of instinct and interest, which they thought the only valid ones, failed to comprehend the full meaning of events. Macaulay, on the other hand, had attempted, with some success, to capture the vital balance between the role of ideas and of interests in history. And, of course, the Whig historians, like Macaulay and his grand-nephew and twentieth-century successor, G. M. Trevelyan, could write in exciting and illuminating fashion, while Namier and his disciples were unconcerned with prose style, as they were with ideas and ideals, and seemed deliberately to cultivate literary awkwardness.

That Macaulay's opinions as a historian and as a liberal statesman were intimately linked has been cited as among his chief faults. Rather than regard this as reprehensible, as do those who think history a thoroughly scientific inquiry, I thought it inescapable. It pleased me that Macaulay had built his political positions on a historical base. How else could a contemplative statesman determine his course? I was gratified, too, that he used his historical subjects to set down the fruits of his own political experience, and this without falling into the error of an ahistorical present-mindedness. For a serious historian, as opposed to a mere antiquarian, could not be indifferent to the problems of his own time and society. The life and the writings of Macaulay, then, supplied me with impressive arguments for a useful interaction of the *vita activa* and the *vita contemplativa*, and of pragmatism and principle.

I

Macaulay was conscious of the efforts made by an elite of contemplative statesmen throughout Western history to unite thought and action, and he identified his own political posture and principles with certain of those figures. What he saw as success in this sphere was not simply the fact of an intellectual in politics: this could prove a disaster, as he well understood. Rather, he admired those who had so merged theory and practice as to have risen above mere doctrinaire and sectarian concerns in the interest of a civilized and improving society. This position left him an admirer of a select pantheon which included Cicero, Machiavelli, Milton, and Burke, and these were joined by a subspecies of scholarly men of action, among whom were Caesar in the ancient world, Lords Somers and Halifax in the seventeenth, and the younger Pitt in the eighteenth century. When still at Cambridge, Macaulay had been warned by his father against radicalism, and at that time he had set his father's worries to rest by assuring him that "my opinions, good or bad," did not come from the Radicals, "but from Cicero, from Tacitus, and from Milton."[2] It is interesting that the young Macaulay could already identify with the republican historian Tacitus who denounced the infamies of the later Caesars, even as he himself would choose, as an English Tacitus, to denounce those of the Stuarts. But his chief models among the ancients were Cicero and Caesar, despite their shortcomings, for he saw the politics of his own time in the light of their examples.

Macaulay's nephew and biographer, Sir George Otto Trevelyan, regretted that his uncle had never written an essay on Cicero with whose political predicament he sympathized, and whose principles he admired. He had especially approved of Cicero's "zeal for popular rights," as it appeared in his oration against Verres, a corrupt proconsul in Sicily. The Roman statesman's great fault was that he had at times acted as the agent of an aristocratic class that he himself really despised.[3] (In "Fragments of a Roman Tale," a story concerning the Catalinarian conspiracy published while the historian was still at Cambridge, Macaulay praised a "moderate"

Caesar, who had opposed both the "oligarchical tyranny," and the demagogic Catalinarians.⁴) The ideal which was to be among the foremost in Macaulay's politics, and even his poetry, was that of the *concordia ordinum*, the harmony between the classes which had been Cicero's chief object in Rome. At the age of twenty, Macaulay struck at revolutionary demagoguery in "A Radical War Song," which depicted the libertine anarchy that would follow an English revolution.⁵ In his once well-known *Horatius*, he described the class harmony that the Rome of the early republic had enjoyed and to which England might aspire, if only the English aristocrats, like the Roman patricians of the early republic, would be prepared to give up everything for their country so that the rich and poor might live "like brothers" in a just society.⁶ This had been Cicero's life-long ideal, and was one of the reasons, Trevelyan observed, though the Roman's practice at times fell short of his principles, that Macaulay regarded Cicero as one of "the foremost men of all the ages."

Machiavelli also occupied a prominent position among Macaulay's heroes. The sixteenth-century Florentine was in many respects his *beau idéal*: "the qualities of the active and contemplative statesman," the essayist declared, were blended "into a rare and exquisite harmony" in the Renaissance writer and politician. Machiavelli was an artist as well as a statesman: his comedy, *Mandragola*, in Macaulay's view, was superior to the plays of Goldini, and inferior only to the best of Molière, while his political writings were far superior to those of an over-praised Montesquieu. Defending Machiavelli against those who had made him seem an incarnation of the Devil, Macaulay brilliantly portrayed the political and personal morality of the northern city-states of Renaissance Italy which made the best of men prefer the qualities of an Iago to those of a blundering and gullible Othello, with whom the less sophisticated audiences of Renaissance England sympathized. Given the climate of opinion in sixteenth-century Italy, there was therefore no personal taint in Machiavelli's espousal of morals which would have utterly defiled a northerner; indeed, the Florentine's "public conduct was upright and honorable." Machiavelli, moreover, understood, as few of his contemporaries did, that Italy's troubles stemmed from the use of mercenary armies composed of men and officers with no interest in the welfare of the state. The solution the Florentine had proposed was the establishment of a citizen army, a militia.[7] How could this diagnosis and remedy fail to delight a Whig whose view of the history of his own country and of all of Europe was, as we shall see, drawn along similar lines? But Macaulay did not depict Machiavelli as a doctrinaire even on this point, but always as a contemplative statesman, acutely conscious of the particular circumstances of each case—a practical Whig, ready to employ the devices of Iago for the sake of liberty.

While still at Cambridge, Macaulay defended Milton against critics who saw him as a reckless revolutionary and the tool of a Cromwellian despotism—this in a dialogue set in 1665 that he had constructed between Milton and the royalist Abraham Cowley. The future historian of the 1688 revolution saw the Puritan poet as the Apostle of Liberty. The earlier revolution was necessary, the Milton of the dialogue argued, because Charles I was not merely a tyrant and a bigot, but because he had proved himself so treacherous and deceitful that no one could feel any security in his promises, though the poet granted the inadvisability of the royal execution. Milton asked Cowley to compare the virtuous and relatively free England during Oliver Cromwell's reign with the base and shameful state of affairs since 1660, and suggested the usefulness of another rebellion. The royalist, arguing the advantages of just one member of the antinomy, could see *anarchism* as the only fruit of a new rebellion, and declared that he himself preferred *despotism*, to which Macaulay's Milton, an advocate of a liberal balance, replied:

> When will rulers learn that, where liberty is not, security and order can never be? We talk of absolute power; but all power hath limits, which if not fixed by the moderation of the governors, will be fixed by the force of the governed. . . . Small, therefore, is the wisdom of those who fly to servitude as if it were a refuge from commotion; for anarchy is the sure consequence of tyranny. That governments may be safe, nations must be free. Their passions must have an outlet provided, lest they make one . . . therefore would I say to all kings, let your demagogues lead crowds, lest they lead armies; let them bluster, lest they massacre. . . . I hold that, as freedom is the only safeguard of government, so are order and moderation generally necessary to preserve freedom.[8]

For Macaulay, as for Milton, revolution was to be avoided, but not at the price of the loss of liberty, which would of itself foment upheaval and lawless bloodshed.

In a celebrated *Edinburgh Review* article on the poet in 1825, which was to make the young essayist famous virtually overnight, Macaulay proclaimed John Milton the embodiment of the union of the contemplative and active lives, as "the glory of English literature" as well as "the champion and martyr of English liberty." The author of *Paradise Lost* had lived at a time of "the great conflict between Oromasdes and Arimanes, liberty and despotism, reason and prejudice" in which "the destinies of the human race were staked on the same cast with the freedom of the English people." While the Revolution had undoubtedly taken many awkward turns, had produced many outrages, such violent events were a necessary consequence of great repression; while the immediate effects of revolution were often "atrocious crimes," in the end "the final and permanent fruits of liberty are wisdom, moderation, and mercy." And Milton's greatest glory was his battle for the most valuable freedom, his struggle against "moral and intellectual slavery," and for "the liberty of the press and the unfettered exercise of private judgement." The Puritan poet had joined the Cromwellians because he saw "free conscience" as their objective. Milton was neither a hot-headed rebel nor an advocate of despotism, but a contemplative statesman who had truly understood the political circumstances of his time. For the choice did not lie "between Cromwell and liberty, but between Cromwell and the Stuarts," and the future historian of that dynasty saw Milton as having chosen well, as was proved by the succeeding reigns of Charles II and James II, thirty years which were "the darkest and most disgraceful in the English annals."[9]

When the *Edinburgh Review* solicited an essay on Edmund Burke from him in 1844, Macaulay turned down the request, observing that there was simply too much to be said on the subject for a single article;[10] certainly, Burke seems everywhere present in the many essays Macaulay devoted to the eighteenth century. A constant, if sometimes submerged, theme of these pieces was the splendor of the principles and the practical wisdom of Burke, and of his admirer, the younger William Pitt. In his article on Warren Hastings, for example, even when taking issue with his hero on the justice of Hastings' impeachment, Macaulay described Burke as "the greatest man then living."[11] Burke was first of all a Whig, and like Macaulay a venerator of the 1688 Revolution. Also, like Macaulay himself, Burke was a man of letters in politics, a contemplative statesman who could write brilliantly about a wide range of subjects, from the principles of aesthetic criticism to those of commercial policy. Though the Tories saw the younger Pitt as the founder of their modern party, Macaulay agreed with Burke who had described him, at least for the first part of his government from 1783 to 1792, as "an enlightened Whig." To be a Whig was above all to be "an honest friend of civil and religious liberty," and this was a test that both Burke and Pitt amply met. In the latter part of his life, in reaction to the excesses of the French Revolution, Pitt was to turn to a course of repression, and to lead a party the principles of which were to become illiberal, harsh, and arbitrary. Yet his earlier interest in freedom of the press, parliamentary reform, and a free trade, and his opposition to the slave trade and life-long championship of Catholic emancipation had earned him Macaulay's devotion. By nature, Pitt had been no friend of "war nor arbitrary government," the Whig essayist proclaimed. Although events had forced such a course upon him, as they had upon Burke who also supported the repressive policies of the 1790s, Pitt, like Burke, was at bottom "a lover of peace and freedom."[12]

Macaulay, in the best Whig tradition, was, as were Burke and Pitt in the 1780s and Milton a century earlier, a friend to religious liberty and an enemy of bigotry. His first speech in parliament, urging the removal of all the barriers to Jewish participation in English political life, is probably his best remembered in this connection. In this address, he anticipated Disraeli's better-known remark when he suggested that when Britain was as "savage as New Guinea," and Athens and Rome were but rude settlements, the Jews had had palaces, fleets, philosophers, historians, and poets.[13] Macaulay sought out bigotry in all its guises: for example, he chided the nonconformists, particularly the Wesleyans, who seemed so ready to use against the Unitarians the arguments and methods the Churchmen employed against dissenters like themselves.[14] "The truth is, that bigotry will never want a pretence," Macaulay observed.[15] In speech after speech, he defended the Irish against the injuries inflicted by centuries of British rule: England governed Ireland as she would a newly-conquered territory in India, he complained, not by teaching respect for the laws, but by military force. In a fierce debate in 1845, he favored the granting of financial support for the Catholic training-college at Maynooth, arguing that though Catholicism might contain religious error, the nation could not permit the millions of Roman Catholics of Ireland to live without the solace offered by religion, or the restraints of religious discipline.[16] The Protestant voters of Edinburgh defeated Macaulay at the next general election for such clearly heretical views.

II

If I can regret Macaulay's not having written an essay on Cicero or Burke, as he had on Milton, Machiavelli, and Pitt, I cannot grieve at his not writing at length on his contemporary, John Stuart Mill. Mill, a thinker I particularly admire, has been much misunderstood, both in his time and in our own, and, in his bits and pieces of comment, Macaulay was most unjust to Mill. For his part, Mill (another unifier of the active and contemplative lives) was less than sympathetic to the Whig historian.

Mill was much more than the doctrinaire Benthamite that Macaulay first thought him, seeing him as sharing the faults of his father, James Mill, concerning whose views on history and politics Macaulay had written two highly critical essays in the 1820s;[17] nor was he the simple-minded defender of individuality he became in the historian's eyes after the publication of *On Liberty*. In fact, the younger Mill had agreed with Macaulay's criticism of his father: history and politics were not to be deduced from psychological principles, and particularly not from such a narrow one as self-interest.[18] (Curiously, the elder Mill's view of historical motivation was akin to that of Namier a century later.) After his father's death, Mill sought to speak for a "neoradicalism" which took all of human nature as its premise, not merely "the ratiocinative faculty" of James's and Bentham's utilitarian Radicalism.[19] In 1859, the Whig historian deplored in his journals that J. S. Mill had wasted "excellent abilities" in his best-known essay, which the Whig historian incorrectly understood as merely a defense of eccentricity in an England in which he felt the quality flourished all too well. "He is really crying 'Fire!' in Noah's flood," Macaulay observed. The historian, moreover, thought such intellectual movements as Comtism, with which Mill had a certain affinity, "absurd,"[20] and could no more have sympathized with Mill's attraction to the positivist view of historical development than he could to the deductive history of the elder Mill.

30

For J. S. Mill, with equal unfairness, Macaulay's vices were those of the common-place Whiggery he associated with the *Edinburgh Review*, which he and his father long believed their principal enemy. Mill saw himself as a Radical Democrat: while he could join Macaulay in his high regard for Cicero, he shortsightedly denounced Milton as an apologist for despotism; his eighteenth-century model was not Burke, but the French *philosophe* Turgot, and his heroes were the Girondists of the French, not the Whigs of the Glorious Revolution.[21] Macaulay, Mill declared, did not understand the French Revolution, which Mill believed the critical event of modern history, even as the more England-centered Whig historian, like his party and its quarterly, saw the Revolution of 1688 in this role.[22] Mill, again unfairly and in line with the Radical stereotype of Whiggery, saw Macaulay and the *Edinburgh* as not able to take seriously any writer "who actually takes decided views, who is positively in earnest, & is capable of downright admiration & even enthusiasm!"[23] Traveling in Italy, in early 1855, Mill read through a collection of Macaulay's *Essays*, and in a letter to his wife, berated their author for his superficiality and for his failure to take into account the historical insights of the German philosophers and the French sociologists. (Only in "mere literature" was Macaulay sound, wrote Mill, noting a passage in an 1830 essay in which the historian had written admiringly of Shelley, whom Mill also admired;[24] Mill could also delight in Macaulay's *Lays of Ancient Rome*, which he had reviewed favorably in 1843.[25])

With such a mutual lack of sympathy between the Mills and the Whig historian, it is surprising that, after Macaulay had become a member of the London-based board of control for India in 1833, he would describe James Mill's *History of India* as "the greatest historical work" to appear in English since that of Gibbon,[26] a tribute which the public a decade and a half later was to give to his own *History of England*. Apparently, the Whig essayist approved of the way in which the elder Mill actually wrote history, even though he had questioned the premises of the utilitarian's historical theory. James Mill, Macaulay observed in 1835, far from writing like a doctrinaire Benthamite, "never fails to bestow praise on those who, though far from coming up to his standard of perfection, yet rose in a small degree over the common level of their contemporaries." This was the way in which a contemplative statesman would

31

write history. This was the way the history of England should be written, Macaulay added.[27] As the Examiner of the East India Company, the chief official in the London-based administration, James Mill had transferred this appreciation of the merits of small improvements to his philosophy for administering India. Mill's policy (agreeing in this with the long-time one of the company) was that of *gradually* bringing India from its benighted condition to a state where she might take her place among civilized nations. To this end, Mill and the Company urged a toleration of native customs even as they sought to eradicate the more shocking ones.

Although he had praised Mill's statesmanlike approach as the historian of India, when Macaulay was in India, from 1834 to 1838, as a member of the Supreme Council, he apparently found the philosophy of gradualism and toleration of native customs offensive. (For each of these five years of service, incidentally, Macaulay was to receive £10,000, and he was able to save £30,000 of this salary, enough to provide himself with financial independence after his return home.) Macaulay's view of India could not help being influenced by the religious faith of his father, Zachary Macaulay, and by the latter's missionizing efforts as the evangelical Governor of Sierra Leone some decades earlier. After his return from India, Macaulay reported to the House of Commons his distress that the Company was prepared to further the native religions, despite their inhumane doctrines and practices, while actually discouraging the activities of Christian missionaries. The Hindus were idolaters, whose gods were "hideous, and grotesque, and ignoble"; in India, "acts of vice are acts of public worship"; the "odious theology" of Hinduism encouraged murder, as in the case of the Thugees, as well as in such vicious institutions as infanticide and suttee. Yet the policy of the government of the East India Company was to consider the toleration of these aberrations as a "profound policy." For Macaulay, on the other hand, to "countenance" Hinduism and "discountenance" Christianity was "to commit high treason against humanity and civilisation."[28]

On this question, posterity has mistakenly labeled Macaulay a bigot, because of his assumption of the superiority of Christianity to the native religion. One may argue that Macaulay saw the Company as guilty of a racial arrogance in its view of Indian possibilities, unjustly condescending in its belief that Hindus could not be more expeditiously disabused of their cruel faith. He certainly believed that England was not fulfilling its civilizing mission in cynically permitting the worship of the savage Kali in order to maintain its Asian rule. This was a Radical, not a Whig position, one hardly befitting a contemplative statesman. In this instance, the Mills knew better.

What J. S. Mill regarded as Macaulay's unstatesmanly and narrowly-English approach was perhaps more evident in his famous—one might even say, notorious—minute on Indian education, of which Mill, as an official of the East India Company, greatly disapproved. Macaulay, soon after his arrival in India, proposed that English replace Sanskrit and Arabic as the language of instruction in the schools, and Lord William Bentinck, the governor general, approved the scheme. This would mean that the classics of English literature would be studied by Indian students and not their own native works, the basis of the system previously in operation. When Macaulay's minute reached London, the directors of the East India Company were horrified. Mill expressed their views in a dispatch which insisted that it was only through the vernacular tongues that the Indian people could be effectively instructed, adding, however, that Macaulay's system might prove useful in training teachers and thus inculcating "the improved ideals and feelings" present in European literature. Privately, the younger Mill scoffed at this example of Macaulay's "statesmanship in India," complaining that all his own patient efforts to further Indian education had been "upset in a week by a coxcombical dilettante litterateur who never did a thing for a practical object in his life."[29] Had he known Mill's views, Macaulay would have bristled to think that a man whom he thought a utilitarian doctrinaire, and whose views had for Macaulay the aura of the study, not the legislature, could dismiss his own Indian policies as the impractical projects of a dabbler.

However, when the first two volumes of Macaulay's *History of England* were published in 1848, Mill found them rather better than he had expected. Macaulay was "a man without genius" who was trying to write history in the manner of people with genius, though, characteristically, without the "painful effort." It would be popular, Mill thought, for it appealed to "shallow people with a touch of the new ideas."[30] After the publication of the second two volumes in 1856, Mill saw Macaulay as ministering "to English conceit": "he

33

is very characteristic & so is his book, of the English people & of his time," not high praise from Mill who disliked the self-satisfied insularity of his countrymen. Mill also objected to Macaulay's caricaturing of characters, and observed that the historian's aiming "at stronger effects than truth warrants" in "disregard of consistency & probability spoils the book even as a work of art." For Mill, Grote's *History of Greece*, though less brilliant, was "far more interesting in its simple veracity & because, instead of striving to astonish he strives to comprehend & explain."[31] Mill was unhappy at Macaulay's failure to learn the "scientific" methods of Guizot, Comte, or Michelet. Less fairly, however, Mill's prejudices against Whiggery caused him to ignore Macaulay's considerable virtues as a historian.

III

The starting point of Macaulay's *History* was a natural one for a Whig: the Glorious Revolution and the establishment of political and religious liberty in the reign of William and Mary. Two previous Whig politicians, both much admired by Macaulay, had already written partial histories of the period—the leader of the party at the end of the eighteenth century, Charles James Fox, and its intellectual mentor in the first third of the nineteenth, Sir James Mackintosh. Both Fox and Mackintosh were men who had joined the intellectual life with one of active politics. As Macaulay had observed in an essay in 1835:

> Both had thought much on the principles of government; yet they were not mere speculators. Both had ransacked the archives of rival kingdoms, and pored on folios which had moldered for ages in deserted libraries; yet they were not mere antiquaries. They had one eminent qualification for writing history: they had spoken history, acted history, lived history. The turns of political fortune, the ebb and flow of popular feeling, the hidden mechanism by which parties are moved, all of these things were the subjects of their constant thought and their most familiar conversation.

Yet as historians and politicians, the two earlier Whigs had had contrasting virtues: Fox was by far the greater orator, but his work on the reign of James II resembled a parliamentary report more than sober and judicious history; on the other hand, if "Mr Fox wrote debates," then "Sir James Mackintosh spoke essays."[32] Macaulay, it is clear, saw himself as possessing potentially greater talents in both these realms.

In the *History*, Macaulay wished to display how "from the auspicious union of order and freedom, sprang a prosperity of which the annals of human affairs had furnished no example"; how England had risen from "a state of ignominious vassalage" to "the place of umpire" among the powers; how her public credit, commerce, and maritime strength had made other empires, ancient and modern, seem insignificant. The historian took as his province the period from the accession of James II in 1685, until "a time which is within the memory of men still living." In fact, however, he brought the narrative only to the death of William III in 1701, in part because he was enthralled by the details of the Glorious Revolution and the post-revolutionary Settlement, in part because he suffered from cardiac difficulties which were to end his life, too soon, in 1859. In the early pages of the work, Macaulay declared his intention of telling the history not only of the statesmen but of the common people (their religions, arts, manners, amusements), and thus "cheerfully bear the reproach of having descended below the dignity of history." Although he would describe "great national crimes and follies," Macaulay was convinced that "the general effect of this checkered narrative will be to excite thankfulness in all religious minds, and hope in the breasts of all patriots."[33]

Perhaps the best known part of the first two volumes was Chapter III, Macaulay's description of the state of England in 1685. It was a remarkable accomplishment, and, in some respects, still serves as a model for social historians. Macaulay saw English history as one of a steady, continuous progress that became "portentously rapid" in the eighteenth century, and achieved an even more "accelerated velocity" in the nineteenth.[34] The picture he drew of England at the accession of James II possessed, as a well-drawn historical tableau must, a dynamic quality, a consciousness of the past as well as of the future growth of population, of the economy, and of knowledge and the sciences. In enlivening prose, Macaulay described the state of the army and the navy, of the upper classes and the yeomanry, of the towns and the spas; he depicted the coffeehouses, the London police, the stage coaches and highwaymen, schools, post office, newspapers, inns; he wrote of the education of women, and the immorality of literature; he set down the wages of the laboring classes and discussed the surprising prevalence of child labor in the seventeenth-century clothing factories.

This last observation prompted Macaulay to suggest that "the more carefully we examine the history of the past, the more reason shall we find to dissent from those who imagine that our age has been fruitful of new social evils"; "that which is new is the intelligence which discerns and the humanity which remedies them." On the so-called "condition of England" question which has intermittently absorbed modern historians, Macaulay thus took the optimistic position, which has come to be regarded as the insensitive position. Aside from his loss of access to the common lands, brought about by the improvement of agricultural methods in the eighteenth century, in Macaulay's view the common man of the nineteenth century had benefited enormously from the progress of civilization. Life was now more secure, health was better provided for, and, in consequence, the life span had increased greatly. The historian spoke of the "mollifying influence of civilization": there were fewer beatings in the workshops, in schools, and within the family; there was an enormous increase in compassion for the criminal and in public entertainment; no one in 1685 had sought to protect the child laborer or the black slave or the Indian widow, as people would a century and a half later. Macaulay rejoiced that his own was "a merciful age" in which "cruelty is abhorred," and observed that while every class had gained from this change, "the poorest, the most dependent, and the most defenceless" had gained the most.[35]

Macaulay took note of the peculiar nostalgia of his countrymen and their belief that the England of the seventeenth century was somehow a more desirable place in which to live than the England of Victoria. We overrate the happiness of past generations, he argued, because we are impatient with the faults of our own; but this very impatience served as a goad to continued improvement. There had been, however, no golden age in the past, "when farmers and shopkeepers breakfasted on loaves, the very sight of which would raise a riot in a modern workhouse," and "when men died faster in the purest country air than they now die in the most pestilential lanes of our towns." Macaulay predicted that in the twentieth century workers would be "little used to dine without meat"; that the average life span would increase by several years; that "numerous comforts and luxuries . . . unknown, or confined to a few," would be enjoyed by "every diligent and thrifty workingman." "And yet," Macaulay concluded, "it may then be the mode to assert that the increase of wealth and the progress of science have benefited the few at the expense of the many"[36]—an accurate prediction!

Insofar as the *History* had a central theme, it was that of the uniqueness of English development, which for Macaulay accounted for the many blessings enjoyed by the subjects of Victoria. What had kept England a limited monarchy, on the pattern that prevailed throughout Europe during the fourteenth and fifteenth centuries, Macaulay inquired, while the monarchies of the continental countries had turned absolute in the sixteenth century? In France and in Spain, where the power of the sword and that of the purse had engaged in mortal combat, the parliaments had yielded their fiscal powers to princes whose armies not only protected their kingdoms from foreigners but imposed an absolute royal authority on all classes within the nation. In England, on the other hand, protected by the Channel from invasion, the parliament had maintained and even extended its power because of the King's increasing dependence on the revenues it raised, and because it had acted to prevent the establishment of a great standing army, by means of which continental monarchs had made themselves supreme.[37] The Cromwellian military despotism had confirmed for Englishmen the supreme importance of resisting the establishment of a standing army, as opposed to a popular militia.[38] That a standing army was a threat to liberty became a leading Whig principle from the seventeenth century onward. In all this, Macaulay argued along the lines followed by Machiavelli over three centuries earlier.

In this great year of European revolutions, 1848, in which the first volumes of his *History* were published, Macaulay saw the "peculiar character" of the Glorious Revolution as a consequence of this special English development. Because the limited monarchy of the Middle Ages had survived, the revolutionary changes of 1688 were limited and relatively peaceful; on the continent, on the other hand, after the revolution of 1789, the rebels against a hated absolute rule were "impatient to demolish and unable to construct," and "the violent action of the revolutionary spirit" was followed by an "equally violent" reaction. If Charles I and Strafford had succeeded in establishing the centralized, bureaucratic state at which they had aimed, and had formed a disciplined royal standing army to repress popular discontent, England, too, would have suffered from such bloody and unproductive uprisings. But English parliamentary institutions had remained vigorous, and England in 1688 consequently experienced a revolution which was "strictly defensive."

The Glorious Revolution had been "a vindication of ancient rights," rather than an uprising based upon doctrines of natural rights, of equality or popular sovereignty, Macaulay argued, following the reasoning of his much-admired Burke. "To us, who have lived in the year 1848, it may seem almost an abuse of terms to call a proceeding, conducted with so much deliberation, with so much sobriety, and with such minute attention to prescriptive etiquette, by the terrible name of Revolution." Yet this least violent of revolutions had confirmed the victory of the popular element in the constitution over the monarchical, and had saved liberty. It had provided toleration for religious Dissenters, laid the foundation for the freedom of the press, and established the bases for an independent judiciary and a greater popular control of the legislature. It had been the fount of "every good law" necessary "to promote the public weal, and to satisfy the demands of public opinion" in the future.

"The highest eulogy which can be pronounced on the revolution of 1688," Macaulay concluded, "is this, that it was our last revolution." Englishmen saw that they could secure necessary improvements constitutionally, without violence. It is difficult to resist quoting the peroration, written in November 1848, after the savage uprisings throughout the continent:

All around us the world is convulsed by the agonies of great nations. Governments which lately seemed likely to stand during ages have been on a sudden shaken and overthrown. The proudest capitals of Western Europe have streamed with civil blood. All evil passions, the thirst of gain and the thirst of vengeance, the antipathy of class to class, the antipathy of race to race, have broken loose from the control of divine and human laws. Fear and anxiety have clouded the faces and depressed the hearts of millions. Trade has been suspended, and industry paralyzed. The rich have become poor; and the poor have become poorer. . . . Europe has been threatened with subjugation by barbarians, compared with whom the barbarians who marched under Attila and Alboin were enlightened and humane. The truest friends of the people have with deep sorrow owned that interests more precious than any political privileges were in jeopardy, and that it might be necessary to sacrifice even liberty in order to save civilization.

Meanwhile, in England, all was different:

> . . . in our island the regular course of government has never been for a day interrupted. The few bad men who longed for license and plunder have not had the courage to confront for one moment the strength of a loyal nation, rallied in firm array round a parental throne. And, if it be asked what has made us to differ from others, the answer is that we never lost what others are wildly and blindly seeking to regain. It is because we had a preserving revolution in the seventeenth century that we have not had a destroying revolution in the nineteenth. It is because we had freedom in the midst of servitude that we have order in the midst of anarchy. For the authority of law, for the security of property, for the peace of our streets, for the happiness of our homes, our gratitude is due, under Him who raises and pulls down nations at his pleasure, to the Long Parliament, to the Convention, and to William of Orange.[39]

Macaulay's principal purpose had been served in the first two volumes of the *History*, but the final three cannot be thought, as has been suggested, entirely anticlimactic. In the second two volumes, published in 1857, Macaulay again revealed himself as one able to paint memorable portraits of the men and events of the age, as in his description of the last days of Judge Jeffreys, the character of the Quaker George Fox, and the terrible slaughter at Glencoe in 1692.[40] Macaulay also displayed an ability to present complex economic questions for the general reader, notably in his brilliant discussion of the origin of the national debt, in the course of which he set down another tribute to Edmund Burke, and in his description of the establishment of the Bank of England.[41] In the fifth volume, published posthumously in 1862, Macaulay was to turn his attention to the controversies concerning the restoration of a sound currency, subjects which he remarked were "not such as have generally been thought worthy to occupy a prominent place in history," but which no historian could now dare to ignore.[42] Nor can we pass over Macaulay's illuminating discussion of the early efforts at parliamentary reform, and his learned as well as entertaining account of the moves to achieve greater liberty of the press.[43]

In the posthumous final volume, Macaulay reopened the question of a standing army, so critical to the main theme of his earlier volumes. The issue, as it was to present itself in 1697, was perceived

39

rather differently from the way it had been previously, for this was a time when, the historian argued, the national interest and a concern for liberty were in delicate balance. Having served as the war secretary in the cabinet of Lord Melbourne after his return from India in 1839, Macaulay could the better appreciate the position of one of the heroes of his *History*, the contemplative statesman, Lord Somers. In past times, Macaulay observed, the hostility to a permanent military force had been both "reasonable and salutary"; in the late 1690s, however, the ancient principle had begun to run counter to the national need. The Whig ideologues—like John Trenchard and his supporters who wished to disband William's army—routinely cited the usual sectarian "claptraps and historical commonplaces" and declared it "a fundamental principle of political science that a standing army and a free constitution could not exist together." They cited the city-states of Greece, the Roman Republic, the Italian republics of the Middle Ages, and the French and Spanish monarchies—even as Macaulay had earlier—as well as the more recent example of Cromwell's model army. Both sides in the controversy agreed that Britain required a military force for its defense, but the wielders of the Whiggish argument saw a popular militia as in all ways preferable to a standing army. The more practical-minded protagonists of a standing army, on the other hand, pointed to the large regular forces kept by France, a past and potential enemy, and warned that if England supported an army, it ought not to be an inefficient militia. But our ancestors, Macaulay observed, "were secure where they ought to have been wary and timorous where they might well have been secure."

Understanding the reasons for the deep antagonism to a standing army, and even to a considerable degree influenced by them, Lord Somers, himself a student of ancient literature, countered the precedents cited by the Whig doctrinaires by historical arguments of his own. He chose to steer a middle course. Somers warned that England had to make "a choice between dangers." What might be a risk when considering her internal policy, might be "absolutely essential to her rank among European Powers, and even to her independence," Macaulay observed, in describing Somers' position. "All that a statesman could do in such a case was to weigh inconveniences against each other, and carefully to observe which way the scale leaned.'' This had been the message of Somers' treatise known as the Balancing Letter in which he had recommended a temporary army, fixed annually by parliament, which would effectively serve the purposes of a regular standing army but would constitute no threat to liberty. This was, of course, the compromise that England finally adopted, one which, in Macaulay's view, had helped to preserve both her freedom and her security. This political expedient had been the amalgam of both principle and the experience of practical political life.[44]

Macaulay regarded the position of Somers and that of another contemplative statesman of the seventeenth century, Lord Halifax, as he did his own. Like Somers, he wished to be ''one who looked on the history of past ages with the eye of a practical statesman, and on the events which were passing before him with the eye of a philosophical historian.''[45] Certainly Macaulay's temper was the pragmatic one of the Balancing Letter: principles, such as the opposition to a standing army, had sometimes to yield to the facts as they were to be found in the particular case of England's new circumstances. This was one of the fruits of Macaulay's union of the active and contemplative lives, as it had been for Somers, and also for Halifax. The latter, we know, has achieved an unsavory reputation as an unprincipled Trimmer. For the Whig historian, however, Halifax, in what some regarded as constant shifts, had behaved with a steady intelligence:

> to have been the foremost champion of order in the turbulent Parliament of 1680, and the foremost champion of liberty in the servile parliament of 1685; to have been just and merciful to Roman Catholics in the days of the Popish Plot, and to [extreme Protestant] Exclusionists in the days of the Rye House Plot; . . . this was a course which contemporaries, heated by passion, and deluded by names and badges, might not unnaturally call fickle, but which deserves a very different name from the late justice of posterity.

Macaulay might well have desired as an appropriate obituary for himself, in his dual role as historian and statesman, what he concluded of Halifax:

> For what distinguishes him from all other English statesmen is this, that, through a long public life, and through frequent and violent revolutions

of public feeling, he almost invariably took that view of the great questions of his time which history has finally adopted."[46]

IV

"Nothing is easier," Macaulay declared in a speech to the House of Commons in 1833, "than to write a theme for severity, for clemency, for order, for liberty, for a contemplative life, for an active life, and so on": "when we come to the real business of life, the value of these commonplaces depends entirely on the particular circumstances of the case."[47] To argue only one side of hoary antinomies was for the rhetorician or the ideologue, not for the contemplative statesman who was Macaulay's ideal. The latter understood the need that both parts of an antinomy be put into balance. He acted on the basis of a right historical reason, even as the good historian never forgot the practical side of politics. Macaulay was a man whose understanding of both history and political realities had taught him to be wary of unbending abstractions that became all too swiftly irrelevant to the facts. Yet an exclusively practical interest in the day-to-day necessities of the State, a concern not informed by historical understanding, was equally dangerous. If the first frequently led to the imposition of a tyranny based on an inflexible ideology, the second, ignorant of history, was likely to repeat its grossest errors, and to incite rebellion.

History had proved that to impose the conceptions of the contemplative upon the active life led to dogmatism and fanaticism. The seventeenth-century Puritan enthusiasts, despite all their virtues, were condemned by Macaulay for their bigoted vision of what God had commanded. Similarly, the philosophical Radicals of the nineteenth-century, in Macaulay's view, might as readily move to a system of repression, erected on a rigid logic, in their effort to secure their moral goal of "the greatest happiness of the greatest number." When the contemplative man turned to political action, he usually found himself unfitted for the thousand acts of petty ruthlessness that the necessities of power imposed. A determined ideologue, however, might adjust all too well, so confident would he be of the truth of his vision. He became a Savonarola, a Calvin, a Robespierre, or a Lenin.

Macaulay, possibly uniquely, seems to have turned to politics primarily so that he might write his *History*, a circumstance which helped to remove him from many of the severities of the contest for power, and to have spared him the intellectual and moral deformities to which that struggle, unalloyed, often gives rise. His parliamentary skills had helped to secure him the independent income necessary to scholarship. His political services, not only on the backbenches but in cabinets, had given him the experience in matters of state to which he had attributed both Fox's and Mackintosh's virtues as historians. Persuaded, as he was, that he had contributed to having eased the path of his country through the difficult days of the 1830s and 1840s, when England was threatened by social upheaval, he wished to erect for posterity a literary monument which would memorably embody the lessons he had learned from historical models, lessons which his career in active politics had confirmed. This was a worthy ambition, and its realization sufficiently compensates for his defects as a writer of history.

Mill was probably right in seeing Macaulay's faults as much like those of his countrymen in the hey-day of the *Pax Britannica*. If, at times, we despair that Macaulay did not have a sufficient sense of the tragic in history, was too complacent in his view of the special position of England or of the benevolent role of the middle-classes, and too naive concerning the inevitability of progress, we can attribute these deficiencies not only to his own temperament, but to the somewhat repellent self-satisfaction of his class and his nation during this period. Not that Macaulay was unaware of the faults of early Victorian society, but his social conscience, clearly different from that of a Carlyle or a Dickens or a Mill, and in good part shaped by his sense of the long sweep of historical development, made it possible for him to achieve what some of his contemporaries, and certainly posterity, thought an unfeeling detachment. That he was correct in seeing the condition of the industrial workers as better than that of their predecessors, for example, or in his view that there would be further improvement, somehow did not and does not excuse an apparent lack of sensitivity to an era, like our own, which prides itself on this quality. Nor, if we are to judge by the success of Dickens, would a display of such sensitivity have deprived Macaulay of the coveted place of his *History* on every lady's boudoir table in his own time.

But Macaulay was the contemplative statesman, not the sentimental reformer. He avoided the great sin of the political intellectual who has become the captive of a sectarian doctrine, whether that creed stemmed from the French Revolution in his day or the Russian in ours. Like Burke who denounced inflexible Jacobin "abstraction" in favor of principle derived from experience, Macaulay saw ideology as subversive of the liberal precepts tested by history and validated by the consensus of the best minds of the past. Because the principles he thought important were not part of a metaphysical system, which an ideological age demands as a sign of seriousness, our somewhat narrow-sighted and present-minded generation has dismissed them as conventional or even hypocritical pieties. But we have not advanced so far that we can easily set aside Macaulay's opposition to tyranny and bigotry, his rejection of an imposed vision of a single Truth, and his devotion to both liberty and order, passions he shared with Milton and Mill. Macaulay was the pragmatic liberal who was guided by the lessons of the past, as well as the historian who understood the realities of politics, an appropriate model for a society which wishes, in its course of improvement, to preserve freedom.

NOTES

1. See, for example, Herbert Butterfield, *The Whig Interpretation of History* (London, 1951).
2. *The Letters of Thomas Babington Macaulay*, ed. Thomas Pinney (Cambridge, Eng., 1974), I, 133.
3. Sir G. O. Trevelyan, *The Life and Letters of Macaulay* (London, 1923), II, 706-14; see also p. 670. The best recent life of Macaulay is John Clive, *Macaulay: The Shaping of the Historian* (New York, 1973).
4. T. B. Macaulay, "Fragments of a Roman Tale" (*Knight's Quarterly Magazine*, June 1823), *Critical, Historical, and Miscellaneous Essays and Poems* (New York, 1895), I, 12, 15, 18 ff. [Hereafter *Essays.*]
5. Lord Macaulay, *Speeches and Poems* (Cambridge, Mass., 1877), II, 241 ff. [Hereafter, *Speeches.*]
6. *Ibid.*, II, 160 (verses 22 and 23).
7. Macaulay, "Machiavelli" (*Edinburgh Review*, Mar. 1827), *Essays*, I, 224, 226 ff., 212, 204-07, 220 ff.
8. Macaulay, "A Conversation between Mr. Abraham Cowley and Mr. John Milton Touching the Great Civil War" (*Knight's Quarterly Magazine*, Aug. 1824), *Essays*, I, 90-96, 100-04.
9. Macaulay, "Milton" (*Edinburgh Review*, Aug. 1825), *Essays*, I, 150, 170, 177 f., 190, 182.

10. See Trevelyan, *Macaulay*, II, 448 and fn.

11. Macaulay, "Warren Hastings" (*Edinburgh Review*, Oct. 1841), *Essays*, II, 628.

12. Macaulay, "William Pitt" (*Encyclopedia Britannica*, Jan. 1859), *Essays*, III, 348-50.

13. Macaulay, "Jewish Disabilities" (House of Commons, Apr. 17, 1833), *Speeches*, I, 157.

14. See Macaulay, "Dissenters' Chapels Bill" (House of Commons, June 6, 1844), *Speeches*, I, 387, 394, 399-403.

15. Macaulay, "Jewish Disabilities," *Speeches*, I, 154.

16. Macaulay, "Maynooth" (Apr. 14, 1845), *Speeches*, I, 432-50; see also "The Church of Ireland" (Apr. 23, 1845), *ibid.*, I, 451-76.

17. See Macaulay, "Mill on Government" (*Edinburgh Review*, Mar. 1829), *Essays*, I, 388-420; also, "Utilitarian Theory of Government" (*Edinburgh Review*, Oct. 1829), *ibid.*, I, 447-75.

18. J. S. Mill, *Autobiography* (New York, 1960), pp. 110-13.

19. See Mill to E. Lytton Bulwer, Nov. 23, 1836, in *The Earlier Letters of John Stuart Mill, 1812-1848*, ed. F. E. Mineka (Toronto, 1963), I, 312.

20. See Trevelyan, *Macaulay*, II, 671.

21. Mill, *Autobiography*, pp. 79 f., 45.

22. Mill to T. Carlyle, May 18, 1833, *Earlier Letters*, I, 155.

23. Mill to Bulwer, Nov. 23, 1836, *Earlier Letters*, I, 311 f.

24. J. S. to Harriet Mill, *The Later Letters of John Stuart Mill, 1849-1873*, ed. F. E. Mineka and D. N. Lindley (Toronto, 1972), I, 332.

25. See Mill to John Sterling, Nov. 1842, *Earlier Letters*, II, 557.

26. See Macaulay, "Government of India" (House of Commons, July 10, 1833), *Speeches*, I, 172.

27. See Macaulay, "Sir James Mackintosh" (*Edinburgh Review*, July 1835), *Essays*, II, 101 f.

28. Macaulay, "The Gates of Somnauth" (House of Commons, Mar. 9, 1843), *Speeches*, I, 331-33.

29. Mill to Henry Taylor, [1837], *Later Letters*, IV, Appendix I, 1969-70 and fn. 3.

30. Mill to Harriet Taylor, Jan. 27, 1849, *Later Letters*, I, 5 f.

31. Mill to Arthur Hardy, Sept. 29, 1856, *Later Letters*, II, 511.

32. Macaulay, "Sir James Mackintosh," *Essays*, II, 83 ff.

33. T. B. Macaulay, *The History of England from the Accession of James the Second* (New York, 1899), I, Chap. I, pp. 1-3. [Hereafter, *History*.]

34. Macaulay, *History*, I, Chap. III, pp. 275 f.

35. *Ibid.*, I, 412, 415-18.

36. *Ibid.*, I, 418-20.

37. *Ibid.*, I, Chap. I, pp. 41 ff.

38. *Ibid.*, I, 115-22.

39. *Ibid.*, II, Chap. X, pp. 643-51.

40. *Ibid.*, III, Chap. XIV, pp. 393-98; IV, Chap. XVII, pp. 136-42; and IV, Chap. XVIII, pp. 300-26.

41. *Ibid.*, IV, Chap. XIX, pp. 426-39; Chap. XX, pp. 595-608. Burke's economic wisdom is discussed on p. 435, and in fn. on p. 438.

42. *Ibid.*, V, Chap. XXI, pp. 81-98, and *passim.*

43. *Ibid.*, IV, Chap. XIX, pp. 439-46; pp. 455-69. See also V, Chap. XXI, pp. 64-69; Chap. XXII, pp. 229-31.

44. *Ibid.*, V, Chap. XXIII, pp. 267-91.

45. *Ibid.*, V, Chap. XXIII, pp. 273 f.

46. *Ibid.*, V, Chap. XXI, p. 8. An excellent discussion of the Whigs and Trimming may be found in Joseph Hamburger, *Macaulay and the Whig Tradition* (Chicago, 1976), pp. 115-65, and *passim.*

47. Macaulay, "Repeal of the Union with Ireland" (Feb. 6, 1833), *Speeches*, I, 138 f.

JOHN HENRY NEWMAN:
THE VICTORIAN EXPERIENCE

MARTIN J. SVAGLIC

Much of the literature of England in the nineteenth and twentieth centuries has been dominated by the search for a balance of intellect and spirit and sensibility that would restore mankind to that harmony and integrity it once enjoyed before the Fall, whenever and in whatever fashion that unhappy event is conceived as occurring. Blake, Wordsworth, Coleridge, Shelley, Arnold, Pater, Henry James, E. M. Forster, and D. H. Lawrence among others, all in their own distinctive ways, illustrate that search. In the conclusion of his essay on Boswell's *Life of Johnson*, Carlyle described its goal as the reconciliation of "the two grand antagonisms of Europe," which he found "embodied under their highest concentration" in Samuel Johnson and David Hume: "They were the two half-men of their time: whoso should combine the intrepid Candour and decisive scientific Clearness of Hume, with the Reverence, the Love and devout Humility of Johnson, were the whole man of a new time." John Stuart Mill found many of the same antipodal tendencies in Bentham and Coleridge and tried to combine them in his own enriched and humanized utilitarianism.

Many Victorians who had no inclination to abandon their Christianity but wished at the same time to retain their rationality and openness to the modern world found an embodiment of this ideal in John Henry Newman. Some of these were his colleagues or disciples in the Oxford Movement who remained in the Church of

England. Others were or more often became Roman Catholics, and many of the latter produced an extraordinary Catholic literary revival lasting almost a hundred years, from the time of the poet Hopkins, who wished to edit Newman's *Grammar of Assent* (Newman politely declined, feeling the book would have to make it on its own), to that of the novelist Muriel Spark, who co-edited a volume of his letters. That unique movement appears to be in abeyance now, perhaps as a result of the crisis of authority in the Roman Church. In any event, what his followers saw in Newman was what T. S. Eliot saw in ranking him only below Pascal as a Christian writer especially "to be commended . . . to those who doubt, but who have the mind to conceive, and the sensibility to feel, the disorder, the futility, the meaninglessness, the mystery of life and suffering, and who can only find peace through a satisfaction of their whole being."[1]

Newman and Mill seemed to some Victorians, at least, the Coleridge and Bentham of their day. As Leslie Stephen put it, "Newman and J. S. Mill were nearly contemporaries; they were probably the two greatest masters of philosophical English in recent times; and the mind of the same generation will bear the impress of their speculation."[2] W. G. Ward, the stormy petrel of the Oxford Movement, was first a disciple of Mill and then for the rest of his life, with whatever disagreements, of Newman. Mark Pattison was first a follower of Newman and then, after Newman's "secession," turned, with much of Oxford, to the sceptical rationalism of Mill: coincident with Newman's departure from Anglicanism came "the appearance of Mill's great work, and Oxford repudiated at once sacerdotal principles and Kantian logic. There was, in the language of the clerical platform, an outbreak of infidelity. For more than a quarter of this century Mill and nominalistic views reigned in the schools."[3]

Newman, however, like his friend Hurrell Froude "an Englishman to the backbone in his adherence to the real and the concrete," was himself well read in Bacon, Locke, and Hume, and has been called a child of the empiricist tradition philosophically.[4] "Mill is not separated from Newman," said Leslie Stephen, "as he was separated from Coleridge or Maurice, by radical differences of intellectual temperament. Newman is, like Mill, a lover of the broad daylight; of clear, definite, tangible statements. There is no danger

48

with him of losing ourselves in that mystical haze which the ordinary common sense of mankind irritates and bewilders. . . ." And he adds significantly: "The resemblance might be extended to another point. Newman has a scepticism of his own, which sometimes coincides with and sometimes exceeds the scepticism of Mill."[5]

In his eighty-fifth year, Newman, whose whole adult life had been devoted to sustaining dogmatic Christianity against the unbelief that grew ever more pervasive in the intellectual world, could say to his future biographer that "it had always seemed to him that the whole quarrel between belief and unbelief turned upon the first principles assumed, and the great difficulty is that you *must* assume something; and yet how are you to prove that our assumptions are right and the infidels' wrong?"

> In trying to prove, you must have assumptions, thus it is vain to attempt to *prove* your assumptions. If a man says to me conscience does not to me carry an intimation of a Holy God, Christianity does not appeal to me as satisfying my highest nature; many of its details seem to be *contrary* to the instincts of my better nature, e.g., eternal punishment and original sin; an eternal destiny seems to me out of proportion to human nature; we are 'over gude for banning and over bad for blessing'—if a man comes to me with these first principles I can't answer him, and I certainly can't prove to him Christianity or Theism are true. I can only say I think differently and that I believe him to be wrong.[6]

Thus when Fitzjames Stephen asked Newman in conversation to give him some "reasonable ground" for believing that "you and your church" are "agents and mouthpiece of Almighty God," Newman "appears to have replied in substance that he could not argue with a man who differed so completely upon first principles." And presumably feeling that he had triumphed, Fitzjames reported that Newman "had absolutely nothing to say."[7]

Of course Newman, who believed that it was as useless to attempt to argue a man into belief as to torture him into it, had his own way of dealing with such doubts and difficulties, or he could hardly have come to be regarded as one of the great modern defenders of Christian orthodoxy. But what should be stressed at the outset is that his strong hold on or at least fascination for so many diverse modern writers is his breathtaking insight into the problems of unbelief implied in Huxley's well-known remark that one could compile a primer of infidelity from his writings. More than one Victorian writer, like A. M. Fairbairn, the principal of Mansfield College, who attacked Newman in the May 1885 *Contemporary Review*, was convinced that Newman was at heart a sceptic who had somehow willed himself into belief. And Newman himself admitted in a famous existentialist passage in the fifth chapter of the *Apologia*, that from a spiritual point of view, the world was a vision to "dizzy and appal," with no reflection of its Creator and only "faint and broken" tokens of a superintending design. Indeed, he said, were it not for the voice of conscience speaking in his heart, he would himself be "an atheist, or a pantheist, or a polytheist."

Few have set down more soberly than Newman the possible foolishness of a commitment to Christianity such as he had called for in his famous sermon "The Ventures of Faith," or more seductively the charms of a life of refined epicurean humanism that he was clearly attracted to and might well have chosen for himself had it not been for the faith in God that he somehow never lost after his first conversion at the age of fifteen. As he told Wilfrid Ward,

> I could talk to you for half an hour . . . on the common sense of worldliness and the folly of other worldliness. This life is secure and before us. The Christian ideal of life is disproportionate to our nature as we see it. It is based on unreal enthusiasm. Let us make sure of what is before us. Let us perfect our nature in all its aspects and not give the abnormal and unnatural preponderance to the ethical aims which Christianity demands. We speak of our nature as testifying to Christianity. But is this true? Is it not only a mood which so testifies? Does not the calm sober study of mankind and of human nature *as a whole* lead us to wish for a *mens sana in corpore sano*, a nature healthy and well developed in its artistic, its intellectual, its scientific, its social capacities, as well as in its moral? Is not the ideal Christian life a very risky venture, based perhaps on a conclusion due to prejudice and fanaticism? This is at least too possible a *hypothesis* to make it wise to venture all in the supposition that Christianity is true and give up the certain pleasures of this life for what is at best so uncertain.[8]

Though he could always remind himself that "man is born for labour, not for self," and that "He who takes his ease in this world, will have none in the world to come," he could nonetheless delightedly realize in imagination a "life in the country in the midst of one's own people, an *otium cum dignitate*" dreamed of by poets from Virgil to Juvenal as "the very type of human happiness."

"If indeed there were no country beyond the grave," Newman

tells us, "it would be our wisdom to make of our present dwelling-place as much as ever we could. . . ."

> Easy circumstances, books, friends, literary companions, the fine arts . . . elegant simplicity, gravel walks, lawns, flower beds, trees and shrubberies, summer houses, strawberry beds, a greenhouse, a wall for peaches, "hoc erat in votis";—nothing out of the way, no hot-houses, graperies, pineries,—"Persicos odi, puer, apparatus,"—no mansions, no parks, no deer, no preserves; these things are not worth the cost, they involve the bother of dependants, they interfere with enjoyment. One or two faithful servants, who last as the trees do, and cannot change their place. . . . We must have acquaintance within reach, yet not in the way; ready, not troublesome or intrusive. We must have something of name, or of rank, or of ancestry, or of past official life, to raise us from the dead level of mankind, to afford food for the imagination of our neighbors, to bring us from time to time strange visitors and to invest our house with mystery. In consequence we shall be loyal subjects, good conservatives, fond of old times, averse to change, suspicious of novelty, because we know perfectly when we are well off, and that in our case "progredi *est* regredi." To a life such as this, a man is more attached, the longer he lives; and he would be more and more happy in it too, were it not for the *memento* within him, that books and gardens do not make a man immortal; that though they do not leave him, he at least must leave them, all but the "hateful cypresses," and must go where the only book is the book of doom, and the only garden the Paradise of the just."⁹

Neither a social conscience devoted to what he called "the improvement of mankind," nor a late developed and somewhat impoverished sensibility would ever have allowed Mill to write quite like this, any more than we would expect to learn of him that he was a violinist who at times had to put down his instrument, as Newman did, to cry out at the pleasure the Beethoven quartets were giving him. Yet Mill and Newman looked at some things, especially the Christians around them, with much the same eye. Both used the same word to describe or to explain the lapses and failures of professed Christians. They simply did not *realize* in imagination the nature and implications of what they claimed to believe, and hence all too often they did not behave like Christians. As Mill put it in *On Liberty*,

> To what extent doctrines intrinsically fitted to make the deepest impression upon the mind may remain in it as dead beliefs, without ever being realized in the imagination, the feelings, or the understanding, is

51

exemplified by the manner in which the majority of believers hold the doctrines of Christianity. By Christianity I here mean what is accounted such by all churches and sects—the maxims and precepts contained in the New Testament. They are considered sacred, and accepted as laws, by all professing Christians. Yet it is scarcely too much to say that not one Christian in a thousand guides or tests his individual conduct by reference to those laws. The standard to which he does refer it, is the custom of his nation, his class, or his religious profession. He has thus, on the one hand, a collection of ethical maxims, which he believes to have been vouchsafed to him by infallible wisdom as rules for his government; and on the other, a set of every-day judgments and practices, which go a certain length with some of those maxims, not so great a length with others, stand in direct opposition to some, and are, on the whole, a compromise between the Christian creed and the interests and suggestions of a worldly life. To the first of these standards he gives his homage; to the other his real allegiance. Christians are not insincere when they say they believe such Christian doctrines as that they should judge not lest they be judged or should love their neighbor as themselves. They do believe them, as people believe what they have always heard lauded and never discussed. But in the sense of that living belief which regulates conduct, they believe these doctrines just up to the point to which it is usual to act upon them. . . . The doctrines have no hold on ordinary believers—are not a power in their minds. They have a habitual respect for the sound of them, but no feeling which spreads from the words to the things signified, and forces the mind to take them in, and make them conform to the formula.

And Mill adds wryly: "When their enemies said of the early Christians, 'See how they love one another' (a remark not likely to be made by anybody now), they assuredly had a much livelier feeling of the meaning of their creed than they have ever had since."[10]

There is virtually nothing in this withering passage which could not have been said by Newman, indeed was not said in one or more of those four o'clock sermons at St. Mary's that were reputed to have put all other sermons out of the market when they were first published in the 1830s, had perhaps the broadest audience of all Newman's works with the possible exception of the *Apologia*, and have been called, with their "piercing and large insight into character and conscience and motives," an instrument more powerful than the Tracts for "drawing sympathy to the [Oxford] movement. . . . without [Newman's] sermons the movement might never have gone on, certainly would never have been what it was."[11] The hearing or reading of his sermons was indeed the most decisive and influential "Victorian experience" of Newman.[12] That Christians do not "realize in their imagination," as Mill put it, the implications of the doctrines of their religion is the vivid perception that supplies the chief impetus to Newman's sermons and underlies much of his theory of religious belief as outlined in the *University Sermons* and the *Grammar of Assent*: the attempt to make the merely notional *real*, whether for Anglicans earlier or Roman Catholics later: "Reading, as we do, the Gospels from our youth up, we are in danger of becoming so familiar with them as to be dead to their force, and to view them as a mere history. The purpose, then, of meditation is to realize them; to make the facts which they relate stand out before our minds as objects, such as may be appropriated by a faith as living as the imagination which apprehends them."[13] His sermons were unforgettably vivid realizations of Gospel truth.[14]

More than twenty years before Mill delineated the all too-typical Christian's failure to act according to his professed beliefs, his easy compromise between his "creed and the interests and suggestions of a worldly life," Newman had said in one of his most remembered sermons:

> Men allow us Ministers of Christ to proceed in our preaching, while we confine ourselves to general truths, until they see that they themselves are implicated in them, and have to act upon them; and then they suddenly come to a stand; they collect themselves and draw back, and say, 'They do not see *this*—or do not admit *that*'—and though they are quite unable to say why that should not follow from what they already allow, which we show *must* follow, still they persist in saying, that they do not see that it does follow; and they look about for excuses, and they say we carry things too far, and that we are extravagant . . . there is no truth, however overpoweringly clear, but men may escape from it, by shutting their eyes; there is no duty, however urgent, but they may find ten thousand good reasons against it, in their own case. And they are sure to say we carry things too far, when we carry them home to themselves.

Reminding his hearers that "faith consists in venturing on Christ's word without seeing," and that the question is "What have we ventured?", he confesses his fear that the answer is really *nothing*:

> I really fear that most men called Christians, whatever they may profess, whatever they may think they feel, whatever warmth and illumination and love they may claim as their own, yet would go on almost as they

53

do, neither much better nor much worse, if they believed Christianity to be a fable. When young, they indulge their lust, or at least pursue the world's vanities; as time goes on, they get into a fair way of business, or other mode of making money; then they marry and settle; and their interest coinciding with their duty, they seem to be, and think themselves, respectable and religious men; they grow attached to things as they are; they begin to have a zeal against vice and error; and they follow after peace with all men. Such conduct indeed, as far as it goes, is right and praiseworthy. Only I say, it has not necessarily anything to do with religion at all; there is nothing in it which is any proof of the presence of religious principle in those who adopt it; there is nothing they would not do still, though they had nothing to gain from it except what they gain from it now: they do gain something now, they do gratify their present wishes, they are quiet and orderly, because it is in their interest and taste to be so; but they *venture* nothing, they risk, they sacrifice, they abandon nothing on the faith of Christ's word."[15]

The cynicism of Newman, elegantly expressed, is never so scathing as La Rochefoucauld's though it is sometimes mordant. It is more like that of Thackeray, whose work he admired, though quite without the sentimentality by which Thackeray often tempered or, as some would say, blunted its force. And it breaks out over the years throughout his works. Aristo's love for his sister Callista, for instance, "was real, but it would not do to look too closely into the grounds of it. . . . Did she lose her good looks, or her amiable unresisting submission to his wishes, whatever they were, she would also lose her hold upon his affections." And Newman adds, in words that, considering his own sometimes troubled family relations, have the ring of experience: "This is not to make any severe charge against him, considering how it is with the common run of brothers and sisters, husbands and wives."[16] Even in his famous joyful Catholic sermon "The Second Spring," he gives us a harrowing picture of the "ordinary winter" of man's moral nature: "Wait till youth has become age; and not more different is the miniature which we have of him when a boy, when every feature spoke of hope, put side by side of the large portrait painted to his honor, when he is old, when his limbs are shrunk, his eye dim, his brow furrowed, and his hair grey, than differs the moral grace of that boyhood from the forbidding and repulsive aspect of his soul, now that he has lived to the age of man. For moroseness, and misanthropy, and selfishness, is the ordinary winter of that spring."[17]

Ordinary but not inevitable since "grace can, where nature cannot" (*O.S.*, p. 176). Nature versus grace is the central dialectic of Newman's thought. It underlies his major works in much the same way, and with much of the same meaning, as the dialectic of mechanics versus dynamics gives form to the work of Carlyle, whom Newman respected, much more, incidentally than Carlyle did him.[18] Nature pulls us toward the earth and scepticism; grace guides us toward God and religion. The "state of the multitude of men is this—their hearts are going the wrong way; and their real quarrel with religion, if they know themselves, is not that it is strict or engrossing or imperative, but that it is religion. It is religion itself which we all by nature dislike, not the excess merely. Nature tends toward the earth, and God is in heaven."[19] Christians are under "the new law, the law of the Spirit of Christ. We are under grace. That law, which to nature is a grievous bondage, is to those who live under the power of God's presence, what it was meant to be, a rejoicing" (*P.S.*, IV, 16).

Still it does mean "a conflict all through life. We have to master and bring under all we are, all we do, expelling all disorder and insubordination, and teaching and impressing on every part of us, of soul and body, its due place and duty, till we are wholly Christ's in will, affections and reason, as we are by profession, in St. Paul's words [2 Cor. x.5], 'casting down imaginations and every high thing that exalteth itself against the knowledge of God, and bringing into captivity every thought to the obedience of Christ' " (*P.S.*, IV, 5).

It is perhaps not too wide of the mark to say that the many volumes of Newman's sermons, both Anglican and Catholic, have four principal concerns: in the earlier sermons especially, the failings or dangers of Evangelicalism, a religion to which he always felt indebted but which he thought was now substituting a preoccupation with one's own heart and salvation for meditation on the life of Christ and the function of the Church as revealed in Scripture: e.g., "Self-Contemplation" (*P.S.*, II); the nature of faith and its relation to reason, as in the *University Sermons* generally; the importance of reflecting on the examples of Christ and the Prophets for the spiritual and moral lessons they supply: e.g., "Obedience Without Love, as Instanced in the Character of Balaam" (*P.S.*, IV); and perhaps especially the easygoing and optimistic religion of the world, denying the seriousness of sin and any real need for spiritual discipline: e.g., "The Religion of the Pharisee the Religion of Mankind" (*O.S.*).

Of the effect of the sermons delivered at Oxford, at least, and they are the great majority of Newman's published sermons,[20] no Victorian has left a better account than the historian James Anthony Froude, a one-time disciple who, following Newman's conversion in 1845, turned to Carlyle, whose biographer he became, without ever losing his great admiration for Newman's abilities and personal character. "No one who heard his sermons in those days," said Froude, "can ever forget them."

> They were seldom directly theological. . . . Newman, taking some Scripture character for a text, spoke to us about ourselves, our temptations, our experiences. His illustrations were inexhaustible. He seemed to be addressing the most secret consciousness of each of us—as the eyes of a portrait appear to look at every person in a room. He never exaggerated; he was never unreal. A sermon from him was a poem, formed on a distinct idea, fascinating by its subtlety, welcome—how welcome! —from its sincerity, interesting from its originality, even to those who were careless of religion; and to others who wished to be religious, but had found religion dry and wearisome, it was like the springing of a fountain out of the rock.

Froude thought that the sermons were probably "the record of Newman's own mental experience. They appear to me to be the outcome of continual meditation upon his fellow-creatures and their position in the world; their awful responsibilities; the mystery of their nature, strongly mixed of good and evil, of strength and weakness. A tone, not of fear but of infinite pity runs through them all; and along with a resolution to look facts in the face; not to fly to evasive generalities about infinite mercy and benevolence, but to examine what revelation has added to our knowledge, either of what we are or of what lies before us."[21]

If Newman's sermons will always be assigned the highest place among his works, as his modern biographer Louis Bouyer believes, or will be read as long as any of his work, as Gladstone thought, one should not therefore conclude that they are read widely today, any more than, if as much as, most of Victorian prose is now read by large numbers of cultivated readers, even in academia. Geoffrey Tillotson found out as much when, in the Introduction to his Reynard anthology of Newman, he said of the famous *Idea of a Uni-*

versity that there could be few educated people who had not read it. He was challenged by the critic Raymond Mortimer to find out if this were so by asking his colleagues at Birkbeck College. He soon found out that it was not.[22] And so I shall attempt to illustrate by quotation some of the preoccupations and merits of Newman's sermons, though realizing how partial a view limitations of space will permit.

Newman's sermons touch on childhood, youth and maturity. The first passage, from one of his less often cited, perhaps, yet most brilliant sermons, is a long one; but it will serve as a shorter quotation could not possibly do to illustrate Newman's method of drawing out in detail the implications of a given situation or fact, his breathtaking psychological acuity, and his frequent anticipation of certain aspects of modern thought that make him still interesting and relevant today when many once famous preachers of his time have been forgotten. The sermon is called "Moral Consequences of Single Sins," and among other things that some readers may be reminded of is a Graham Greene story, "The Basement Room" (*The Fallen Idol* in Carol Reed's skillful but radically altered film version), a story illustrating Greene's idea that in the early years he "would look for the crisis, the moment when life took a new slant on its journey towards death," that as A.E. put it in "Germinal": "In the lost boyhood of Judas/Christ was betrayed."[23] The analogical reasoning of the sermon is another instance of Butler's pervasive influence on Newman's works.

Reflecting on the "probable influence upon us of sins committed in our childhood, and even infancy, which we never realized or have altogether forgotten," Newman proceeds:

> . . . mysterious as it is that infants and children should suffer pain, surely it is not less so that, when they come to years of reason, they should so forget it, as hardly to be able to believe, when told of it, that they themselves were the very sufferers; yet as sickness and accidents then happening permanently affect their body, though they recollect nothing of them, there is no extravagance in the idea that passing sins then contracted and forgotten for ever afterwards, should so affect the soul as to cause those moral differences between man and man which, however originating, are too clear to be denied. And with the fearful thought before us of the responsibility attaching to the first years of our life, how miserable it is to reflect on the other hand that children are commonly treated as if they were not responsible, as if it did not matter

what they did or were. They are indulged, humoured, spoiled, or at best neglected. Bad examples are set them; things are done or said before them, which they understand and catch up, when others least think it, and store in their minds, or act upon; and thus the indelible hues of sin and error are imprinted on their souls, and become as really part of their nature as the original sin in which they were born.

[To such] single or forgotten sins . . . as I have described them, are not improbably to be traced the strange inconsistencies of character which we often witness in our experience of life. I mean, you meet continually with men possessed of a number of good points, amiable and excellent men, yet in one respect perhaps strangely perverted. Perhaps they are weak and over-indulgent toward others, perhaps they are harsh, perhaps they are obstinate, perhaps they are perversely wedded to some wrong opinion, perhaps they are irresolute and undecided,— some fault or other they have, and you lament it, but cannot mend it, and are obliged to take them for what they are. . . . Men are sometimes so good and so great, that one is led to exclaim, Oh that they were only a little better, and a little greater!

[This is true even] with the better sort of Christians; they are deformed in stature, they are not upright, they do not walk perfectly with God. And you cannot tell why it is. . . . when you come to know them well, there is in them this or that great inconsistency.

This consideration moreover tends to account for the strange way in which defects of character are buried in a man. He goes on, for years perhaps, and no one ever discovers his particular failings, nor does he know them himself; till at length he is brought into certain circumstances, which bring them out. Hence men turn out so very differently from what was expected; and we are seldom able to tell beforehand of another, and scarcely ever dare we promise for ourselves, as regards the future. The proverb, for instance, says power tries a man; so do riches, so do various changes of life. We find that after all, we do not know him, though we have been acquainted with him for years. We are disappointed, nay sometimes startled, as if he had almost lost his identity; whereas perchance it is but the coming to light of sins committed long before we knew him (*P.S.*, IV, 40–44, passim).

Though Newman was an admirer of Southey, particularly for the heroic *Thalaba*, and had high regard (though with reservations) for Coleridge, whose apologetic in some ways resembled his own, he was not especially fond of Wordsworth, disliking what struck him as "sacerdotal pretension."[24] Yet one of his favorite poems was and remained the "Ode: Intimations of Immortality," about which such great admirers of Wordworth as Coleridge, Mill, and Arnold all had serious reservations. Presumably it reminded him of the "Platonic" side of his own childhood, when he used to wish that the *Arabian Nights* were true and fancied that he himself might be an angel in a world only deceptively real; and it lamented so memorably the extinction of the visionary gleam by the attractions and preoccupations of life in this world, a favorite theme of Wordsworth and of Newman in his sermons.

"We have most of us by nature," he says, "longings more or less, and aspirations, after something greater than this world can give."

> Youth, especially, has a natural love of what is noble and heroic. We like to hear marvellous tales, which throw us out of things as they are, and introduce us to things as they are not. We so love the idea of the invisible that we even build fabrics in the air for ourselves, if heavenly truth be not vouchsafed us. . . . we imagine some perfection, such as earth has not, which we follow, and render it our homage and our heart. Such is the state more or less of young persons before the world alters them, before the world comes upon them, as it often does very soon, with its polluting, withering, debasing, deadening influence, before it breathes on them, and blights and parches, and strips off their green foliage, and leaves them, as dry and wintry trees without sap or sweetness. But in early youth we stand with our leaves and blossoms on which promise fruit . . . we have not yet come to think, though we are in the way to think, that all that is beyond this world is after all an idle dream.[25]

By the time they have grown into their mature years, most men, if they think seriously of the subject at all, have pretty well accepted the religion of the world, which "considers that all men are pretty much on a level, or that, differ though they may, they differ by such fine shades from each other, that it is impossible, because forsooth it would be untrue and unjust, to divide them into two bodies, or to divide them at all."

> Each man is like himself and no one else; each man has his own opinions, his own rule of faith and conduct, his own worship; if a number join together in a religious form, this is an accident, for the sake of convenience; for each is complete in himself; religion is simply a personal concern; there is no such thing really as a common or joint religion, that is, one in which a number of men, strictly speaking, partake; it is all a matter of private judgment. Hence as they sometimes proceed even to avow, there is no such thing as a true religion or a false; that is true to each, which each sincerely believes to be true; and what is true to one, is not true to his neighbour. There are no special doctrines necessary to be believed in order to salvation; it is not very difficult to be saved; and most men may take it for granted that they shall be saved. . . . There is

no such place as hell, or at least punishment is not eternal. Predestination, election, grace, perseverance, faith, sanctity, unbelief, and reprobation are strange ideas, and, as they think, very false ones. This is the cast of opinion of men in general, in proportion as they exercise their minds on the subject of religion, and think for themselves; and if in any respect they depart from the easy, cheerful, and tranquil temper of mind which it expresses, it is when they are led to think of those who presume to take the contrary view, that is, who take the view set forth by Christ and His Apostles.[26]

The world, then, lives by nature and not by grace. "In truth the world does not know of the existence of grace; nor is it wonderful, for it is ever contented with itself, and has never turned to account the supernatural aids bestowed on it."

Its highest idea of man lies in the order of nature; its pattern man is the natural man. . . . It sees that nature has a number of tendencies, inclinations, and passions; and because these are natural, it thinks that each of them may be indulged for its own sake, so far as it does no harm to others, or to a person's bodily, mental, and temporal wellbeing. It considers that want of moderation, or excess, is the very definition of sin, if it goes so far as to recognise that word. It thinks that he is the perfect man who eats, and drinks, and sleeps, and walks, and directs himself, and studies, and writes, and attends to religion, in moderation. The devotional feelings and the intellect, and the flesh, have each its claim upon us, and each must have play, if the Creator is to be duly honoured. It does not understand, it will not admit, that impulses and propensities, which are found in our nature, as God created it, may nevertheless, if indulged, become sins, on the ground that he has subjected them to higher principles, whether these principles be in our nature, or be superadded to our nature. . . . Concupiscence, it considers, may be indulged, because it is in its first elements natural (*Mix.*, pp. 148–49).

On more secular matters, introduced in his sermons by way of illustrations, Newman could also be stimulating and prophetic. Fearful, like Carlyle and Mill, of the growing influence of uneducated public opinion, in the relative infancy of journalism and long before the mania for polls of one kind or another, he could say, in an early sermon "Unreal Words":

. . . there cannot be a more apposite specimen of unreality than the way in which judgments are commonly formed upon important questions by the mass of the community. Opinions are continually given in the world on matters, about which those who offer them are as little qualified to judge as blind men about colours, and that because they have never exercised their minds upon the points in question. This is a day in which all men are obliged to have an opinion on all questions, political, social, and religious, because they have in some way or other an influence upon the decision; yet the multitude are for the most part absolutely without capacity to take their part in it. In saying this, I am far from meaning that this need be so—I am far from denying that there is such a thing as plain good sense, or (what is better) religious sense, which will see its way through very intricate matters, or that this is a fact sometimes exerted in the community at large on certain great questions; but at the same time this practical sense is so far from existing as regards the vast mass of questions which in this day come before the public that (as all persons who attempt to gain the influence of the people on their side know well) their opinions must be purchased by interesting their prejudices or fears in their favour—not by presenting a question in its real and true substance, but by adroitly colouring it, or selecting out of it some particular point which may be exaggerated, and dressed up, and be made the means of working on popular feelings. And thus government and the art of government becomes, as much as popular religion, hollow and unsound (*P.S.*,V, 3.).

More questionable, perhaps, and paradoxical as coming from one who was both poet and novelist and the author of a Platonic essay like "Poetry, with Reference to Aristotle's Poetics," is the opinion Newman occasionally expressed about literature in general, setting him apart from the romantic idealizers like Shelley or even the humanists like Matthew Arnold. "Literature is almost in its essence unreal," he says, "for it is the exhibition of thought disjoined from practice. . . . Mere literary men are able to say strong things against the opinions of their age, whether religious or political, without offence; because no one thinks they mean anything by them. They are not expected to go forward to act upon them, and mere words hurt no one." (*P.S.*, V, 3.) And much the same could be said for the effect produced on the reader: the danger is that the reading will substitute for the doing.

There is in most of these sermons a note of austerity, almost of fear and trembling, which was unquestionably a part of Newman's nature, a permanent residue of early Calvinist influence. The Catholic Baron von Hügel thought Newman personally lacked the note of joy common in saints. And even the moderate Calvinist preacher and educator of Edinburgh, Alexander Whyte, who had the deepest regard for the sermons, thought that many of them were the last thing he would give to a troubled sinner since Newman did not suf-

61

ficiently emphasize the justifying act of the Redeemer. But von Hügel had little personal contact with Newman, and then only when he was very old; and of course Newman did not share Whyte's evangelical view of justification. Dean Church always found Newman a delightful house guest and companion, even in his later years, and J. A. Froude and others have testified to his general good humor in earlier life. Here, too, as in other matters, the Newman who was from childhood and youth both Platonist and Aristotelian, believer and skeptic, combined opposite traits and tendencies. "Christianity, considered as a moral system," he said, "is made up of two elements, beauty and severity; whenever either is indulged to the loss or disparagement of the other, evil ensues."

In heathen times, Greek and Barbarian in some sense divided these two between them; the latter were the slaves of dreary and cruel superstitions, and the former abandoned themselves to a joyous polytheism. And so again, in these latter times, the two chief forms of heresy into which opposition to primitive truth has developed, were remarkable, at least in their origin three hundred years ago, and at times since, the one for an unrefined and self-indulgent religiousness, the other for a stern, dark, cruel spirit, very unamiable, yet still inspiring more respect than the other.[27]

A more optimistic side of Newman, demonstrating his ability to reconcile opposites, his spiritual if not political democracy, and his appreciation of deep friendship may be seen in one of his most impressive sermons, "The Greatness and Littleness of Human Life," in which he says that the "very greatness of our powers makes this life look pitiful; the very pitifulness of this life forces on our thoughts to another; and the prospect of another gives a dignity to this life which promises it; and thus this life is at once great and little, and we rightly contemn it while we exalt its importance." Our present state in this "attractive but deceitful world" is, indeed,

. . . precious as revealing to us, amid shadows and figures, the existence and attributes of Almighty God and His elect people: it is precious because it enables us to hold intercourse with immortal souls who are on their trial as we are. It is momentous, as being the scene and means of our trial; but beyond this it has no claims upon us. "Vanity of vanities," says the Preacher, "all is vanity." We may be poor or rich, young or old, honoured or slighted, and it ought to affect us no more, neither to elate us nor depress us, than if we were actors in a play, who know that the characters they represent are not their own, and that though they may appear to be superior one to another, to be kings or to be peasants, they are in reality all on a level. The one desire which should move us should be, first of all, that of seeing Him face to face, who is now hid from us; and next of enjoying eternal and direct communication, in and through Him, with our friends around us, whom at present we know only through the medium of sense, by precarious and partial channels, which give us little insight into their hearts (P.S., IV, 222–23).

The phrase "amid shadows and figures" would reappear by Newman's request more than fifty years later as the inscription on his tombstone: *"Ex umbris et imaginibus in veritatem."*

"Joy and gladness," Newman insists, are also "characteristics of the Christian, according to the exhortation in the text, 'Rejoice in the Lord always!, . . .'" While "fearing greatly and trembling greatly at the thought of the Day of Judgment . . . is a great duty, yet the command so to do cannot reverse the command to rejoice. . . . It is as clear a duty to rejoice in the prospect of Christ's coming as if we were not told to fear it. The duty of fearing does but perfect our joy; that joy alone is true Christian joy, which is informed and quickened by fear, and made thereby sober and reverent." If a man tries "both to fear and rejoice, as Christ and His Apostles tell him . . . in time he will learn how," even if he cannot explain in words his fulfillment of "the paradox which Scripture enjoins." ("Equanimity," *P.S.*, V, 65–67.)

However amiable the paradoxical Newman may have ordinarily been to his pupils and those who knew him well, his deepest joy was in solitude, as Oriel's Provost, Edward Copleston, had sensed in Newman's early days there. On crossing his path one day, we are told in the *Apologia*, Copleston said to him in the words of Cicero, *"Nunquam minus solus quam cum solus."* And the Newman who thought that ultimately there were "two and two only absolute and luminously self-evident beings in the world," one's self and one's Creator, provided his own gloss on Copleston's words in the sermon just quoted: ". . . the Christian has a deep, silent, hidden peace, which the world sees not—like some well in a retired and shady place, difficult of access. He is the greater part of his time by himself, and when he is in solitude, that is his real state. What he is when left to himself and to his God, that is his true life. He can hear himself; he can (as it were) joy in himself, for it is the grace of God within him, it is the presence of the Eternal Comforter, in which he joys. He can bear, he finds it pleasant, to be within himself at all times—'never less alone than when alone.'" (*P.S.*, V, 69-70.) In 1852, after a week's rest alone at a friend's house in Limerick, Newman could write to another friend: "The quiet set me up. It is the only thing for me ever. I have never tired of being by myself since I was a boy."[28]

In addition to the eight volumes of *Parochial and Plain Sermons* (1834-1843), Newman also published while at Oxford *Sermons on Subjects of the Day* (1843), of the same general character as the earlier sermons, but containing on publication passages of a more personal tone or nature influenced by developments in the Oxford Movement that he ordinarily avoided touching on in the pulpit: e.g., the sermons (XXI-XXIV) preached on Sundays from November 28 to December 19, 1841, after receiving what he called in the *Apologia* the three blows which broke him; the sermons that especially upset Charles Kingsley ("The Apostolical Christian" and "Wisdom and Innocence"); and especially the haunting "Parting of Friends." In 1843 appeared also his last such volume, *Fifteen Sermons Preached Before the University of Oxford*, a series he had begun as early as 1826 and dealing with the problem he saw as central to his spiritually troubled and divided age: the relations between faith and reason and the possibility that men in general could reach a rational conviction of religious truths. These sermons for many years drew relatively little attention, according to Newman himself some seventeen years later.[29] However, they were to culminate in 1870 in the last of his four chief works, *An Essay in Aid of a Grammar of Assent*, to which much more attention was paid and to which we shall return later.

The final sermon in the *University Sermons* volume was "The Theory of Developments in Religious Doctrine," which was to grow in two years into his last book as an Anglican, another of his major works, *The Development of Christian Doctrine* (1845), broken off when he felt convinced enough of the general argument to join the Roman Catholic Church in October of that year. Under the circumstances, the book naturally attracted great attention, the last of Newman's works to do so until the *Apologia*. He regarded it as a "hypothesis" to account for a difficulty, the differences between modern Catholicism and the primitive Church, differences (e.g., in such matters as the growth of papal authority and the increasing devotion paid to the Virgin Mary) felt long in his own case and so often cited by Protestants as an insuperable objection to Rome.

Newman argued by analogy that the process of development in living ideas that we see in civil life, for example, in the growth of states or the changes of a constitution, developments political, logical, historical, and so on, may likewise be expected in Christianity, Scripture itself showing development through the Old and into the New Testaments. Development is the "process, whether it be longer or shorter in point of time, by which the aspects of an idea are brought into consistency and form. . . ."[30] The view on which the essay was written, Newman maintains,

> . . . has at all times, perhaps, been implicitly adopted by theologians, and, I believe, has recently been illustrated by several distinguished writers of the continent, such as De Maistre and Möhler: viz. that the increase and expansion of the Christian creed and Ritual, and the variations which have attended the process in the case of individual writers and Churches, are the necessary attendants on any philosophy or polity which takes possession of the intellect and heart, and has had any wide or extended dominion; that, from the nature of the human mind, time is necessary for the full comprehension and perfection of great ideas; and that the highest and most wonderful truths, though communicated to the world once for all by inspired teachers, could not be comprehended all at once by the recipients, but, as being received and transmitted by minds not inspired and through media which were human, have required only the longer time and deeper thought for their full elucidation. This may be called the *Theory of Development of Doctrine . . .* (*Dev.*, pp. 29-30).

Thus in Christianity, "[t]aking the Incarnation as its central doctrine, the Episcopate, as taught by St. Ignatius, will be an instance of political development, the *Theotokos* of logical, the determination of the date of our Lord's birth of historical, the holy Eucharist of moral, and the Athanasian Creed of metaphysical." (*Dev.*, p. 54.)

The second and much larger part of the *Essay* sets up and applies seven tests whereby a true development of an idea may be distinguished from a corruption:

(1) Preservation of type, as in the child being father of the man. Newman argues that the pagan world saw Christianity in much the same unflattering terms as the modern world does Catholicism.

(2) Continuity of principles—Languages, institutions, states have their own distinctive principles: e.g., Pericles in his "Funeral Oration" tells us that the Athenian Commonwealth was "carried on, not by formal and severe enactments but by the ethical character and spontaneous energy of the people." (*Dev.* p. 184.) So Catholicism proclaims the principles of dogma and the supremacy of faith.

(3) Power of assimilation—As plants assimilate more or less foreign material in any habitat in which they grow, so Catholicism assimilated temples to saints, images, incense, and so on from pagan religions.

(4) Logical sequence of ideas—As the private judgment of Luther led ultimately in Newman's view to the infidelity of Strauss, so in Catholicism the idea of penance, for instance, leads to the doctrine of purgatory.

(5) Anticipation of its future—The Russians as mere pirates anticipated their later aims towards Constantinople. So in a Church believing that matter is essentially good and that Christ rose in the flesh and carried that flesh with him into heaven, developed the veneration of the bodies and relics of saints and belief in their resurrection from the dead. (*Dev.*, p. 402).

(6) Conservative action upon its past—as in Blackstone's observation that when society is once formed, government results to keep it in order. So the honors paid to Mary have historically resulted in protecting the doctrine of the Incarnation, though to the superficial view it might seem otherwise.

(7) Chronic vigour—As the vigor of the American union shows the republican principle still alive, so the Church has united "vigour with continuance, that is, in its tenacity" (*Dev.*, p. 206).

By applying such tests in detail to ecclesiastical history, Newman grew convinced that the Roman "additions" were indeed true developments and not the corruptions evident in heresies of various kinds, that indeed "to be deep in history is to cease to be a Protestant."

I have briefly outlined the argument of the *Essay on Development* because the book does not seem to be well known or at least widely read in the contemporary university. (Of course this is a rather crude outline of an acute and sophisticated work, and says little or nothing about Newman's methods of reasoning on historical and religious questions, though some of these will be briefly touched on presently in discussing the closely related *Grammar of Assent*.) But the book was very well known in Victorian England, as the many reviews, several of them book-length, indicate. A partial list of these has been provided by Owen Chadwick, of which he says that "Mozley's reply is the most convincing, Palmer's the most learned and Milman's the most amusing."[31]

The noisiest and long the most persistent, at any rate, was that of the feisty American convert from Unitarianism, Orestes Brownson, who reacted against the American Unitarian citing of Newman's work as proof that the doctrine of the Trinity was a later development. He himself rigidly held Bossuet's view of development, without any appeal to the history the great Bishop believed it rested on. Newman's view, he said, was that the Church "at first cannot take in all revealed truth. She has it all stowed away somewhere, but she only partially apprehends it. As time goes on, individuals differently circumstanced view it under different particular aspects and from opposite poles; as new controversies arise, bold and obstinate heretics start up, some clamorous for one particular aspect, and some for another, she is able to enlarge her view, to augment the number of her dogmas, and tell us more truly what is the revelation she has received." And Brownson thundered:

And this we are to say of a Church we are defending as authoritative and infallible, and which we hold has received the formal commission to teach all nations whatsoever our Lord commanded his Apostles! In plain words, was the Church able to teach truly and infallibly the age of Saints Clement and Polycarp, or of Saints Julian and Irenaeus, the whole Catholic faith, on any and every point which could be made,—or was she not? If she was, there can have been no development of doctrine; if she was not, she was not then competent to discharge the commission she received? Was what she then taught the faithful sufficient for salvation? Is not what was then sufficient all that is really necessary now? If so, and if she teaches doctrine now which she did not then, or insists on our believing now what she did not then, how will you exonerate her from the charge brought by Protestants, that she added to the primitive faith, and teaches as of necessity to salvation what is not necessary. . . . Moreover where are these developments to stop?[32]

Eventually Brownson made his peace with Newman, who even invited him to become a Professor in the new Catholic University in Dublin, an offer he declined and one which some thought rather craven on Newman's part. But by that time Brownson, after reading Newman's story of a convert called *Loss and Gain*, had changed his mind about Newman's orthodoxy and had written him to apologize for his earlier misunderstanding.[33]

J. B. Mozley, who later became Regius Professor of Divinity at Oxford and whom Dean Church regarded as "after Mr. Newman, the most forcible and impressive of the Oxford writers (*Oxford Movement*, p. 293), was, until his own theological views changed somewhat, long active in support of the Oxford Movement and editor of its organ, *The Christian Remembrancer*, in the January 1847 number of which he reviewed Newman's *Development*. Recalling the Anglo-Catholic view that Protestantism may diminish or dilute Christian truth, whereas "the Roman system . . . in various doctrines, keeping the original type . . . has introduced an exaggerated corruption of it," Mozley charged that in concentrating on "the *destruction* of the special laws or principles of a development" as 'the corruption of an idea' and that only, Newman largely ignored "the whole notice of corruption by excess. Corruption being defined to be loss of type, it follows that exaggeration, which is not this, is not corruption. . . . Whereas . . . the ordinary charge maintained by English divines against the Roman system is . . . that of exaggeration, and abuse in exaggeration, we have here a definition of corruption which excludes exaggeration from its meaning. . . . [Newman] has only to say that Roman doctrines have not destroyed or reversed the ideas and feelings in which they arose . . . and immediately no absence whatever of measure in extent of expansion, growth, development can make corruptions of them. They are secure by the definition, and have a pledge of faultlessness which no controversialist can touch."[34] Though he read some of his critics, according to Chadwick (p. 164), "it must be said at once that none of their criticisms, not even the reluctant but powerful examination to which Mozley subjected the essay, had the least effect upon Newman's mind. There is no scrap of evidence that he later altered a single line in response to any of these early Anglican critics.''

As for the agnostic view of Newman's development, T. H. Huxley took a line similar to James Mill's after the latter had read Butler's *Analogy of Religion* and decided that it was decisive not only against the Deists but against the Christians and all other believers as well. Butler was, of course, a most profound influence on Newman, who argued analogically throughout the *Essay on Development*, as when he says, for instance, "it is not a greater difficulty that St. Ignatius [of Antioch] does not write to the Asian Greeks about Popes, than that St. Paul does not write to the Corinthians about Bishops. And it is a less difficulty that the Papal supremacy was not formally acknowledged in the second century, than that there was no formal acknowledgment on the part of the Church of the doctrine of the Holy Trinity till the fourth. No doctrine is defined till it is violated.'' (*Dev.*, p. 151)

Agreeing with Newman's similar argument in his second *Essay on Miracles* (1842–1843) that it is difficult or impossible logically to draw a line between acceptance of the miracles of the Bible and those of Church history—that if one may be true, all may be true, and if one false, all false, Huxley describes it as a method of reasoning "applied to the confutation of Protestantism with so much success by one of the acutest and subtlest disputants who have ever championed Ecclesiasticism—and one cannot put his claims to acuteness and subtlety higher.'' Of Newman's remark in the *Essay of Development* that "the Christianity of history is not Protestantism'' and that "to be deep in history is to cease to be a Protestant,'' Huxley says:

> I have not a shadow of doubt that these anti-Protestant epigrams are profoundly true. But I have as little that, in the same sense, the "Christianity of history is not'' Romanism; and that to be deeper in history is to cease to be a Romanist. The reasons which compel my doubts about the compatibility of the Roman doctrine, or any other form of Catholicism, with history, arise out of exactly the same line of argument as that adopted by Dr. Newman in the famous essay which I have just cited. If, with one hand, Dr. Newman has destroyed Protestantism, he has annihilated Romanism with the other; and the total result of his ambidextral efforts is to shake Christianity to its foundations.[35]

Of the next two of Newman's four major works, *The Idea of a*

University and the *Apologia pro Vita Sua*, little need be said here, though for very different reasons. The former was first published in Dublin in 1852 as *Discourses on the Scope and Nature of University Education*, with a second and somewhat revised edition in London in 1859, and a third edition in London in 1873, enlarged to include the *Lectures and Essays on University Subjects* published separately at first in 1858. The final title was *The Idea of a University Defined and Illustrated*. It appears to have attracted little attention: ". . . The Discourses, the Lectures and Essays, and finally the *Idea* itself were all passed over in the columns of the leading Victorian periodicals, apart from two reviews in the two principal Catholic journals, the *Rambler* and the *Dublin Review*."[36] This may seem strange considering such familiar encomia as Walter Pater's ("the perfect handling of a theory") and later that of Arthur Quiller-Couch: "Of all the books written in these hundred years there is perhaps none you can more profitably thumb and ponder." But one must remember that the book was first rather obscurely published in Dublin and, more important, that it appeared before the triumph of the *Apologia* had done so much to rehabilitate Newman's reputation in non-Catholic England.

Richard Simpson's review of the earlier version in the *Rambler* (II, 1853) was highly enthusiastic, but the ultramontane W. G. Ward criticized the book (*Dublin Review*, n.s. 21, 1873) for insufficient emphasis on religion and for over-valuing intellectual culture. An interesting reaction came from Mark Pattison, saying that "Nothing can be grander than the development of the idea [of education]" in Newman's volume and quoting his view that "all knowledge whatever is taken into account in a university, as being the special seat of that large philosophy which embraces and locates truth of every kind, and every method of attaining it."

Thus thought Newman in 1852. Are we to suppose that this magnificent ideal of a national institute, embracing and representing all knowledge, and making this knowledge its own end, was the wisdom of riper years —a vision which grew up in Newman's mind in the course of the twenty or more years which elapsed between the Oriel tutorship and the Dublin presidency? Perhaps so; it required much time and mental enlargement for any of us, who were brought up under the old eight-book system of an Oxford college of 1830, to rise to the idea of a university in which every science should have its proper and appointed place. Newman may have been no exception. At any rate, during the time of his Oriel tutorship, there is no sign that he had any loftier conception of the duties of a tutor than his friends H. Froude and Mozley. . . . Religion was evidently to Newman in 1830, not only the first but the sole object of all teachings. There was no thought then . . . of a genealogical chart of all the sciences; there was not even the lesser conception of education by the classics, as containing the essential elements of humanism.

Some of this is probably true enough, for no doubt Newman grew with the years, and he did admit to being rather "fierce" in the early days of the Movement. But considering the tributes of later Oxonians like J. A. Froude to Newman's breadth and balance, it does seem to be extreme. Of course one must remember that Pattison was writing in the heat of an almost Swinburnian reaction against the "triumph of the church organization over the wisdom and philosophy of the Hellenic world . . . , which, to the Humanist, is the saddest moment in history"; and that to him, the teachers of the classics at Oxford, including Newman, "had sided with the enemies of humanism" (*Memoirs*, pp. 95–96).

If little need be said of the *Idea* because for a long time little was said, even less need be said about the *Apologia* because the book itself and the story of its triumph, proclaimed by the leading journals of the day, are so well known. A sampling of the principal reviews is provided in the present writer's Introduction to the O.E.T. edition of the *Apologia* (1967, p. xliii–lii). However, after examining some fifty contemporary reviews of the book from a variety of less well-known sources, Vincent Blehl pointed out that the chorus of praise was less widely echoed than one would gather from Wilfred Ward's *Life of Newman*. Blehl describes the situation as "exceedingly complex, subtle, and nuanced,"[37] which it may well have been. In reading over his excerpts from contemporary reviews, however, one gets the impression that a good many of the journals simply reached conclusions determined by their own religious or philosophical bent, a fact which is hardly surprising at almost the same time Arnold was pleading for disinterestedness in "The Function of Criticism at the Present Time" and lamenting the domination of England's political and religious life by party spirit.

As Blehl says, "The *Westminster Review*, for example, used the *Apologia* to advocate a liberal, rationalistic attitude towards religion. . . . The reviewer argued that it was illogical for Protestants to attack Newman for taking refuge in the authority of Rome since they take refuge in the external authority of the Bible. 'Men need depend neither on the Bible nor on the Pope.' The alternative to the principle of authority is not unbelief but the principle of freedom" (Blehl, p. 57, citing the American ed. of *WR*, LXXXII [Oct. 1864], 176-77). The *Evangelical Witness and Presbyterian Review* (III [Sept. 1864] 228-29) praised the frankness of the *Apologia* but concluded that "it is painful and revolting in its details—the narrative of the gradual darkening of a man's soul to the light," leaving Newman "ten times worse off" than by Kingsley's accusation. Anglican reviews were generally favorable to Newman's personal sincerity and honesty, while naturally regretful about his departure from the Church of England. Of these the review in the *Quarterly* by Samuel Wilberforce, as I have pointed out elsewhere (*Apologia*, ed. Svaglic, Introduction, p. 1) was probably the most significant, laying the foundation for the psychological interpretation of Newman so common in subsequent biographies of Newman and studies of the *Apologia*: "that sensitive, ill-understood soul," the causes of whose "defection are, we think, clearly shown to have been the peculiarities of the individual, not the weakness of the side which he abandoned."

The last of Newman's major works, *An Essay in Aid of a Grammar of Assent* (1870), brings us back to the point at which we began, to the sermons and to John Stuart Mill. Since the first of the *University Sermons*, preached at Oxford in 1826, Newman had been grappling with the problem of what he called the logical cogency of faith, more specifically, the problem growing ever more troublesome since the Enlightenment of how if religion is reasonable and intended for all, every man and not merely the empirical scientist or learned philosopher could arrive at a rational acceptance of belief: of the kind of unwavering faith so constantly praised in Scripture, as when Christ said to his doubting disciple: "Because thou hast seen me, Thomas, thou has believed; blessed are they that have not seen and have believed." Of the *Grammar* itself, Newman said apropos of an attack for its non-scholastic mode of reasoning by the Jesuit periodical *The Month*: "My book is to show that a right moral state of mind germinates or even generates good intellectual principles. . . . I am sensible it may be full of defects, and certainly characterized by incompleteness and crudeness, but it is something to have started a problem, and mapped in part a country, if I have done nothing more" (Ward, *Life*, II, 270–71).

A Grammar of Assent is a fairly long and difficult book, especially at the outset, though if the reader persists, he will be rewarded by what Aldous Huxley was to call a psychological analysis of human thought "among the most penetrating and certainly the most elegant ever made."[38] Newman himself gives an outline of the structure of the book in the opening of Chapter X (p. 384), and this appears to have been the basis for what is surely the best brief account of the *Grammar* available, the special study in the *Dictionnaire de Théologie Catholique*, part of a magisterial article by the Oratorian Fathers Bacchus and Tristram on all the works of Newman, Anglican and Catholic.

It would be impossible to treat the *Grammar of Assent* at length here, but perhaps a passage on the supremacy of faith in the *Development of Christian Doctrine*, for the more detailed elucidation of which Newman refers us to the *University Sermons* and the *Grammar*, might serve as an epitome. The principle, Newman says, is of the following kind:

> That belief in Christianity is itself better than unbelief; that faith, though an intellectual action, is ethical in its origin; that it is safer to believe; that we must begin with believing; that as for the reasons of believing, they are for the most part implicit, and need be but slightly recognized by the mind that is under their influence; that they consist moreover rather of presumptions and ventures after the truth than of accurate and complete proofs; and that probable arguments, under the scrutiny and sanction of a prudent judgment, are sufficient for conclusions which we even embrace as most certain, and turn to the most important uses.

2

> Antagonistic to this is the principle that doctrines are only so far to be considered true as they are logically demonstrated. This is the assertion of Locke, who says in defence of it,—"Whatever God hath revealed is certainly true; no doubt can be made of it. This is the proper object of Faith; but, whether it be a divine revelation or no, reason must judge." Now if he merely means that proofs can be given for Revelation, and that Reason comes in logical order before Faith, such a doctrine is in no sense uncatholic; but he certainly holds that for an individual to act on Faith without proof, or to make Faith a personal principle of conduct for themselves, without waiting till they have got their reasons accurately drawn out and serviceable for controversy, is enthusiastic and absurd.

'How a man may know whether he be a lover of truth for truth's sake is worth inquiry; and I think there is this one unerring mark of it, viz. the not entertaining any proposition with greater assurance than the proofs it is built on will warrant. Whoever goes beyond this measure of assent, it is plain, receives not truth in the love of it; loves not truth for truth's sake, but for some other by-end.'

3

It does not seem to have struck him that our "by-end" may be the desire to please our Maker, and that the defect of scientific proof may be made up to our reason by our love of Him. It does not seem to have struck him that such a philosophy as his cut off from the possibility and the privilege of faith all but the educated few, all but the learned, the clear-headed, the men of practised intellects and balanced minds, men who had leisure, who had opportunities of consulting others, and kind and wise friends to whom they deferred. How could a religion ever be Catholic, if it was to be called credulity or enthusiasm in the multitude to use those ready instruments of belief, which alone Providence had put into their power? On such philosophy as this, were it generally received, no great work ever would have been done for God's glory and the welfare of man. The "enthusiasm" against which Locke writes may do much harm, and act at times absurdly; but calculation never made a hero (*Dev.*, pp. 327–28).

Newman's 1841 letters to the *Times*, published as "The Tamworth Reading-Room," will also throw some light on this passage.

The Lockean principle of "not entertaining any proposition with greater assurance than the proofs it is built on will warrant" is the heart of the matter. If one demanded proof of a demonstrative or empirical sort, as it was the natural tendency of science to do, then of course unwavering religious faith was virtually unattainable. The subject was on Newman's mind again in the 1850s—he had meant to write a magnum opus on the problem—because of the growing prestige of the sciences at Oxford, where John Stuart Mill's *System of Logic, Ratiocinative and Inductive*, promising a "connected view of the principles of evidence, and the methods of scientific investigation," had pretty well superseded Whately's *Elements of Logic*. Newman began a study of Mill's *Logic* in May, 1857,[39] perhaps partly to deal with the problems being raised in what turned out to be a correspondence of more than twenty years with his agnostic friend, the engineer William Froude, F.R.S., the brother of William and James Anthony, whose wife and two of whose children Newman received into the Roman Catholic Church.

Newman read, marked, and annotated most of the first volume of Mill's *Logic*, but left the pages of the second uncut, having apparently learned as much as he felt he needed to know.

The correspondence with Froude was a kind of rehearsal for *A Grammar of Assent*. Froude set out the tone and problem in a most impressive letter of December 29, 1859, characterized by its editor as "a statement, probably as succinct as any in existence, of those principles of thinking and investigating which actuated the best of the liberal minds of the mid-nineteenth century. Much of it appears today as truisms, but one has only to search out passages on a similar theme in Huxley's writing, to recall how far from general acceptance was this attitude of mind at the time."[40] Succinct it may be, but since it is some eight passages long, it cannot be quoted here. However, one may see in the following passage the Lockean principle reasserted and carried even further than Locke envisioned, a principle also eloquently expressed earlier that same year in Mill's *On Liberty:*

> I will at least endeavour to convey to you as distinctly as I can that rule or principle of thought which . . . seems to hold my mind in the most complete antagonism to Catholicism. More strongly than I believe anything else I believe this—that [on?] no subject whatever—distinctly not in the region of the ordinary facts with which our daily experience is consonant—distinctly not in the domain of history or of politics, and yet again *a fortiori*, not in that of Theology, is my mind, (or as far as I can take the mind of any human being,) capable of arriving at an absolutely certain conclusion. That though of course some conclusions are far more certain than others, there is an element of uncertainty in all.
>   . . . For myself, in every province of thought and action, I am content to take as my motto the words: "Ever learning and never able to come to a knowledge of the truth."

As for John Stuart Mill:

> The beliefs which we have most warrant for, have no safeguard to rest on, but a standing invitation to the whole world to prove them unfounded. If the challenge is not accepted, or is accepted and the attempt fails, we are far enough from certainty still; but we have done the best that the existing state of reason admits of; we have neglected nothing that could give the truth a chance of reaching us; if the lists are kept open, we may hope that if there be a better truth, it will be found when the human mind is capable of receiving it; and in the meantime we may rely on having attained such approach to truth, as is possible in our day.

75

This is the amount of certainty attainable by a fallible being, and this the sole way of attaining it (*Collected Works*, XVIII, 232).

The effect on Newman of such principles as Froude's might easily be inferred from his remark in the *Apologia* (p. 30) that if every conclusion were to be considered as doubtful or "an opinion, which it is safe indeed to obey or to profess, but not possible to embrace with full internal assent, then the celebrated saying, 'O God, if there be a God, save my soul, if I have a soul!' would be the highest measure of devotion:—but who can really pray to a Being, about whose existence he is seriously in doubt?"

There are only two points that I would like to stress here about the *Grammar*. First, the book is directed toward those who are initially prepared for religious inquiry by the truths of natural religion, which for Newman was not at all the same kind of argument as Paley's from the design evident in nature. The world was made before sin and gives no evidence of redemption. The testimony of nature to religion, by which is meant "the knowledge of God, of His Will, and of our duties towards Him" comes from "our own minds, the voice of mankind, and the course of the world, that is, of human life and human affairs" (*Grammar*, p. 389). The most authoritative source is our conscience, our sense of right and wrong, which often gives a burdensome sense of guilt but also convinces us that some higher being is responsible for our feelings and inclines us to long and look for a clearer revelation of His will. When the Scriptures are presented to such a sincere inquirer, he finds they answer to his spiritual needs and reveal the God he has looked for. This is the process illustrated for a popular audience in Newman's second novel of conversion, *Callista*.[41] If one approaches the subject of religion with a show-me attitude, denying or at least doubting Newman's first principle (assumed) of the existence of conscience, there is no real point to going on, which may explain Newman's silence before Fitzjames Stephen. Pascal and Montaigne will never come to the same conclusion.

Second, Newman's argument for the acceptance of Revelation and the Church is, like that in *Development*, basically analogical. We have no formally logical or empirical evidence in everyday life for many things about which we are certain. There is surely a surplusage of belief over evidence, Newman liked to point out in

Lockean phrase, that we shall die. What was the evidence in Newman's day (before aerial photography) that Britain was an island? A multitude of greater or lesser evidences—what Newman called probabilities—cumulating to produce certainty or rather what Newman called certitude. If we arrive at our certitudes this way in daily life and its mundane affairs, why should we not also do so in the matter of religion? He summarized the argument in the *Apologia:*

> My argument is in outline as follows: that that absolute certitude which we were able to possess, whether as to the truths of natural theology, or as to the fact of a revelation, was the result of an *assemblage* of concurring and converging probabilities, and that, both according to the constitution of the human mind and the will of its Maker; that certitude was a quality of propositions; that probabilities which did not reach to logical certainty, might suffice for a mental certitude; that the certitude thus brought about might equal in measure and strength the certitude which was created by the strictest scientific demonstration; and that to possess such certitude might in given cases and to given individuals be a plain duty, though not to others in other circumstances . . . (*Apologia,* p. 31).

The question of how the Victorians received all this has not yet, I think, been examined in sufficient detail;[42] but even to treat briefly of the material available would require more space than I have here. One interestingly ambivalent reaction came from James Anthony Froude in *Fraser's Magazine*, of which he was then editor. He never read a book, he says, "unless the *Ethics* of Spinoza be an exception, which is less convincing in proportion to its ability. You feel that you are in the hands of a thinker of the very highest powers; yet they are the powers rather of an intellectual conjuror than of a teacher who commands your confidence. . . . unless you bring a Catholic conclusion ready made with you to the study, you will certainly not arrive at it" (81, n.s. 1 [May, 1870], 562).

Of course by now Froude had become an ultra-Protestant nationalist, as the *History of England* (Kingsley's review of which provoked the *Apologia*) vividly revealed. The fact that a gifted recent convert like Hopkins wished to edit the *Grammar* suggests that it did draw some people, at least, to "a Catholic conclusion." And Froude himself, though he wished to warn Protestants against the "Catholic mistake" of strangling themselves in "dogmatic formulas," was quite willing to trust Newman on "the facts of nature." He says indeed of the *Grammar:* "Nowhere in the English language will be found the reasons for believing in a moral power as the supreme ruler of the universe, drawn out more clearly or persuasively. . . . He lays the facts of personal experience before us; he indicates the conclusion at which they point: and when the conclusion is conceded, the obligations of obedience follow" (pp. 580 and 565).

To the present writer, the most searching of the contemporary discussions of Newman's epistemology was that of Leslie Stephen, who agreed with Newman to a considerable extent: "If every condition which in fact determines belief were taken to be therefore a condition of logical belief, we should sanction every possible error. If, on the other hand, logical conditions were regarded as the sole causes which in fact determine belief, we should certainly have, as Newman conclusively shows, a most inadequate view of the way in which belief, and even sound belief, is in fact originated and propagated." So long as Newman remains within these limits, "his theory appears to be as unassailable as it is admirably expounded" (*An Agnostic's Apology*, pp. 208–09).

But for Stephen the upshot of Newman's personalism, the "pith" of *A Grammar of Assent*, is that "rational agreement is impossible" (239):

> . . . if Newman is asked why he accepts his own solution, he can only reply that, as a matter of fact, it convinces his "illative sense," and that he believes it would convince the illative sense of other people, provided that they have a conscience, that they interpret it in the way that he does, and that the arguments are fairly set before them. To which one can only say that, undoubtedly, if any man is precisely in Newman's state of mind, and has precisely the same arguments put before him, he will come to precisely the same conclusion. But any attempt at a common measure of truth as an "objective test," is explicitly pronounced impossible; and thus we are once more landed in complete scepticism (236–37).

The way to escape from such scepticism while admitting experience as the ultimate test of truth is, for Stephen, to interpret *securus iudicat orbis terrarum* in a much wider sense than Newman takes it in the *Apologia*. The safest opinions are the most rational, and the test of their rationality is that they have commended themselves to independent thinkers everywhere: "There is no infallible guide and no complete and definitive system of universal truth . . ." (240-41). And if Stephen and his school were, as Newman feared, more and more to carry the day, it would, of course, mean that faith in the Biblical sense was for modern man impossible.

In discussing Newman, almost the only thing agreed on by most Victorians of whatever school was the perfection of his literary style. Gladstone, Matthew Arnold, Froude, Pater, George Eliot, Hardy, Wilde, Joyce, Saintsbury, and many others all paid tribute to his artistry. The most pointed and convincing explanation of its appeal, however, remains that of the late Victorian American literary critic Lewis E. Gates, a professor of English literature at Harvard: ". . . for the trained student of literary method much of the surpassing charm of Newman's work is due to the possibility of finding in it, on analysis, a continual victorious union of logical strenuousness with the grace and ease and charm of a colloquial manner and idiom. This victory is so easily won as to seem something by the way; but the student and analyst knows that it is the result of rare tact, finely disciplined instinct, exquisite rhetorical insight and foresight, and extraordinary luminousness and largeness of thought." Without minimizing his readiness "to meet an opponent fairly on the grounds of debate," Gates recognized with Saintsbury the effect of subtle musical beauty [running] elusively through" Newman's prose: "Newman understood perfectly the symbolic value of rhythm and the possibility of imposing upon a series of simple words, by delicately sensitive adjustment, a power over the feelings and the imagination like that of an incantation."[43] And that, no doubt, is one of the principal reasons why to this day, many readers are still moved even to tears, like George Eliot long ago, by the final words of the great *Apologia*, "perhaps . . . the most beautiful piece of prose," according to Gates, "that Newman ever wrote."

NOTES

1. *Selected Essays* (New York, 1950), p. 368.
2. *An Agnostic's Apology*, 2nd ed. (London, 1903), pp. 168-69.
3. *Memoirs* (London, 1885), p. 166.

4. See J. M. Cameron, *The Night Battle* (London, 1962), p. xi, and "Newman and the Empiricist Tradition," in *The Rediscovery of Newman: An Oxford Symposium*, ed. John Coulson and A. M. Allchin (London, 1967), pp. 79–96. Edward Sillem lists in no particular order but with the first four as most important, "seven main sources to which Newman was particularly indebted throughout his life: (a) the Aristotelian sources; (b) the philosophy of the Noetics of the Oriel Common Room; (c) the *Analogy of Religion* of Joseph Butler; (d) the cosmic Platonism of the Alexandrian Fathers; (e) the natural philosophies of Isaac Newton and Francis Bacon, and the advances made in Mathematics by contemporary Mathematicians; (f) the Empiricism of Locke and Hume; (g) the associationist theories in psychology derived from Abraham Tucker and Sir Joshua Reynolds, which were systematized by William Paley" (*The Philosophical Notebooks of John Henry Newman*, ed. Sillem, 2 vols. [New York, 1969], I, 149. In one form or another empiricism dominates these sources.

5. *An Agnostic's Apology*, pp. 178–79.

6. Wilfred Ward, *Life of John Henry Cardinal Newman* (2 vols., London, 1912), II, 491–92.

7. See Leslie Stephen, *Life of Sir James Fitzjames Stephen*, 2nd ed. (London, 1895), pp. 190–200.

8. Ward, *Life*, II, 492.

9. Newman, *Historical Sketches*, III, 62–63, and Ward, *Life*, II, 337–38. Unless otherwise noted, all quotations of Newman's works are from the standard Longman's edition (39 vols., London, 1898–1903).

10. *Collected Works of John Stuart Mill*, XVIII, ed. J. M. Robson (Toronto, 1977), 248–49.

11. R. W. Church, *The Oxford Movement* (London, 1891), p. 113.

12. Though sermons were widely read in Newman's day, they did not ordinarily go through more than one edition of a thousand copies. "Newman's volumes of parochial sermons went through five, four, and three large editions, only his sixth volume in 1842 being limited to two editions, owing to his leaving the Church of England in 1845." In a letter of 1849 Newman himself said: "I *do* think that my influence among persons who have *not* seen me has been indefinitely greater than among those who have" (See C. S. Dessain, *John Henry Newman*, 2nd ed. [London, 1971], p. 45). In answer to a question about which of Newman's writings would be read in a hundred years, Gladstone replied in 1879, "all his parochial sermons." He had earlier said of Newman's influence at its height (in 1836–41), "I do not believe that there has been anything like [it] in Oxford . . . since Abelard lectured in Paris" (Dessain, p. 44, citing M. E. Grant Duff, *Notes from a Diary*, 1873–1881 [London, 1898], II, 140).

13. *Grammar of Assent*, p. 79.

14. *Realizations*, ed. V. F. Blehl, S. J. (London, 1964) is, in fact, the title of an attractive and convenient collection of the thirteen parochial and plain sermons which Newman himself in a letter to Ambrose St. John of Jan. 26, 1846, called his best: "The Strictness of the Law of Christ" (1837, in *Parochial and Plain Sermons* (hereafter *P.S.*), IV, No. 1); "Obedience without Love, as Instanced in the Character of Balaam" (1837, *P.S.*, IV, 2); "Love, the One Thing Needful" (1839,

P.S., V, 23); "The Ventures of Faith" (1836, *P.S.*, IV, 20); "The Weapons of Saints" (1837, *P.S.*, VI, 22); "Unreal Words" (1839), *P.S.*, V, 3); "Remembrance of Past Mercies" (1838, *P.S.*, V, 6); "Christ Hidden from the World" (1837, *P.S.*, IV, 16); "The Greatness and Littleness of Human Life" (1836, *P.S.*, IV, 14); "Waiting for Christ" (1840, *P.S.*, VI, 17); "Subjection of the Reason and Feelings to the Revealed Word" (1840, *P.S.*, VI, 18); "Equanimity" (1839, *P.S.*, V, 5); and "Peace in Believing" (1839, *P.S.*, VI, 25).

15. *P.S.*, IV, 201–02.

16. *Callista*, p. 305.

17. *Occasional Sermons*, p. 166. Hereafter *O.S.*

18. One of Carlyle's more fatuous remarks was that Newman had "not the intellect of a moderate-size rabbit." (But see D. A. Wilson, *Carlyle to Threescore and Ten* [London, 1929], pp. 450–51.) But that, no doubt, was due to Newman's alarmingly conservative attempt to re-tailor "Hebrew old clothes" instead of taking the modern path of a John Sterling, a hero of Mill also.

19. Why did not St. Augustine join the Catholic Church sooner? ". . . he saw that truth was nowhere else; but he was not sure it was there. He thought there was something mean, narrow, irrational, in her system of doctrine; he lacked the gift of faith. Then a great conflict began within him,—the conflict of nature with grace; of nature and her children, the flesh and false reason, against conscience and the pleadings of the Divine Spirit, leading him to better things" (*Discourses to Mixed Congregations*, p. 54. Hereafter *Mix.*)

20. Ten out of thirteen volumes thus far published, partly because it was not the Catholic custom to deliver sermons from a MS.

21. *Short Studies on Great Subjects*, new edition, 4 vols. (London, 1886), IV, 282–83 and 284.

22. See Geoffrey and Kathleen Tillotson, *Mid-Victorian Studies* (London, 1965), p. 239.

23. See "The Lost Childhood" in Greene's *Collected Essays* (New York, 1969), pp. 13 and 19.

24. For some of Newman's literary tastes, see Ward, *Life*, II, 353–55.

25. See "The Weapons of Saints," *P.S.*, VI, 317. Also "Intellect the Instrument of Religious Training," *O.S.*

26. "Nature and Grace," *Mix.*, pp. 147–48.

27. *Sermons on Subjects of the Day*, p. 120.

28. Meriol Trevor, *Newman, The Pillar of the Cloud* (New York, 1962), p. 609.

29. See *Letters and Diaries of John Henry Newman*, ed. C. S. Dessain, XIX, 254.

30. *Development*, p. 38.

31. J. B. Mozley, *The Theory of Development* (London, 1878), reprinted from the *Christian Remembrancer* of January, 1847; William Palmer, *The Doctrine of Development and Conscience* (London, 1846); and H. H. Milman, "Newman on the Development of Christian Doctrine," *Quarterly Review*, March, 1846, reprinted in *Savonarola, Erasmus, and Other Essays* (London, 1870).

Chadwick makes admirably clear the difference between the earlier view of development held by the very influential Bossuet and the Gallican School that the Church is *semper eadem*, never making 'new' articles of faith but only making clear what she has always "explicitly, consciously, and continuously believed"; the scholastic view that in defining a doctrine, the Church was not adding to but only "displaying more clearly the inner content of the revelation, explicating what was implicit"; and Newman's version, which even in the revised 1878 edition of *Development* "still taught that Christianity was an idea which makes impressions, and that developments are aspects of the original idea slowly elicited . . . that the Church had been unconscious of truths which she had later defined . . . that dogma grew by 'incorporation' or 'assimilation.' " See Owen Chadwick, *From Bossuet to Newman/The Idea of Doctrinal Development* (Cambridge, 1957), pp. 236, 19, 23, and 191.

32. *Brownson's Quarterly Review*, III (1846), 360–61.

33. See Meriol Trevor, *Newman/Light in Winter* (New York, 1963), p. 54.

34. *The Theory of Development*, pp. 34–36.

35. *Science and Christian Tradition* (London, 1894), pp. 343–44.

36. See *The Idea of a University*, ed. with introduction and notes by I. T. Ker (Oxford, 1976), p. xxviii.

37. V. F. Blehl, S.J., "Early Criticism of the *Apologia*," in *Newman's Apologia: A Classic Reconsidered*, ed. Blehl and F. X. Connolly (New York, 1964), p. 48.

38. *Proper Studies* (London, 1927), p. xix.

39. Sillem, *The Philosophical Notebooks*, II, 224–25.

40. Gordon Huntington Harper, *Cardinal Newman and William Froude, F.R.S./ A Correspondence* (Baltimore, 1933), p. 116.

41. For a good account of Newman's "philosophy of mind" and its reflection in his novels and 'autobiography,' see Thomas Vargish, *Newman/The Contemplation of Mind* (Oxford, 1970).

42. For a brief survey and evaluation of the principal attacks on Newman's theory of belief, especially what the author calls "the most telling . . . Anglican-agnostic attack of 1864–1892," (Fitzjames and Leslie Stephen, J. A. Froude, Principal Fairbairn, T. H. Huxley, and E. A. Abbott), see J. F. Cronin, *Cardinal Newman: His Theory of Knowledge* (Washington, D.C., 1935), pp. 72–113.

43. Lewis E. Gates, "Newman as a Prose-Writer," *Three Studies in Literature* (New York, 1899), pp. 67 and 96.

JOHN STUART MILL
A POST-HOLOCAUST RETROSPECT

"The French philosophes *of the eighteenth century were the example we sought to imitate, and we hoped to accomplish no less results. No one of the set went to so great excesses in this boyish ambition as I did. . . ."*

John Stuart Mill, Autobiography

"The dream which Western man conceived in the eighteenth century, whose dawn he thought he saw in 1789, and which, until August 2, 1914, had grown stronger with the progress of enlightenment and the discoveries of science—this dream vanished finally for me before those trainloads of little children."

Francois Mauriac,
foreword to Night, by Elie Wiesel

EDWARD ALEXANDER

Recently I heard a survivor of Auschwitz speak for two hours about her experience of Nazi terror from the time that she and her family were arrested in Hungary in 1944 and deported to the death factories until the day of her liberation at the end of the war. She spoke movingly but also precisely of the murder of her whole family, of the obliteration of the world she had known, of the destruction of her innocence: "In the camps," she said, "I learned that men are born evil." In the ensuing question period, one student asked whether, during her decades in the United States, she had experienced any "insensitivity" on the subject of the Holocaust. "I have experienced," she replied, "almost nothing except insensitivity, because for thirty years nobody would listen to my story." To epitomize what she meant, she told an anecdote about a very close friend of hers, a lawyer for the American Civil Liberties Union. "During all the twenty-five years of our friendship," she said, "he had never wanted to hear about my life during the war years. It was too painful—too painful, that is, for him. I remembered this recently when he was holding forth at our home on the subject of the vigorous support by the ACLU of the right of the Nazi Party of America to demonstrate in Skokie. He quoted John Stuart Mill and spoke of the sanctity of the First Amendment and expressed his impatience with the Jewish inhabitants of Skokie because they wanted to prevent the Nazis from marching past their houses." The Jewish inhabitants of Skokie are, of course, themselves mostly survivors of the death camps. This ACLU stalwart and self-proclaimed devotee of Mill had studiously protected himself from learning anything of the experience and inner life of the people whom he now berated for the insufficiency of their devotion to "freedom."

What struck me about the story was not primarily the feeble inadequacy of ACLU ideology to deal with a case like that in Skokie. Many commentators have remarked on the inanity or worse of a policy which defended a Nazi march through a community of survivors of Hitler as "symbolic political speech" and exhorted the local residents to draw their blinds and hide indoors while the Nazis tramped past inciting their murder. Others had remarked on the double standard of the ACLU, and on its politicization, and openly asked whether "it is time for the American Civil Liberties Union to undertake a test case for a Jew who views himself directly assailed by a program calling for his murder."[1]

What was far more disturbing to me in this woman's remarks was the implied question about the relevance of John Stuart Mill, a writer to whom I had devoted a considerable amount of time, attention, indeed loyalty over many years, to the Holocaust, the systematic destruction of European Jewry. Indeed, this survivor's remarks immediately reminded me of a remark made to me several years ago by one of the leading Mill scholars in the world when she was visiting our campus as a Phi Beta Kappa lecturer. After the seminar she conducted on *On Liberty*, Mill's most influential work, we continued to discuss privately the question of whether *On Liberty* was a representative or an aberrant work in Mill's *corpus* until she noticed—from the books on my desk—that I was immersed in reading about the Holocaust. "Oh, forgive me," she said, "alongside *that* subject everything having to do with John Stuart Mill is trivial."

Yet if we are to speak of Mill's "contemporary relevance," as the contributors to this volume have been asked to do, we can hardly evade the question of the link between the liberalism that claims descent from Mill and the central event of our times. Antisemitism and the "final solution" of the Jewish question are not "merely" Jewish concerns. In her classic study of modern totalitarianism published in 1951, Hannah Arendt pointed out that "the Jewish question and antisemitism, relatively unimportant phenomena in terms of world politics, became the catalytic agent first for the rise of the Nazi movement and the establishment of the organizational structure of the Third Reich, in which every citizen had to prove that he was *not* a Jew, then for a world war of unparalleled ferocity, and finally for the emergence of the unprecedented crime of genocide in the midst of Occidental civilization." The destruction of the Jews involved not only Jewish victims and German criminals, not only what a Christian theologian has called the mass apostasy of millions of baptized Christians, but also the destruction of European civilization itself. If most people, including most historical scholars, refuse to face up to the enormity of this event, that, asserted Arendt, is because "there is a great temptation to explain away the intrinsically incredible by means of liberal rationalizations. In each one of us, there lurks such a liberal, wheedling us with the voice of common sense."[2]

The actual involvement of European liberalism with the development of antisemitic ideology is not my concern here. In the introductory chapter of *On Liberty* Mill explicitly dissociates himself from the statist tendencies of European liberalism, the whole thrust of which had, in his view, become to identify the interest and will of democratically elected rulers with the interest and will of the nation itself. "The nation did not need to be protected against its own will. There was no fear of its tyrannising over itself."[3] It would not have surprised Mill to learn that modern antisemitism originated in the German Liberal Party just after his death in 1873, or that by the eighties (under the leadership of Georg von Schoenerer) the Liberals had begun to organize the first closely knit university students' organizations on the basis of open antisemitism.

Whether Mill could have understood what was objectionable and dangerous in the attitude of liberal *friends* of the Jews like Wilhelm von Humboldt, whose ethical idealism is celebrated in Chapter III of *On Liberty*, is a more delicate question. For Humboldt considered the disappearance of the Jews as an ethnic group a condition for taking up the cause of their "emancipation." In this attitude, he was representative of the Enlightenment and the French Revolution, which professed its readiness to grant to the Jews as citizens everything, but to the Jews as Jews nothing. These harried people were asked to choose between their individual identity as "human beings" and their collective identity as members of their own people. Now, with the wisdom of hindsight, we can recognize the insidious link between this liberal principle and Hitler's insistence that every single person in Europe had to prove that he was *not* a Jew in order to be considered "human" and receive the basic human right, the right to live.

Even in the aftermath of the Holocaust, orthodox liberalism has generally shown itself incapable of recognizing, much less comprehending, what it was that happened in the Holocaust. Liberal discourse about the Holocaust—as Hannah Arendt implies in her reference to "liberal rationalizations"—typically treats the plan to murder every single member of the Jewish people as a crime against "humanity" and "life" itself, thus making of the destruction of the Jews a blurred and indiscriminate example of "man's inhumanity to man." This is partly a historical error, an obfuscation of the difference between the terrible crimes committed by the Nazi regime against Poles, Russians, Czechs, Gypsies, on the one hand, and Jews on the other. Yehuda Bauer, the foremost living scholar of the Holocaust, stresses "the difference between forcible, even murderous, denationalization, and wholesale, total murder of every one of the members of a community."[4] The Jews alone were singled out to die for the sole "crime" of having been born.

This historical error is not accidental, but derives directly from the metaphysical premises of modern liberalism. In her essay "A

86

Liberal's Auschwitz," Cynthia Ozick writes that "the liberal is a humanist—which is to say, he is an anthropomorphic idolator; his god is called *humanity*. And because he is a humanist, the liberal is also an egalitarian—which is to say, he is a leveler: like death."[5] The modern liberal who, in contemplating Auschwitz and Treblinka and Majdanek, weeps over "mankind" and "humanity" but not the Jews, is the true heir of his Enlightenment ancestors who would grant to the Jews as citizens or as "men" everything but to the Jews as Jews nothing—not even their deaths.

For Cynthia Ozick, the liberal's preference of abstraction to specificity is, like his anthropomorphic idolatry, a function of his spiritual hollowness. Liberalism, as a child of the Enlightenment, has always faced the problem of how to make systematic negation, fashioned to destroy an oppressive reigning philosophy, into the organic basis of a living culture. A recent critic of the Enlightenment shrewdly observes that "enlighteners have spent the past two centuries seeking out what they oppose, and, in quiet times, studying ways to turn the instruments of attack into philosophies in order to discover what it is they favor."[6] Indeed, the Skokie affair itself produced a stunning illustration of this problem in one of the few subjectively honest responses to the affair among those who took the "liberal" side in the controversy. The leader in the *New Yorker*, a magazine famous for the sophisticated confusion of its political utterances, came to the predictable ACLU conclusion that, paradoxical though it might seem, the best way of opposing the Nazis in the long run was to support them in the short run. But then the writer, in a burst of candor, said:

> In short, freedom's strange emptiness—its maddening refusal to favor the body or the soul, to choose between tolerable and intolerable music, or even to tip the scales of the political system against unfreedom and in favor of itself—is not a flaw in freedom but, rather, its essence. Just this lack is its most precious treasure, just this emptiness its surest foundation.[7]

Such a statement summons from the vaults of death not only the spectre of Weimar Germany, where liberalism did a most admirable job of *not* tipping the scales against freedom's enemies, but the spectre of John Stuart Mill himself. It serves to remind us just how far modern liberalism has departed from the spirit of its founder, who did indeed celebrate the freedoms of the secular society, but expressed dread of, and sought means to forestall, its emptiness.

The Skokie "affair" sharpened the uneasiness which my readings in the Holocaust had already aroused about Millite liberalism, and made me cast a retrospective glance over my experience of Mill during a period of almost twenty years. For a number of reasons— resistance to a full awareness of one's past innocence and shame at revealing it not least among them—it never occurred to me to share the fruits of this retrospective examination with others until the editor of this volume asked me precisely to discuss my own "involvement" with Mill and my changing responses to him over many years of study. Whether the conclusions I draw from my own "subjective" experience of Mill will be a mere exercise in self-awareness (and perhaps self-correction) or will recommend themselves to others as well is a question to be answered by the readers of this volume. Of one thing, at least, we may be certain: the constant calling into question of the first principles of liberalism would surely recommend itself to John Stuart Mill. For he believed that however true any doctrine may be, "if it is not fully, frequently, and fearlessly discussed, it will be held as a dead dogma, not a living truth."[8]

In the first period of my interest in Mill, which extended from the late fifties, when I was in my early twenties, to the mid-sixties, he was for me primarily the Mill of Chapters II and III of *On Liberty*, the apologist for nearly unbridled liberty of thought and discussion, and for individuality of character, even to the point of eccentricity. He struck me as the most articulate spokesman since Milton for the perennially beleaguered intellectual whose heretical ideas incurred the disapprobation and often punishment of official society, of temporal authority unjustly extending its arm into the spiritual and intellectual realm. Like most "thinking" teenagers of the fifties, I held the conviction that McCarthyism was an enormous danger to the liberty and democracy of this country, a far greater danger than the communism which it pretended to battle. At Columbia College, where I was an undergraduate, professorial wisdom had it that the true inheritor of the totalitarianism of Nazi Germany was not the Soviet Union or its satellites but the "Cold War ideologists" and McCarthyites of the United States. Liberalism, often so defined as to make socialism its natural accompaniment, was the reigning orthodoxy at Columbia, and I was far from immune to its influence. Perhaps out of deference to Mill's own insistence on the desirability of a devil's advocate, the standardized social-science curriculum at Columbia for the first two years of college did allow for the reading of one dissenter every year—an anti-liberal like Arnold or an anti-socialist like F. A. Hayek—so that it was possible, however difficult, to believe that somebody besides the ignorant, anti-intellectual majority of the citizenry called into question the first principles of liberalism and socialism.

The liberalism inculcated at Columbia was distinctly the twentieth-century version, with its very un-Millite receptivity to governmental interference in the economy and in education. It would have come as a shock to me if, in those days, I had come upon Mill's warning that "a general State education is a mere contrivance for moulding people to be exactly like one another: . . . in proportion as it is efficient and successful, it establishes a despotism over the mind, leading by natural tendency to one over the body." Mill's *Principles of Political Economy*, one of the four classics of laissez faire economic theory, with its insistence that "Wherever competition is not, monopoly is" and that "monopoly, in all its forms, is the taxation of the industrious for the support of indolence, if not of plunder,"[9] had I read it as an undergraduate, would also have struck me as remarkably illiberal for a founding father of what we were taught to think of as liberalism. Indeed, it *did* come as a shock to me, when I began to write about Mill, to discover that not only his Examiner essays of 1831, "The Spirit of the Age," but also his correspondence with Harriet Hardy Taylor, had been collected and edited by none other than F. A. Hayek, one of the most articulate and contentious advocates of a free-market economy as against the welfare-state ideology of modern liberalism.

Nevertheless, we who believed that the essential concern and conflict of modern America was the struggle of a minority of liberal intellectuals, doggedly devoted to free speech, against an unthinking majority, who lived only according to custom, prejudice, and conformity, were not wrong to find in Mill our most eloquent spokesman. Northrop Frye has correctly pointed out that the underlying opposition, posited as almost a permanent one, in *On Liberty*, is between the majority of people living in what Burke had called a continuum of habit and prejudice, and the much smaller liberal opposition, a highly individualized group who are said to initiate all wise and noble things.[10] If you shared such assumptions about the plight of democratic society in the United States, it was also natural to respond sympathetically to the schemes which Mill at various times in his career propounded for diluting the power of the numerical majority in democratic societies, for the simple reason—so it seemed to Mill—that "the great majority of voters, in most countries, and emphatically in this, would be manual labourers."[11] Mill's *Considerations on Representative Government* despaired of the operation of equal and universal suffrage unless it were combined with the proportional representation of all minorities. The scheme he himself preferred, however, was plural voting, in which everyone would have a voice, but not an equal one. When I first read *Representative Government*, I not only shared the common liberal illusion of those days that "we" were outnumbered and beleaguered by "them," but I had not yet myself become a member of the academic community, not yet lived among those officially certified to be what Mill calls "superior . . . in knowledge and intelligence" to the rest of the community and therefore entitled to two or even more votes. Neither had I much attended to the startling revelations of the disproportionate role played by professors and intellectuals in the establishment and running of concentration camps, death factories, and all the other institutions of totalitarian rule. Perhaps because he never taught or even studied at a university, never entered a learned profession, and worked mostly in isolation, Mill could believe that "wherever a sufficient examination, or any serious conditions of education, are required before entering on a profession, its members could be admitted at once to a plurality of votes."[12] One does not need to be a fanatical believer in "one man, one vote, one vote, one value" to recognize that as between this proposal and the suggestion sometimes made (for example, by Eric Hoffer) that professors should not be allowed to vote at all, the latter is by far the more prudent.

When, in this first stage of my attraction to him, I read Mill along with the other Victorian thinkers, his liberalism served me as a kind of litmus paper for the detection of what was dangerous, dogmatic, and in some cases (most notably Carlyle's) violent in their thought. The seemingly self-evident truth of Mill's claim, in the Introductory chapter of *On Liberty*, that advanced thinkers had, throughout history, "occupied themselves rather in inquiring what things society ought to like or dislike, than in questioning whether its likings or dislikings should be a law to individuals,"[13] was confirmed in my readings of Mill's contemporaries. Carlyle derided individual liberty at every opportunity, preferring a well-fed Gurth bound in a brass collar to a hungry one at liberty, and explosively rejecting *On Liberty* itself with "As if it were a sin to control, or coerce into better methods, human swine in any way; . . . Ach Gott im Himmel!" Newman represented the Catholic Church as believing that "unless she can, *in her own way*, do good to souls, it is no use her doing anything." Ruskin boasted that "My own teaching has been, and is that Liberty, whether in the body, soul, or political estate of men, is only another word for Death, and the final issue of Death, putrefaction." Arnold, though very far from a strident opponent of individual liberty, saw it as no more than a piece of machinery, like coal or population, and was not notably distraught when accused of violating its spirit. When his sister Jane told him he was becoming as dogmatic as Ruskin, he "told her the difference was that Ruskin was 'dogmatic and wrong.' "[14]

In varying degrees all of these thinkers were heretics within Victorian society, even so sober a figure as Arnold taking pleasure in the awareness of how frequently he had "startled" Oxford with his "heresies." But Mill pointed out, in *On Liberty*, that heretics, with whom he tended naturally to sympathize, were in respect of liberty no better than the established authorities who badgered or censored or oppressed them. For they aspired precisely to bring the rest of mankind around to their own way of thinking rather than making common cause with heretics generally, in defense of freedom itself. Starting from the principle that all silencing of discussion, and all interference with individual behavior that does not primarily concern other people, are assumptions of infallibility, Mill argued in *On Liberty* (and elsewhere) for complete liberty of expressing and publishing opinions, for the liberty of "doing as we like, subject to such consequences as may follow," and for the liberty of "combination among individuals . . . for any purpose not involving harm to others."[15]

It was in the middle and late sixties that my relationship to Mill's work and personality began to undergo a change, arising from a variety of causes, and not easy to define. Under the pressure of de-

91

mands for racial quotas in admission and hiring and for organized opposition to American involvement in the Vietnam War, academic communities everywhere demonstrated that their liberalism was highly selective and often blatantly political. With remarkable ease, universities yielded themselves to the seeming exigencies of politics (sometimes to merely trendy idolatries), and the academy was soon the very last place in America where one could find freedom of speech. Rather it had become the instrument for inculcating and enforcing what Lionel Trilling once called the "orthodoxies of dissent."[16] I marveled at the way the majority of the university community continued to pay a kind of ritual obeisance to the libertarian doctrines of Mill while doing the will of explicitly anti-democratic enemies of tolerance and of Mill like Noam Chomsky and Herbert Marcuse, who spoke before large and adoring campus audiences. Chomsky insisted that "By entering the arena of argument, by accepting the presumption of legitimacy of debate on certain issues, one has already lost one's humanity."[17] Herbert Marcuse, as early as 1965, condemned tolerance on the ground that it is a veil for subjection, a rationale for maintaining the status quo, and demanded that "regressive" elements of the population be suppressed lest they impede social liberation. In something of an understatement, Irving Howe remarked at the time that "Such theories are no mere academic indulgence or sectarian irrelevance; they have been put to significant use on the American campus as rationalizations for schemes to break up meetings of political opponents and as the justification for imaginary *coups d'etat* by . . . enraged intellectuals."[18]

Since Mill was a progressive and a social reformer as well as a lover of liberty, I returned to his work to see how he reconciled the principles of liberty with the exigencies of practical political action. He did not disappoint me. Indeed, in the essay called "Civilization," he pays particular attention to the problem of sectarian teaching in the universities of England, and asserts that this evil will never be removed by altering the form of sectarianism taught, for "the principle itself of dogmatic religion, dogmatic morality, dogmatic philosophy, is what requires to be rooted out; not any particular manifestation of that principle."[19] It was precisely his own ability to rise above disagreements over particular issues to shared first principles that enabled him to learn so much from Coleridge and other conservative thinkers. The primacy of principle over party now seemed to me one of the strongest elements in Mill's work. The party might be one's own, might in addition be—or proclaim itself to be—the party of Humanity and Altruism. But if it invoked the dogmatic principle, Mill was as firm in his rebuke of it as he had been when his political and philosophical antagonists acted on their assumption of infallibility.

Mill, I now recognized, had gone further yet in placing liberty above reformism. He had gradually come to see that it is precisely in our most generous wishes and most moral passions rather than in the selfish ones that the greatest dangers to liberty and the human spirit lie. His account of the origin of *On Liberty* locates the chief threat to liberty and individuality, not in governments, but precisely in movements of social reform. Writing from Rome in 1855 he told Harriet that "On my way here . . . I came back to an idea we have talked about, and thought that the best thing to write and publish at present would be a volume on Liberty. So many things might be brought into it and nothing seems more to be needed—it is a growing need too, for opinion tends to encroach more and more on liberty, and almost all the projects of social reformers of these days are really liberticide—Comte's particularly so."[20] Mill was indebted to Comte for many things, including a theory of history, the so-called law of the three stages, the conception of altruism (Comte's word), the theoretical groundwork of sociology, and above all the Religion of Humanity, in which the great benefactors of the human race were to inspire the religious devotion formerly called forth by supernatural figures. But by the time he came to compose his definitive estimate of Comte and positivism (published in 1865) Mill admitted that the dogmatic principle had rooted itself in positivist sociology. Comte, believing that the time had arrived for the final truths of sociology to be formulated and applied, had acquired a powerful conviction of his own infallibility and proposed the establishment of an intellectual dictatorship, headed by himself, to enforce distinctions between indispensable and merely frivolous intellectual pursuits and to direct all the mental resources of a nation to the solution of the most pressing question of the moment.

Within *On Liberty* itself, Mill several times insists that the spirit of liberty and the spirit of reform are not the same, and are perhaps even naturally incompatible. He sees England as a country by no means averse to change, so long as everyone changes at once.

> The spirit of improvement is not always a spirit of liberty, for it may aim at forcing improvements on an unwilling people; and the spirit of liberty, in so far as it resists such attempts, may ally itself locally and temporarily with the opponents of improvement; but the only unfailing and permanent source of improvement is liberty, since by it there are as many possible independent centres of improvement as there are individuals.

Social reformers are an impatient and therefore frequently intolerant lot. Mill knew them at first hand, had indeed been nurtured by them and even trained up as their secret weapon. From personal experience he knew that "spontaneity forms no part of the ideal of the majority of moral and social reformers, but is rather looked on with jealousy, as a troublesome and perhaps rebellious obstruction to the general acceptance of what these reformers, in their own judgment, think would be best for mankind."[21]

If reformers in general were, in Mill's view, prone to the temptations of *liberticide*, revolutionary socialists were committed to it in principle. Of socialism, as of the Religion of Humanity, Mill was a qualified adherent, but just as he opposed the establishment of the latter through suppression of opinion and intellectual dictatorship, so did he oppose the institution of the former through insurrectionary violence. Both were violations of what he understood to be the moral code of liberalism. What made revolutionary socialism still more terrifying than its explicit doctrines was the emotional character of the revolutionaries. In his posthumously published "Chapters on Socialism" Mill maintained that the introduction of socialism by the revolutionaries' taking over the whole property of the country "could have no effect but disastrous failure." But the prospect of such failure and the bloodshed it would bring would be no deterrent, but rather an incentive to the revolutionaries. Spectacular and bloody failure would bring to them "only the consolation that the order of society as it now exists would be involved in the common ruin—a consolation which to some of them would probably be real, for if appearances can be trusted the animating principle of too many of the revolutionary Socialists is hate."[22]

The firmness with which Mill condemned reformers who invoked the aid of tyranny, and socialists who wedded their cause to terror (and came to prefer terror to the cause), his ability to recognize barbarism dressed in the slogans of liberation, made him seem the perfect antidote to the sleazy opportunism and selective morality of late-sixties progressivism. On a few occasions, in print and on the lecture platform, I had the temerity to prescribe this antidote to others. Rarely did it find acceptance, except among certain of the more senior members of the academic community. One of my old professors, for example, told me that when his younger colleagues accused him of having become, by virtue of his old-fashioned liberal opposition to violence and his unresponsiveness to progressive fashion, an anachronism, he would reply by pointing out that "young Alexander" held the very same retrograde views. More typical of the reaction to the Mill who preferred liberty to "improvement" was the professor at Boston University who said, or rather shouted, to me that nothing could be less immediate to the needs of our historical moment than "another elitist-fascist snob like Yeats and Eliot." The fist which he waved at me, I can still recall, was clenched symbolically around a copy of the *New York Review of Books*, which had by 1968 already become what Ruth Wisse calls "the *Women's Wear Daily* of the American intelligentsia."[23]

It was in reaction to an atmosphere created by intellectual desperadoes like Marcuse, Chomsky, and I. F. Stone that I began to teach Mill, as I still do, as that rarest of all creatures, the radical who is able to dissent from the conformity of dissent and to be truthful with himself about his own politics. This was the Mill who, despite having been trained by his father and Bentham to believe that in the total mobilization of virtue for the purpose of reforming the world lay the only prospect of happiness for himself and others, awakened from this "dream" in 1826 at the behest of a terrifying question: "Suppose that all your objects in life were realized; that all the changes in institutions and opinions which you are looking forward to, could be completely effected at this very instant: would this be a great joy and happiness to you?" I would ask students to imagine contemporary versions of Mill's question, to suppose that their own desiderata were realized, that Vietnam was united under a Communist regime and Israel was reduced to sandy wastes, and international busing was mandated by the U.N., and then to ask

95

themselves whether "this would be a great joy and happiness to you?" Few students, even in those days, could fail to appreciate the unique force of Mill's candor in allowing "an irrepressible self-consciousness distinctly [to answer] 'No!' "[24] Few could fail to respond to his discovery in literature of the means of rescue from the desert of political abstraction.

It was comforting to me to discover that Mill could be decisively set apart from his wayward disciples, and effectively invoked against the totalitarian tendencies of radicalism. Yet the quarrel with others served also to exacerbate the quarrel with oneself. Millite liberalism, after all, had once been, for most of the now militantly illiberal academics, a kind of substitute religious faith. How much, I now asked myself, could such a faith be worth if its central doctrines were hastily hidden from view at the first emergency which tested them? Was it not, after all, true that liberty in itself, being only a procedure rather than a good, could never be elevated above things of intrinsic value and made the basis of a philosophy of life and society? The rapid disintegration of academic liberalism (and liberals) under pressure from leftist bullying was provoking the more thoughtful liberal philosophers like Emil Fackenheim to ask whether contemporary events did not indicate that "secularist liberalism itself stands in secret need of Biblical inspiration for its liberalism. If bereft of this inspiration, or subjugating and thus perverting it, may secularism not become illiberal and totalitarian or even a demonic pseudo-religion?"[25] I began, in short, to return to the essentially religious critique of Millite liberalism made by his Victorian contemporaries, and especially by Matthew Arnold. Only now, instead of using Mill's liberalism as a standard by which to judge Arnold's doctrine of culture, I was more inclined to use Arnold's culture as a touchstone for judging the spiritual sufficiency of Mill's liberalism.

Arnold's criticisms of Mill seemed to me especially potent because they were not entangled in peculiarly "Victorian" issues, but penetrated to the most enduring questions that separate liberal from idealist modes of thought. When Carlyle and Ruskin accused Mill of fostering anarchy under the cloak of liberty, they were attacking his laissez-faire political economy as much as his doctrines of free speech (for which Ruskin even expressed a grudging admiration before he wrote *Unto this Last*). It was Arnold alone who recognized that the real, the permanent danger implicit in Mill's world view was that of *spiritual* anarchy, of what Arnold also called Atheism. Except when he takes offense at Mill's references to the Church of England as nothing more than "the dominant sect" in English religion, Arnold chooses to challenge Mill on the enduring questions of whether there is such a thing as a truth that can be known and made to prevail, and of whether man or God is ultimately the measure of all things.

In Arnold's view Mill was wholly blind to one indispensable dimension of human experience: religion. "How short," he facetiously asked Clough in 1848, "could Mill write Job?" In other words, could a man whose entire education and philosophy were predicated on the desirability of realizing "the greatest happiness of the greatest number" appreciate the wisdom that was inseparable from suffering? Could this advocate of individual freedom and untrammeled self-development appreciate the ambiguous self-assertion of the Job who says: "Behold, he will slay me; I have no hope; but I will defend my (godly) ways before Him." (13:15) The implication of Arnold's question is that a utilitarian liberal devoid of artistic feeling as well as religious sensibility could make nothing of Job except a logical outline. Arnold was also quick to pounce upon what seemed to him the unconscious acknowledgement, in Mill's *Autobiography*, of the power of religion from one of the enemies of religion: "Mr. Mill tells us . . . that his father 'looked upon religion as the greatest enemy of morality.' Eighteen pages farther on, where he is descanting on the lamentable absence, in English society, of any high and noble standards of conduct, he adds that this absence prevails everywhere '*except among a few of the stricter religionists.*' "[26]

To *On Liberty* Arnold at first responded with cautious approval, recommending it to his sister as "worth reading attentively, being one of the few books that inculcate tolerance in an unalarming and inoffensive way." But by 1863 Arnold felt called upon to criticize *On Liberty* because it attacked the negativism of Christian morality and recommended a philosophical, which is to say a man-made, morality, over a religious, or revealed, one. This, in Arnold's view, showed a misunderstanding of the emotional springs of action, a

97

failure to recognize that a purely rational morality can appeal only to the few, not to the many—and is not likely to appeal to anybody on a death bed.[27]

In *Culture and Anarchy*, Arnold condemned Mill as a "rabbi," and probably took the title of his second chapter "Doing as One Likes," from Mill's argument in *On Liberty* for the liberty of "doing as we like, subject to such consequences as may follow." Although rarely mentioned by name, Mill appears to be a target throughout Arnold's work. His contention that past thinkers have grossly erred in inquiring what things society should like or dislike instead of questioning whether those likes and dislikes should be a law to individuals is countered by Arnold's insistence that "culture indefatigably tries, not to make what each raw person may like, the rule by which he fashions himself; but to draw ever nearer to a sense of what is indeed beautiful, graceful, and becoming, and to get the raw person to like that." What Arnold deplores as British Atheism is illustrated by a quotation from the *Times* that comes almost verbatim from Mill's *Liberty*: " 'It is of no use,' says the *Times*, 'for us to attempt to force upon our neighbours our several likings and dislikings.' " All the social and political manifestations of anarchy denounced by Arnold derive from the spiritual anarchy of Millite liberalism, "a kind of philosophical theory . . . widely spread among us to the effect that there is no such thing at all as a best self and a right reason having claim to paramount authority."[28] Mill ought not to have been surprised—he was—at "Matthew Arnold enumerating me among the enemies of culture."[29] According to Arnold's definition culture did not consist only of knowledge, even prodigious knowledge, like Mill's, but of the perfection of reason —"right reason"—under the aegis of authority.

Yet despite these severe criticisms of Mill, Arnold recognized that he was something more than a garden-variety liberal, and took pains to set him apart from his disciples, from those "in whom there appears scarcely anything that is truly sound or Hellenic at all." Arnold's concessions to Mill do have something of the condescending air of Ruskin's well-known praise of Mill for "inadvertently disclaiming the principles which he states, and tacitly introducing the moral considerations with which he declares his science has no connection." Yet it is clear that they are more than a rhetorical gesture designed to show Arnold's flexibility and concessiveness. They represent a genuine respect of the kind that Mill could evoke from even his most resolute enemies. It was because, for all his shortcomings, Mill had attained to the perception of certain truths about human nature that he was, "instead of being, like the school from which he proceeds, doomed to sterility,—a writer of distinguished mark and influence, a writer deserving all attention and respect." Mill was neither the great spirit nor the great writer that his admirers supposed, yet "was a singularly acute, ardent, and interesting man, . . . capable of following lights that led him away from the regular doctrine of philosophical radicalism."[30]

That the school of Enlightenment radicals—"philosophical radicals," as they once were called—was "doomed to sterility" everything in my mature experience now seemed to confirm. In the twentieth century the liberalism of Mill's followers had either taken a leftward turn into statism, or had ended in the empty self-contradiction of the "honest doubters," like the well-known author of the following:

> All the previous ages . . . had something they could take for granted. . . . We can be sure of nothing; our civilization is threatened, even the simplest things we live by. . . . In our present confusion our only hope is to be scrupulously honest with ourselves, so honest as to doubt our own minds and the conclusions they arrive at. Most of us have ceased to believe, except provisionally, in truths, and we feel that what is important is not so much truth as the way our minds move toward truths.[31]

That is to say, there are no truths, but it is terribly important that we search for them in the most scrupulous way.

Yet I remained convinced that Mill had indeed, as Arnold said, followed lights that kept him from the dark corridors in which other philosophical radicals lost themselves. One of these lights had revealed to Mill, decades before Arnold's critique, that the philosophy of the Enlightenment was destructive of the essence of culture. In his essays on Bentham and Coleridge, essays which F. R. Leavis long ago singled out as more indispensable to knowledge of Victorian literature than *Sartor Resartus* or *Unto this Last*,[32] Mill preceded Arnold in making "the philosophy of human culture" the vital center of conservative, religious, and idealistic philosophy, just as it was the great deficiency in infidel Enlightenment radicalism. Not even Arnold (who frequently expresses admiration for Voltaire) ever spoke so harshly of the spiritual emptiness of Enlightenment monism, naturalism, and relativism as did the Mill of 1840 who wrote of the exponents of "the French philosophy":

> To tear away was . . . all that these philosophers, for the most part, aimed at: they had no conception that anything else was needful. At their millennium, superstition, priestcraft, error and prejudice of every kind, were to be annihilated; some of them gradually added that despotism and hereditary privileges must share the same fate; and, this accomplished, they never for a moment suspected that all the virtues and graces of humanity could fail to flourish, or that when the noxious weeds were once rooted out, the soil would stand in any need of tillage.[33]

The conservatives, on the other hand, understood that every living culture, every society committed to continuance, is held together by something more than "freedom," something which does not come into existence by itself, but through human cultivation. Coleridge and the philosophers of his school had grasped the root meaning of the word and the idea of *culture*. Mill, at least in 1840, was entirely in sympathy with the Coleridge who, when his liberal friend Thelwall expressed the view that it was "very unfair to influence a child's mind by inculcating any opinions before it should have come to years of discretion, and be able to choose for itself," at once led Thelwall into his garden:

> I . . . told him it was my botanical garden. "How so?" said he, "it is covered with weeds."—"Oh," I replied, "*that* is only because it has not yet come to its age of discretion and choice. The weeds, you see, have taken the liberty to grow, and I thought it unfair in me to prejudice the soil towards roses and strawberries.[34]

The conservatives, with their respect for history and for the collective experience of the human race, grasped what Mill calls the three requisites of a civil society, one in which men obeyed as citizens, not as slaves. The first was a system of education in which "one main and incessant ingredient was *restraining discipline.*" The second requisite of permanent political society as defined by the conservatives and approved by Mill, was "the feeling of allegiance, or loyalty," the establishment in the very constitution of the State of "*something* which is settled, something permanent, and not to be called in question." The third requisite of a stable polity and culture was "a strong and active principle of cohesion among the members of the same community or state."[35]

100

In reweaving the fabric of Mill's thought to make it proof against the onslaught of Arnold's criticism, I found that the essays on Bentham and Coleridge were the strongest and most durable elements. They represented no mere "compromise" between the conservative idealism of Coleridge and the radical utilitarianism of Bentham, but a creative union of vital forces at war with each other, then and now. They were a pure exercise of mind, operating free of attachment to sect and party, a perfect realization of what Arnold was later to call "disinterestedness." In them resonates the ideal which Mill had, according to his autobiography, been striving to achieve since the early 1830s, the union of the best qualities of the critical with the best qualities of the organic periods of history in the future society of Europe. Far from celebrating what the *New Yorker* rhapsodically calls the "strange emptiness" of freedom, Mill looked beyond the unnatural "transitional" era in which he lived, to a society which would incorporate not only "unchecked liberty of thought, unbounded freedom of individual actions in all modes not hurtful to others; but also, convictions as to what is right and wrong, useful and pernicious, deeply engraven on the feelings by early education and general unanimity of sentiment. . . ."[36]

This perfect balance between freedom and conviction posited in the Bentham-Coleridge essays was an idea that eluded Mill nearly as often as it did the world for which he wrote. The excessive stress on the blessings of dissent and uncertainty in *On Liberty*, the arrant dogmatism and intolerance of Mill's championship of women's rights, serve in opposite ways as reminders that Mill did not always achieve the perfection of his own ideal. But I was now convinced that he came closest to realizing the balance he recommended for society as a whole when, in these dazzling essays of 1838 and 1840, he undertook to show that the great radical and the great conservative of his time, "these two sorts of men, who seem to be, and believe themselves to be, enemies are in reality allies. The powers they wield are opposite poles of one great force of progression."[37]

Mill's thought model was almost invariably a debate, either between individuals or between historical periods. Typically, he linked a theory of controversy and of the way to extract the whole truth from "the noisy conflict of half-truths" with a theory of history. Thus Bentham and Coleridge were made the spokesmen of historical epochs as well as of philosophical schools. History was a perpetual oscillation between conflicting modes of thought, a process in which progress consisted in approaching closer to the center of equilibrium. This newly-structured apologia for Mill satisfied me until I came to study the Holocaust. It was only then that I began to have doubts about what Mill calls the "historical" method of seeking truth, and about the source of that spiritual authority he invokes as a necessary complement to freedom of expression.

Prior to the twentieth century, the nearest parallel to the Holocaust, both in actuality and in Mill's perception of history, was the Reign of Terror of the French Revolution. Here, for a brief time and on a small scale, a sentence of death was pronounced and executed upon a class of people for no other "crime" than that of having been born into a certain class, the aristocracy. (Parenthetically, it may be noted, the aristocracy shared certain strongly-held life-principles with the Jews: both were inter-European, even international in their loyalties; for both, national allegiances often took second place to allegiance to a family scattered over Europe; both, moreover, "shared a conception that the present is nothing more than an insignificant link in the chain of past and future generations."[38]) I had always had a vague sense that, despite Mill's insistence that the French Revolution was a watershed event in history, its place in his historiography and his political ethos was something of a mystery, and perhaps a mystery with a meaning. I therefore decided to re-examine all his historical writing, using the French Revolution as a kind of litmus paper for detecting the moral underpinning of Mill's historiography.

According to the young Mill's historical theory, the outbreak of the French Revolution was the first spectacular manifestation of Europe's entry into an age of transition. Reading its history at age seventeen, he "learnt with astonishment, that the principles of democracy . . . had borne all before them in France . . . and had been the creed of the nation." For the next decade Mill immersed himself intellectually and emotionally in the revolution. Sometimes he would identify himself with the early revolutionists and dream of becoming "a Girondist in an English Convention"; at other times, "the French *philosophes* of the eighteenth century" were the example he and his friends sought to imitate.[39] By 1832 the largest segment of his private library consisted of materials on the revolution, and everybody reported that it was his favorite subject of con-

versation. Henry Crabb Robinson reported that Mill "is deeply
read in French politics, and bating his . . . unmeaning praise of
Robespierre . . . and . . . the respect he avowed for the virtues of
Mirabeau, he spoke judiciously enough about French matters. . . ."[40]

In 1828 Mill made the French Revolution the subject of his final
and most ambitious article for the original *Westminster*, a detailed
rebuttal of that part of Scott's *Life of Napoleon* which gives a history of the revolution. This elaborate defense of the early revolutionists against Scott's Tory calumnies was for Mill both "a labour
of love" and the natural reaction of one who intended writing the
history of the revolution against the premature effort of a biased
and ignorant interloper. Mill at this time believed that he alone of
all living Englishmen could do justice to the subject, a considerable
claim in view of the fact that early in this essay he lays it down that
no one short of a universal genius can adequately convey so unprecedented and unimaginable an event.[41]

One might suppose that in April 1828 the Mill who had recently
recovered from his mental crisis by an exercise of literary imagination would seek in imaginative literature an instrument for fathom-
ing a historically unique event, incredible not only to those who did
not witness it, but often even to those who, having acted or witnessed, tried to record their experiences "when the genuine impression of the present events" had faded and they had returned to the
realm of normal experience. Yet Mill asserts that Scott's novelistic
gifts are among his prime disqualifications for writing the history
of the revolution. Mill assumes a disjunction between objective
chronology of naked facts and a novelistic presentation of them,
which he derides as "dressing up" of reality according to the writer's
bias. A still more serious shortcoming of the novelistic approach to
the events of the French Revolution is that of moral judgment.
Scott's history presents the revolutionists as free moral agents, fully
responsible for their misdeeds. Ignoring the contingent nature of
human actions, Scott "blames men who did the best they could, for
not doing better; treats men who had only a choice of inconveniences, as if they were the masters of events."[42]

Mill does not, by deploring Scott's propensity for moral judgment, seek to exonerate the Terrorists. He refers to "the opprobrium
which is justly due to the terrorists alone," and to the absolute
separation between "all the more ardent and enthusiastic partisans

103

of the Revolution" and "the party called the Terrorists." Yet it is also true that he tries to keep the Terror and the moral ambiguities linked with it decently out of view, that he flirts with the liberal "idea" that everybody is guilty of a crime except the person who happens to commit it, and that he wants to see the whole revolution as a "great experiment" in the laboratories of history and human nature.[43]

Why, then, having invested tremendous amounts of time and energy in study of the revolution, having convinced himself that the cause of human improvement itself hinged upon vindication of the revolutionary experiment and that England too would feel the revolutionary "hurricane," did Mill abandon the project of writing the history of the revolution and consign it, along with many of his books on the subject, to Carlyle? His own explanation was that he found it impossible to declare to English readers that Christianity was historically, perhaps even biologically, obsolete and unsuited to the species in its present state of development. "One could not, *now*, say this openly in England, and be read at least by the many . . . *A propos* I have been reading the New Testament; properly I can never be said to have *read* it before." That Mill should simultaneously own up to the secret vice of gospel-reading and complain of Christian prejudice against truth-telling suggests that it was his own doubts about the adequacy of a purely historical judgment of historical events rather than those of the public that kept him from writing the history. If Christianity had indeed been, in Mill's words of 1833, "the greatest and best thing which has existed on this globe,"[44] was not one forced to question the view that the French Revolution was a great milestone in an infinitely progressing historical sequence? Or was progress distinct from improvement?

These questions pressed upon Mill's mind in 1833. History, he now argued, had both a scientific and a moral aspect. As a scientific enterprise, it "exhibits the general laws of the moral universe . . . and enables us to trace the connexion between great effects and their causes"; as a moral enterprise, it displays "the characters and lives of human beings, and calls upon us, according to their deservings or to their fortunes, for our sympathy, our admiration, or our censure." Yet the French Revolution challenged the historian's ability to reconcile his scientific and moral functions. In an angry review of Alison's *History of Europe* Mill calls the revolution

104

"one turbulent passage in a progressive revolution embracing the whole human race" and derides the historian exclusively concerned with "the degree of praise or blame due to the few individuals who . . . happened to be personally implicated in that strife of the elements." The figure implies that the revolution was as irresistible as —what he had already called it in 1831—a "hurricane," and as little liable to moral judgment. Admitting that the revolution immersed itself in "Immediate Evil", Mill seeks refuge in the idea that it served the cause of improvement towards which history seems to be aiming. As for the moral questions raised by the Terror, Mill pleads that "We have not now time or space to discuss the quantum of the guilt which attaches . . . to the . . . revolutionary governments, for the crimes of the revolution." Yet he feels constrained to confess that "Much was done which could not have been done except by bad men." A few months earlier he had so far forgotten his devotion to the scientific aspect of history as to complain of French historians of the revolution that they had arrived at "the annihilation of all moral distinctions except *success* and *not success.*"[45]

The strife between the scientific and moral principles in Mill's speculations on revolution is not primarily a conflict between the "radical" and the "conservative" Mill. That an amoral progressivism could coexist with Mill's newly-discovered reverence for conservatism is indicated in the language and sentiments of the following 1831 letter to Sterling:

> If there were but a few dozens of persons safe (whom you & I could select) to be missionaries of the great truths in which alone there is any well-being for mankind individually or collectively, I should not care though a revolution were to exterminate every person in Great Britain & Ireland who has £500 a year. Many very amiable persons would perish, but what is the world the better for such amiable persons. But among the missionaries whom I would reserve, a large proportion would consist of speculative Tories. . . .[46]

The real argument is between two differing views of the source of authority for these "great truths." The "scientific" Mill tends towards the historicist view that history is the sole source and arbiter of truth and values; the Mill leavened by suffering and by literature seeks a more absolute and eternal basis of intellectual and spiritual authority without ever finding it.

The years immediately following the abandonment of the French Revolution project were for Mill years of intense speculation on the nature of the historical enterprise. During the late thirties and the forties he began to substitute perpetual antagonism for perpetual movement as his metaphor for history. From Coleridge especially he learned that the well-being of society and politics demanded a balanced antagonism between radical and conservative sympathies, the interests of progression and permanence, with each party to this fruitful conflict tempering its opposite. The Enlightenment thinkers and their revolutionary disciples had forgotten that without contraries there is no progression. Their intolerance of the conservative party to the historical dialogue found its natural expression in the enormities of Robespierre and Saint-Just. These organizers of terror persuaded themselves (as did the originators of modern totalitarianism) that they murdered not as criminals but as executors of death-sentences passed by history itself upon unprogressive classes and ideas. What other conviction, asks Mill in 1838, "could lead any man to believe that his individual judgment respecting the public good is a warrant to him for exterminating all who are suspected of forming any other judgment, and for setting up a machine to cut off heads, sixty or seventy every day, till some unknown futurity be accomplished, some Utopia realized?"[47] Mill had come to the recognition that utopianism is not love but precisely hatred of mankind.

Hannah Arendt, in her magisterial study of the subject of totalitarianism, has located its origins in "the tremendous intellectual change which took place in the middle of the last century . . . in the refusal to view or accept anything 'as it is' and in the consistent interpretation of everything as being only a stage of some further development." She shows how totalitarian movements built themselves upon the idea of a "law of nature" that eliminated everything unfit to live or a "law of history" that eliminated unprogressive classes in the "class struggle." Those who impede the movement of History or Nature are the objective enemies of the natural or historical process which has passed judgment over inferior races, individuals "unfit to live," dying classes and decadent peoples. According to totalitarian ideology, as perfected by Hitler and Stalin, the practitioners of terror are subjectively innocent because "they do not really murder but execute a death sentence

106

pronounced by some higher tribunal. . . . Terror is lawfulness, if law is the law of the movement of some suprahuman force, Nature or History."[48]

I confess that, in this most recent rereading of Mill, I very much wanted to find conclusive evidence that he eventually rejected historicist notions of inevitable forces which override human will and render moral judgment pointless. But I found that alongside the exhortations to the will which flow from his belief that in this world we make our own good, or our own evil, were to be found invocations of the principle of historical law and inevitability. In the forties Mill continued to equate historical with natural causes, though he was now more likely to speak of raging rivers, which man can harness to his use, than of hurricanes, which he cannot.

What kept Mill—fortunately, in my view—from being a consistent historicist was his experience of literature, the proper role of which in historiography had troubled him from the time of his attack on Walter Scott. After being "cured" of his spiritual illness by Wordsworth, Mill associated literary experience with the joy and wisdom that derive from stationariness. From the poets and novelists one learned little or nothing of the law of historical progress, but one could gain moral and psychological knowledge of what Mill in the *Autobiography* calls "the perennial sources of happiness." Since Mill's historical theory insisted that the laws of historical evolution required validation by correspondence with the laws of human nature to become scientific, literature posed the question of whether human nature matches the (supposedly) progressive character of European history. Mill's progressive theory both of history and of the human intellect was contradicted by his deep-seated conviction in the stationary character of human nature. What kept laws of history from becoming laws of nature was not a flaw in Victorian historiography—as the youthful Mill had supposed—but a flaw in human nature itself. This grim discovery invades Mill's writings in the fifties. In 1853 he praises the Greeks because they "decided for an indefinite period the question, whether the human race was to be stationary or progressive," but "that the former condition is far more congenial to ordinary human nature . . . experience unfortunately places beyond doubt. . . ." *On Liberty* assumes that truth often fails to survive persecution, that history makes appalling "mistakes," and is often the record of wrong triumphant. In 1854 Mill confided to his diary: "It seems to me that there is no progress, and no reason to expect progress, in talents or strength of mind. . . . But there is great progress . . . in feelings and opinions. If it is asked whether there is progress in intellect the answer will be found in the two preceding statements taken together."[49]

These unresolved antinomies indicate that Mill's retreat from the organic and necessitarian view of history was a partial, yet substantial, one. That he had hit upon one of the most dangerous elements in nineteenth-century thought, one whose full destructiveness would become apparent only in our own time, is evident in his growing reluctance to accept "natural" metaphors for historical action. In the essay "Nature," written between 1850 and 1854, Mill returns briefly to the Reign of Terror and compares it, as he had done twenty years earlier, to "a hurricane and a pestilence." But the point of the comparison has entirely changed. Previously, Mill had used the analogy to "explain" the Terror as the agent of a historical progression as inevitable as a natural force. Now his aim is to reveal the moral enormity of political murderers who masquerade as the innocent executors of a law of nature: "Pope's 'Shall gravitation cease when you go by?' may be a just rebuke to any one who should be so silly as to expect common human morality from nature. But if the question were between two men, instead of between a man and a natural phenomenon, that triumphant apostrophe would be thought a rare piece of impudence. A man who should persist in hurling stones or firing cannon when another man 'goes by,' and having killed him should urge a similar plea in exculpation, would very deservedly be found guilty of murder."[50]

I believe that now, in the aftermath of the Holocaust, and for some time to come, Mill's exploration of the relation between history and terror, rather than his advocacy of liberty, individuality, sex reform and electoral reform, should compel the attention of scholars and students. Mill never wholly freed himself from the belief that the "law" of historical progression is of necessity a law of improvement. But to the extent that he incorporated into his thought an ability, which he had gained from the poets, to imagine the world as always in its beginning, the influence of historicism over his mind waned. His retreat from historicism arose from a recognition that human beings, to be truly free, had to be liberated from the service of history and nature as well as from the service of the state. He saw that a principle of progression which assigned to whole groups of human beings the role of raw material for the development of a more nearly perfect "mankind" was a crime against the human status itself.

NOTES

1. Marie Syrkin, "Sadat, Skokie & Cosmos 954," *Midstream*, 24 (March 1978), 66.

2. Hannah Arendt, *The Origins of Totalitarianism*, 3 vols. (New York: Harcourt, Brace, and World, 1951), I, x; III, 137-38.

3. J. S. Mill, *On Liberty*, in *Autobiography and Other Writings*, ed. Jack Stillinger, Riverside Edition (Boston: Houghton Mifflin, 1969), p. 353.

4. Yehuda Bauer, *The Holocaust in Historical Perspective* (Seattle: University of Washington Press, 1978), p. 35.

5. Cynthia Ozick, "A Liberal's Auschwitz," in *The Pushcart Prize: Best of the Small Presses*, ed. Bill Henderson (Yonkers, New York: Pushcart Press, 1975), p. 125.

6. Robert J. Loewenberg, "The Theft of Liberalism," *Midstream*, 28 (May 1977), 24.

7. *New Yorker*, August 21, 1978, p. 17.

8. *On Liberty*, in *Autobiography and Other Writings*, p. 383.

9. Ibid., p. 453; J. S. Mill, *Principles of Political Economy*, ed. J. M. Robson (Toronto: University of Toronto Press, 1965), II, 794.

10. Northrop Frye, "The Problem of Spiritual Authority in the Nineteenth Century," in Richard Levine, ed., *Backgrounds to Victorian Literature* (San Francisco: Chandler, 1967), pp. 129-30.

11. J. S. Mill, *Considerations on Representative Government*. Everyman Edition (London: J. M. Dent, 1910), p. 283.

12. Ibid., p. 285.

13. *On Liberty*, in *Autobiography and Other Writings*, p. 357.

14. Alexander Carlyle, ed., *New Letters of Thomas Carlyle*, 2 vols. (London, 1904), II, 196; John Henry Newman, *Lectures on Difficulties of Anglicans*, Lecture VIII, 1850; John Ruskin, *Works of John Ruskin*, ed. E. T. Cook and A. Wedderburn, 39 vols. (London, 1903-12), XXVIII, 402; Matthew Arnold, *Letters of Matthew Arnold*, ed. G. W. E. Russell, 2 vols. (New York, 1900), I, 233.

15. *On Liberty*, in *Autobiography and Other Writings*, p. 362.

16. Lionel Trilling, *The Liberal Imagination* (New York: Viking Press, 1950), p. 7.

17. Noam Chomsky, *American Power and the New Mandarins* (New York: Pantheon Books, 1968), p. 17. In this connection, it is worth noting that Chomsky has recently (1980-81) been among the most vigorous defenders of Robert Faurisson's inalienable right to propagate, from a university chair, the Nazi lie that the Holocaust is a Zionist invention. He has also written a preface to the English edition of the book in which this French professor sets forth his "argument." Apparently,

since Chomsky takes an "agnostic" view on the question of whether the Jews of Europe really were murdered, he does not fear that his "humanity" is endangered by neo-Nazism. Either he is a late convert to Millite liberalism or his zeal for free speech swells in proportion to the anti-Zionism of the speaker.

18. Irving Howe, "The New York Intellectuals," *Commentary*, 46 (October 1968), 45.

19. J. S. Mill, "Civilization," in *Dissertations and Discussions*, 2 vols. (London, 1859), I, 201.

20. F. A. Hayek, *John Stuart Mill and Harriet Taylor* (Chicago: University of Chicago Press, 1951), p. 216.

21. *On Liberty*, in *Autobiography and Other Writings*, pp. 417, 404.

22. J. S. Mill, "Chapters on Socialism," *Essays on Economics and Society* (Toronto: University of Toronto Press, 1967), p. 749.

23. Ruth Wisse, "The Anxious American Jew," *Commentary*, 66 (September 1978), 50.

24. *Autobiography*, in *Autobiography and Other Writings*, p. 81.

25. Emil Fackenheim, "On the Self-Exposure of Faith to the Modern-Secular World," *Daedalus*, 96 (Winter 1967), 199.

26. *Letters of Matthew Arnold to A. H. Clough*, ed. H. F. Lowry (London and New York: Oxford University Press, 1932), p. 75; Matthew Arnold, *A French Eton* (London: Macmillan, 1904), p. 122.

27. *Letters of Matthew Arnold*, I, 111; Matthew Arnold, *Lectures and Essays in Criticism*, ed. R. H. Super (Ann Arbor: University of Michigan Press, 1962), pp. 133–34.

28. Matthew Arnold, *Culture and Anarchy*, ed. J. Dover Wilson (Cambridge: Cambridge University Press, 1960), pp. 50, 120.

29. *Later Letters of John Stuart Mill*, ed. F. E. Mineka and D. N. Lindley, 4 vols. (Toronto and London: University of Toronto Press, 1972), III, 1324.

30. Matthew Arnold, *Dissent and Dogma*, ed. R. H. Super (Ann Arbor: University of Michigan Press, 1968), p. 126; *Lectures and Essays in Criticism*, p. 136; *A French Eton*, p. 100.

31. Bonamy Dobrée, *Modern Prose Style* (Oxford: Clarendon, 1934), p. 220.

32. F. R. Leavis, Introduction to *Mill on Bentham and Coleridge* (London: Chatto & Windus, 1959), p. 1.

33. J. S. Mill, "Coleridge," in *Autobiography and Other Writings*, pp. 273–74.

34. *Table Talk*, in *Inquiring Spirit: A Coleridge Reader*, ed. K. Coburn (New York: Minerva Press, 1968), p. 75.

35. "Coleridge," in *Autobiography and Other Writings*, pp. 275–77.

36. *Autobiography*, in *Autobiography and Other Writings*, p. 100.

37. "Coleridge," in *Autobiography and Other Writings*, p. 289.

38. Arendt, *The Origins of Totalitarianism*, I, 31.

39. *Autobiography*, in *Autobiography and Other Writings*, pp. 40, 66.

40. *The Diary of Henry Crabb Robinson: An Abridgment*, ed. D. Hudson (London: Oxford University Press, 1967), p. 114.

41. *Autobiography*, in *Autobiography and Other Writings*, p. 79; "Scott's *Life of Napoleon*," *Westminster Review*, 9 (April 1828), 256.

42. "Scott's *Life of Napoleon*," pp. 275, 258, 276.

43. Ibid., pp. 275, 296, 312n, 262-63.

44. *Earlier Letters of John Stuart Mill*, ed. F. E. Mineka, 2 vols. (Toronto and London: University of Toronto Press, 1963), I, 182.

45. J. S. Mill, "Alison's History of the French Revolution," *Monthly Repository*, 7 (August 1833), 513, 515-16; *Earlier Letters*, I, 139.

46. *Earlier Letters*, I, 84.

47. J. S. Mill, "Poems and Romances of Alfred de Vigny," *London and Westminster Review*, 29 (April 1838), 39.

48. *The Origins of Totalitarianism*, III, 162-63.

49. *Autobiography*, in *Autobiography and Other Writings*, p. 89; "Grote's History of Greece," *Edinburgh Review*, 98 (October 1853), 428; *Letters of John Stuart Mill*, ed. H. S. R. Elliot, 2 vols. (London: Longmans, Green and Co., 1910), II, 359.

50. J. S. Mill, *Essays on Ethics, Religion and Society*, ed. J. M. Robson (Toronto and London: University of Toronto Press, 1969), pp. 384-85.

The final segment of this essay includes some paragraphs from my much lengthier discussion of Mill's ideas about history in "The Principles of Permanence and Progression in the Thought of J. S. Mill," in *James and John Stuart Mill: Papers of the Centenary Conference*, ed. J. M. Robson and Michael Laine (Toronto: University of Toronto Press, 1976), pp. 126-42.

ADVENTURING WITH DARWIN[1]

PHILIP APPLEMAN

After 1859, when Charles Darwin published *The Origin of Species,* Western civilization experienced a collective intellectual adventure, slowly (and sometimes painfully) adapting to a radically new perception of how human beings understand and relate to the world. That adventure continues today, and it is often reflected, in microcosm, in our individual lives. Since my own adventures with Darwin have paralleled the larger experience, I am going to take the liberty of invoking my memories in order to discuss some of the ways in which Darwinism has shaped, and is still shaping, our view of the world.

I

In a rather Shandean way, it was relevant to my own experience of Darwin that I was conceived in the same month that John Thomas Scopes was arrested and indicted by a grand jury for the crime of teaching evolution to the schoolchildren of Dayton, Tennessee; and that in due course I was born in Kendallville, Indiana, in the year that the legislature of the state of Mississippi duplicated the Tennessee anti-evolution law. My memory of those events is imperfect; but by the time I started school, the anti-evolutionary laws had spread to Arkansas and (by legislative resolution) to Florida. There had been agitation for similar laws all around the country; and high school and college teachers had been fired for mentioning evolution in the classroom. By the time I learned to read, textbook publishers had already got the message: the word "evolution" and the name of Darwin had been deleted from virtually all public-school textbooks and continued to be banned, partly by law and partly by self-censorship, for four decades. The public schools of my home town were no different from most others in America: in twelve years of public education, including a high school course in biology, I never heard the name of Charles Robert Darwin. Across the nation, the invisible government of church fathers and school boards had, in effect, abolished a natural law from the schools. It was, in retrospect, a rather astonishing feat, the educational equivalent, of, say, the Flat Earth Society abolishing gravitation.

So when I was eighteen, my fifty-eight classmates and I, like many thousands of our contemporaries around the country, graduated from high school, profoundly ignorant of one of the most basic facts of life: the perpetual functioning of organic evolution. World War II was in progress then, so most young men my age went immediately into the army, where we learned very little else of any value; and after the war I joined the Merchant Marine for a spell, which, as it happened, was to have a considerable effect on my education. For after two years of college, where I finally did hear about Darwin, I returned to the Merchant Marine, eager for free time to read and to reflect on the flood of new ideas that college had turned loose on me.

In 1948, before the paperback revolution, the only cheap and easily available editions of the classics of literature, science, and philosophy were the Everyman and the Modern Library editions. Fortunately, there was a Modern Library Giant with *The Origin of Species* and *The Descent of Man* in one volume: exactly one thousand pages of small print. I still have the book, a bit dog-eared from thirty years of travel and use, and much underscored with the smudgy blue first-generation ballpoint pens I carried to sea.

I read that book in noisy mess rooms, surrounded by cribbage-playing seamen. I read it in my bunk at night, the persistent bed-lamp sometimes infuriating my surly watchmates. I read it on deck in the sunny waters of the Mediterranean, meanwhile collecting extra hazard pay because stray floating mines were still sinking ships there. The 1948 marginalia reinforce my memory of being interested in the mechanisms of natural selection: the smudgy blue lines draw attention to Darwin's pondering of the lapse of time in evolution; to his remarks on differentiation of parts and specialization; on the possible causes of variation; on unity of type and the conditions of existence; on transitional links; on the significance of rudimentary organs.

But the more detailed marginalia indicate that what most held my attention, in both *The Origin* and *The Descent*, was the information bearing upon the relation of human beings to the rest of nature, and the philosophical implications of evolution. Chapter 1 of *The Descent of Man* ("The Evidence of the Descent of Man from Some Lower Form") is systematically outlined and heavily underlined in that blue ink. So is the part of Chapter 2 relating to the Malthusian rationale for natural selection. And so are large parts of Chapter 6 dealing with our descent from "lower animals," with what those animals must have looked like, and with Darwin's marveling over the "glory" of the human presence while at the same time remaining openly skeptical of the notion of a benevolent God or the possibility of special creation.

I'm sure it is difficult for anyone reared in a more enlightened time and place to imagine the sense of exhilaration in a young person schooled in Midwestern fundamentalism, reading Darwin and understanding evolution for the very first time. But I recall that experience vividly: the sense of overwhelming sanity that emerged from Darwin's clearly thought out and clearly written propositions; the sense of relief at being finally released from a constrained allegiance to the incredible creation myths of Genesis; the profound sense of satisfaction in knowing that one is truly and altogether a part of nature.

There is a lot of time for reading on a ship, and I read much more on the cold North Atlantic that year: Plato, Montaigne, Kant, Nietszche, Schopenhauer, Bergson, James, Dewey, and others, most of them in those handy Modern Library volumes. Some of them spoke to me with force, but none with the compelling authority of Darwin's vision. Reading Darwin made all the other thinkers, especially the older ones, seem obsolete. In his recent book *The Selfish Gene*, Richard Dawkins has this to say:

> We no longer have to resort to superstition when faced with the deep problems: Is there a meaning to life? What are we for? What is man? After posing the last of these questions, the eminent zoologist G. G. Simpson put it thus: "The point I want to make now is that all attempts to answer that question before 1859 are worthless and that we will be better off if we ignore them completely."[2]

114

That is the way I felt about it, too, pondering the winter stars in the long night watches in 1948.

II

Five years later I had graduated from Northwestern University, done graduate work at the University of Michigan and a Fulbright year at the University of Lyon, France—literally in the shadow of a colossal statue of the local dignitary, Lamarck—and was back at Northwestern, casting about for a dissertation subject. I had already been impressed with how extensively the idea of evolution had affected the literary criticism of late nineteenth-century France. The English critics accepted such abstract notions more gingerly than the French did; nevertheless, they too began to perceive literature in evolutionary ways. Walter Bagehot and Leslie Stephen, for instance, both thought they recognized the operation of something like natural selection in literature, the appearance of new strains of writing causing the extinction of older ones. John Addington Symonds held that since literature, like everything else, exists in process, one must look at literature with reference to its antecedents, its environment; he believed that the critic would then see literature passing through stages of growth and decline, like any organism, and that this outlook would help to illuminate lesser works and put the greater ones in useful perspective. And Walter Pater's criticism was shaped by his perception of evolution as both an empirical and a genetic shaping force. Literature, in the perspective of this new and influential science, could be viewed either impressionistically ("What is this work of art to *me?*) or historically ("Every intellectual product must be judged from the point of view of the age and people in which it was produced"). The two approaches seem to be incompatible; but Pater spent his life as a critic managing somehow to hold them in suspension, attempting (as Michael Field put it) to "seize the vitality of the present in any moment of the past."[3]

There is a fusing agent in the theory of evolution, a welding power that blends present with past in causal and meaningful relationships and forces us to be more aware of the multiplicity and yet the interrelation of all sorts of experience. The post-Darwinian critic, Pater's experience implies, simply does not have the option of being "either" isolated and personal "or" historical and tradi-

115

tional; nor may he stack the one on the other like building blocks. If any metaphor will do at all, it is Darwin's vision of life: we are "all netted together."⁴ The responsible critic must keep past and present, tradition and texture, history and imagery "netted together," for it is not any one of these alone, but all of them at once, which make the power and richness, the value, of the work of art.

III

My adventures with Darwin had by this time gone further than I had once expected them to; but as it turned out, they had only begun. A revolutionary world view, it goes by definition, will affect one's ideas on every subject. I had become aware of evolution as a straightforward biological fact; soon, however, it had altered my personal philosophy; then it prompted a literary investigation. Next it became the source of a historical and social study. Arriving at Indiana University in 1955, I was asked to lecture on social Darwinism. The subject interested me, but of course it had already been much explored. Still, the subject was so broad that there were many fresh ways of thinking about it.

For my part, I was fascinated by the blandly self-serving assumptions of social Darwinism, by the contradictions between that philosophy and others of our accepted and respectable social philosophies, and by the anomalies generated by those contradictions. The publication of *The Origin of Species* and the American Civil War were almost simultaneous, and in the years following those two traumatic events, the United States was industrializing very rapidly. The late nineteenth century became the pre-eminent period in our history of the Rugged Individualist, the Robber Baron, the Captain of Industry, the accumulators of great wealth. It was also a period of sweatshops, of union-busting, of goon squads and strike-breaking massacres, of a dollar a day for working people, of tenements without sanitation, of widespread malnutrition.

It was not simple, in a "Christian society," to reconcile such contradictions. The economic establishment had, since the beginnings of the industrial revolution, been casting about for sanctions, for justifications. Manchester political economy had been a powerful sanction for the establishment, emphasizing as it did the necessity for untrammelled individual enterprise, the automatic enlightenment of self-interest, and the "iron" laws of economics. ("There is no more possibility of defeating the operation of these laws," Carnegie once said, "than there is of thwarting the laws of nature which determine the humidity of the atmosphere or the revolution of the earth upon its axis."[5]) Curiously enough, there were religious sanctions, too, for had not material things always been corrupting to people, and was it not therefore self-evident that the lower classes had to be kept poor to be kept virtuous—and, paradoxically, could not the virtuous and industrious among the poor expect to be rewarded, even in this world? ("He that gets all he can honestly," Ben Franklin had declared, "and saves all he gets will certainly become rich, if that Being who governs the world, to whom all should look for a blessing on their endeavors, doth not, in His wise providence, otherwise determine." To which a railroad president added, a century later: "The rights and interests of the laboring man will be protected and cared for by the Christian men to whom God has given control of the property rights of the country."[6]

And always, in the nineteenth century, there was that court of last resort, the sanction of Progress, in whose name all contradictions were resolved—or ignored.

But in natural selection the economic establishment found a massive sanction which gathered into one grand synthesis all of the previous ones and added to them its own profound, "scientific" prestige. Natural selection and the struggle for existence lent authority to laissez faire economics (the state, said Herbert Spencer, should refrain from action calculated to interfere with the struggle for existence in the industrial field[7]); absorbed the older religious sanctions (the "laws" of natural selection, said one economist, were "merely God's regular methods of expressing his choice and approval"[8]); and seemed to make Progress inevitable (evolution, said Spencer, "can end only in the establishment of the greatest perfection and the most complete happiness"; "Progress," he said, "is not an accident, but a necessity"[9]).

Among American economists, the most thoroughgoing advocate of these views was William Graham Sumner, whose reading of Spencer in the early 1870s convinced him that Spencer was right in seeing the world as "a harsh, exacting nature, enforcing a bitter struggle for the meager goods available to humankind. To him the laws of individual and social existence were simple and rigorous. Rewards and punishments are meted out with impartial justice. Property, the enjoyment of family life, health, social preference go to the fit, while poverty, disease, and starvation are the lot of the unfit." And thus "the millionaires are a product of natural selection, acting on the whole body of men to pick out those who can meet the requirement of certain work to be done."[10] This is conservative social Darwinism, in a nutshell.

The Captains of Industry were quick to pick up this Darwinistic vocabulary. "The growth of a large business," said John D. Rockefeller (speaking to a Sunday-school class), "is merely a survival of the fittest. . . . The American Beauty rose can be produced in the splendor and fragrance which bring cheer to the beholder only by sacrificing the early buds which grow up around it. This is not an evil tendency in business. It is merely the working-out of a law of nature and of God."[11] Similarly, James J. Hill held that "the fortunes of railroad companies are determined by the law of the survival of the fittest."[12] And Carnegie once warned his lieutenants, upon his break with the Steel Pool, that "a struggle is inevitable and it is a question of the survival of the fittest."[13]

Carnegie was the most introspective and easily the most articulate of the Rugged Individualists. He was strongly attracted to Spencer's theories, and his own speech and writings became full of Spencer's phraseology. He quickly adopted Spencer's easy optimism about progress; he believed firmly that the "fit" who survived in the struggle were the "best," and that these people would lead the rest to certain progress. "The exceptional man in every department," he said, "must be permitted and encouraged to develop his unusual powers, tastes, and ambitions in accordance with the laws which prevail in everything that lives or grows. The 'survival of the fittest' means that the exceptional plants, animals, and men which have the needed 'variations' from the common standard, are the fructifying forces which leaven the whole."[14]

But there were all sorts of anomalies in this use of the evolutionary sanctions: anomalies of language, for instance. To scientists, the word "natural" meant simply "the way things occur in nature"; but used by the apologists for social Darwinism, it always implied "the way things ought to be." "Survival" was similarly converted into a term of generalized approbation—so persistently that William James was prompted to object: "The entire modern deification of survival *per se*, survival returning to itself, survival naked and abstract, with the denial of any substantive excellence in *what* survives, except the capacity for more survival still, is surely the strangest intellectual stopping-place ever proposed by one man to another."[15] The most abused of all of the evolutionary terms, however, was the word "fit." Spencer and Sumner insisted that the wealthy must be the "fit," for obvious reasons, and conversely, that the poor must be the "unfit," since the latter were, as Spencer held, the "stupid, vicious, or idle," or, to use Sumner's words, the "negligent, shiftless, inefficient, silly, and imprudent." The fallacies of this terminology are obvious and have often been objected to. T. H. Huxley insisted that the biologically "fittest" were by no means always the "highest" order of creatures, and G. G. Simpson has pointed out that, inchoately in Darwin and definitely for neo-Darwinians, "fittest" means simply: leaving the most descendants over a number of generations. Lester Ward, from a less biological, more moralistic point of view, observed that Sumner's definition of the "fit" was based on the "fundamental error that the favors of this world are distributed entirely according to merit."[16]

It stands as at least a qualified tribute to the humanity of human beings that many people simply would not accept the callousness of conservative social Darwinism, however much it attempted to justify itself by the appeal to "scientific" prestige. Richard Tawney once argued that one sees the true character of a social philosophy most clearly in "the way it regards the misfortunes of those of its members who fall by the way."[17] Those who fell by the way in late nineteenth-century America were assured by the conservative apologists that this was their "natural" lot, that "science" proved that they were the unavoidable by-products of a beneficent Struggle for Existence, without which there could be no Progress; but meanwhile, people with less emotional investment in maintaining the economic status quo were questioning whether the implications of evolution were really as somberly deterministic as the conservatives made out. As early as the 1870s some zoologists had been investigating the implications of cooperation, as well as competition, in the natural world, and in 1902 Peter Kropotkin was to publish his *Mutual Aid*, revealing that he had

> failed to find—although I was eagerly looking for it—that bitter struggle for the means of existence, *among animals belonging to the same species*, which was considered by most Darwinists (though not always by Darwin himself) as the dominant characteristic of struggle for life, and the main factor of evolution. . . . On the other hand, wherever I saw animal life in abundance . . . I saw Mutual Aid and Mutual Support carried on to an extent which made me suspect in it a feature of the greatest importance for the maintenance of life, the preservation of each species, and its further evolution.[18]

And he generalized, from this pattern, that

> it is not love and not even sympathy upon which Society is based in mankind. It is the conscience—be it only at the stage of an instinct—of human solidarity. It is the unconscious recognition of the force that is borrowed by each man from the practice of mutual aid; of the close dependency of every one's happiness upon the happiness of all; and of the sense of justice, or equity, which brings the individual to consider the rights of every other individual as equal to his own. Upon this broad and necessary foundation the still higher moral feelings are developed.[19]

Thomas Henry Huxley had already made the distinction, in his Romanes lecture of 1893, that "the ethical progress of society depends, not on imitating the cosmic process, still less in running away from it, but in combating it."[20] "Social progress," he said, "means a checking of the cosmic process at every step and the substitution for it of another, which may be called the ethical process; the end of which is not the survival of those who may happen to be the fittest, in respect of the whole of the conditions which obtain, but of those who are ethically the best."[21]

By the end of the century, then, there were developing some serious demurrers to narrowly conservative Darwinistic social thought. Some naturalists were broadening the evolutionary view of life to show that nature was not always and simply competitive. And some social and ethical thinkers were attempting to demonstrate that even though ruthless competition does exist in nature, it is not therefore necessarily a proper pattern for human behavior.

IV

I have noted that a Darwinian coloration gradually tinted many of my perceptions. The process continued in the late 1950s, as the centennial year of *The Origin of Species* approached. William Madden, Michael Wolff, and I (joined, a little later, by Donald Gray and George Levine) had by then established a new journal called *Victorian Studies*, and we planned a special Darwin issue for 1959. We also planned another volume to commemorate that *annus mirabilis*, which we called *1859: Entering an Age of Crisis*. At the same time I was asked to lecture on Darwin and modern literature. The evolution of my Darwinian perspectives continued. Rereading modern literature from a Darwinian point of view, I was struck by how much less explicit the evolutionary idea has been in twentieth-century literature than it was in nineteenth-century literature. However, there have been some exceptions: for instance, one of the alleged effects of Darwinian assumptions on modern literature was the claim that Darwin's ideas have eroded human values and therefore destroyed high tragedy in our century. Joseph Wood Krutch wrote in *The Modern Temper* (1929):

> Three centuries lay between the promulgation of the Copernican theory and the publication of the *Origin of Species*, but in sixty-odd years which have elapsed since that latter event the blows have fallen with a rapidity which left no interval for recovery. The structures which are variously known as mythology, religion, and philosophy, and which are alike in that each has as its function the interpretation of experience in terms which have human values, have collapsed under the force of successive attacks and shown themselves utterly incapable of assimilating the new stores of experience which have been dumped upon the world. With increasing completeness science maps out the pattern of nature, but the latter has no relation to the pattern of human needs and feelings.

This situation, Krutch said,

> precludes tragedy because "the Tragic Fallacy depends ultimately upon the assumption which man so readily makes that something outside his own being . . . confirms him in his feeling that his passions and his opinions are important. . . . We can no longer tell tales of noble men because we do not believe that noble men exist."[22]

Looking about us from the perspective of the last decades of the twentieth century, we can recognize the symptoms of Krutch's diagnosis. Nevertheless, the case as he states it can hardly be the whole story. For one thing, we ought to consider the negative instances. If Darwin destroyed twentieth-century tragedy, who then was responsible for the palpable failure of early nineteenth-century

121

tragedy, or for the failure of eighteenth-century tragedy? In fact, the occurrence of high tragedy has always been far rarer than its nonoccurrence; to expect every age to produce a Sophocles or a Shakespeare is overoptimistic.

For another thing: it is not simply axiomatic that a physically mechanistic world is necessarily a morally valueless one. Those who propose that it is, seem to regret that natural selection is an automatic process, that it acts independently of teleological considerations, and that it, together with Mendelian genetics, makes such a satisfactory explanation of organic evolution; and they sometimes attempt to ignore all this and postulate instead some sort of "will" or "preference" or "emergent evolution." Since Darwin, however, reasonable people have simply had to abandon naturalistic teleology—one cannot, any more, look to nature for revealing patterns of goal-directed process. Or, to put it another way, goal-direction in nature must now be divorced from final causes or preternatural factors. However, as John Herman Randall, Jr., pointed out,

> nature is once more for us, as for the Greeks, full of *implicit* ends and ideals, full of "values," just because it is now an affair of processes, of means effecting ends, of things that are "necessary for," "better" and "worse for" other things. It contains so much "natural teleology," in terms of which its various factors can be "evaluated." It takes but a single flower to refute the contention that there are no "values" in nature, no achievement of ends through valuable means. We may even say it is obviously "good for" the planet to go round the sun. Of course, neither the flower nor the planet "finds" it good: only men "find" anything. But surely it does not follow that because only men find anything good or bad, better or worse, what they find is not found. The finding is a genuine cooperation with nature.
>
> It is such a nature our best post-Darwinian knowledge and thought now reveal to us.[23]

I would propose not that Darwinism has killed human values and therefore great and tragic art in our time, but something nearer the reverse: that since Darwin, we have been forced, in art as in life, to mature to finiteness. I mean maturing as human beings not simply by realizing that there are no usable absolutes for us—for that mere realization is still a kind of adolescence—but by accepting our finiteness and learning to live with it with some degree of sanity and integrity.

Oedipus, Antigone, and Lear are not great tragic figures simply because they stand in relation to the gods as flies to wanton boys, after all, but because of their own impressive human characters. And we have not stopped defending our uniqueness. If we are unique because of a certain type of brain rather than some supernatural prerogative, and if we have chosen a perhaps disagreeable scientific fact in preference to a pretty illusion, the case is nevertheless the same: our uniqueness, our dignity, remain important to us. Twentieth-century literature taken as a whole—despite absurdity, disillusion, black humor, anti-heroism, existential angst, and cosmic nausea—remains a human-centered, human-valued literature. We need not look for the tragic spirit only in drama. The greatest of the modern writers in all genres—Dickinson, Lawrence, Joyce, Faulkner, Camus, Woolf, Yeats, Frost, Brecht, Beckett— have kept aspiring humanity as at least the implied focus of their work, so that even when we read as a gray failure, we are still the ghostly negative of an implicitly positive picture.

V

After the centenary excitement of 1959, I turned back to writing poetry, which was then, and still is, my principal vocation. In addition, however, I was following Darwin's lead by interesting myself in Malthusian perceptions about overpopulation. During two years of travel and study, much of it in Asia, I developed a personal view of that vast and continuing problem, which was published in 1965 as *The Silent Explosion*, with a helpful foreword by a generous and distinguished Darwinian, Julian Huxley. (Eleven years later I edited Malthus' *Essay on the Principle of Population*, motivated by much the same sense of the disturbing pertinence of Malthus' observations on population growth.)

By 1968, when the W. W. Norton Co. began a new series of Critical Editions in the History of Ideas, I was pleased to be invited to prepare the initial volume, on Darwin. I was grateful for that prompting to return to Darwin once more; to explore the pre-Darwinian context of biological and philosophical ideas from which Darwin's work had emerged; to do some pruning on the lengthy Darwinian tomes to make them more attractive to undergraduate students; and to review the many works of science, theology, philosophy, history, sociology, and literature that represent the varied influences of the Darwinian idea upon nineteenth-century and

123

twentieth-century thought. The resulting book appeared in 1970. By 1979, the first edition of *Darwin* had been used in hundreds of colleges around the country, had gone through a dozen printings, and was already partially out of date. A new edition had to be prepared, because in the decade since *Darwin* was first planned and compiled, the biological sciences had brought forth a great deal of original, important, and often highly controversial research, and much of this work had consciously Darwinian origins, as the following examples indicate.

1. The continuing discoveries of hominid fossils in East Africa have pushed back proto-human evolutionary history millions of years farther into the past. Discussing these new additions to the fossil record, Richard Leakey writes in *Origins* (1977):

> Perhaps more prophetic than anything else in *The Descent of Man* was its suggestion that the African continent was the cradle of mankind. Darwin reasoned that "in each great region of the world the living mammals are closely related to the extinct species of the same region. It is, therefore, probable that Africa was formerly inhabited by extinct apes closely allied to the gorilla and chimpanzee; and as these two species are now man's nearest allies, it is somewhat more than probable that our early progenitors lived on the African continent than elsewhere." The current accumulation of fossil evidence strongly supports Darwin's hunch. . . .[24]

2. Recombinant DNA research, or "gene splicing" as it is more conveniently called, is a technique first successfully used in 1973. It is "in essence a method of chemically cutting and splicing DNA, the molecular material which the genes of living organisms are made of. It enables biologists to transfer genes from one species to another, and in doing so to create new forms of life."[25] Thus a revolutionary development in biological science has opened the door to unprecedented evolutionary manipulation and also to unpredictable evolutionary risks. In *The Ultimate Experiment* (1977), a book about gene splicing, Nicholas Wade writes, "The fusion of Darwin's theory with Watson and Crick's discovery [of the structure of DNA] has provided a remarkable insight into the evolutionary history of life. . . . Living species . . . are all the product of some three billion years of evolution. . . . [But] man can now create a new species . . . and dump it into the system without notice."[26]

124

3. Ethology is the study of animal behavior; it emphasizes the interplay of genetic and environmental influences, and thus, as one recent commentator says, "Its point of departure and of rest is in the theory of evolution."[27] Konrad Lorenz and two other founders of ethology were awarded a Nobel Prize in 1973, bringing to a new level of public consciousness provocative ideas about our evolutionary inheritance from allegedly aggressive forebears. These ideas have been popularized by books with titles like *The Naked Ape, The Territorial Imperative,* and *The Imperial Animal*—"pop ethology," as Stephen Jay Gould calls them. Actually, Lorenz's Nobel Prize was awarded not for his speculations on human aggression but for solid ethological work on other species; nevertheless, in his best-known book, the central question is, "What is the value of . . . fighting?" And he comments: "It is our duty to ask this Darwinian question."[28]

4. The comparatively new discipline of sociobiology is, according to its chief spokesman, Edward O. Wilson,

> defined as the systematic study of the biological basis of social behavior in every kind of organism, including man, and is being pieced together with contributions from biology, psychology, and anthropology. There is of course nothing new about analyzing social behavior, and even the word "sociobiology" has been around for some years. What is new is the way facts and ideas are being extracted from their traditional matrix of psychology and ethology . . . and reassembled in compliance with the principles of genetics and ecology.
>
> In sociobiology, there is a heavy emphasis on the comparison of societies of different kinds of animals and of man, not so much to draw analogies . . . but to devise and to test theories about the underlying hereditary basis of social behavior.[29]

Sociobiology is now becoming an established academic discipline, buttressed by Wilson's landmark compilation of research, *Sociobiology* (1975), and it has been both highly praised and sharply criticized by other biologists. In the first chapter of his massive book, Wilson refers to "the neo-Darwinist evolutionary theory—the 'Modern Synthesis' as it is often called," and he observes: "It may not be too much to say that sociology and the other social sciences, as well as the humanities, are the last branches of biology waiting to be included in the Modern Synthesis."[30] Later he adds, "Sociobiology will perhaps be regarded by history as the last of the disciplines to have remained in the 'unknown land' beyond the route charted by Darwin's *Origin of Species*. . . . Now let us proceed to a deeper level of analysis based at last on the principle of natural selection."[31]

5. Students of human intelligence have for a decade been caught up in a continuing controversy over possible race-related and class-related genetic factors in intelligence. John C. Loehlin, Gardner Lindzey, and J. N. Spuhler, writing in 1975 about the origins of this subject, noted that "Darwin's . . . emphasis upon the continuous and orderly development of new forms of life from other forms and the decisive role played by fitness, or reproductive advantage, was from the beginning linked to behavioral as well as physical attributes and thus directly relevant to social scientists."[32]

6. Recent work with primates has established that chimpanzees and gorillas are sufficiently intelligent to learn at least the symbolic rudiments of human languages; this raises far-reaching ethical questions about the "human" treatment of "nonhuman" beings. In *The Dragons of Eden*, Carl Sagan, discussing the evolution of intelligence, wrote in 1977:

> There is an arresting passage in Charles Darwin's *Descent of Man*: "The difference in mind between man and the higher animals, great as it is, certainly is one of degree and not of kind. . . . If it could be proved that certain high mental powers, such as the formation of general concepts, self-consciousness, et cetera, were absolutely peculiar to man, which seems extremely doubtful, it is not improbable that these qualities are merely the incidental results of other highly-advanced intellectual faculties; and these again mainly the results of the continued use of a perfect language."[33]

7. Alarmed by the successful efforts of religionists to have the doctrine of separate creation included in science textbooks, American biological scientists have increasingly felt obliged to issue public statements in support of the principle of evolution by natural selection and in opposition to the insertion of religious ideas in science texts. In 1977, two hundred professional scholars, most of them professors of biology in American universities, signed a position paper affirming that "the evidence for the principle of evolution has continued to accumulate . . . including the further confirmation of the principle of natural selection and adaptation that Darwin and Wallace over a century ago showed to be an essential part of the process of biological evolution."[34]

126

VI

What this persistent contemporary invocation of Darwin's work and words makes clear is that Darwin is not one of those pioneers of science who are no longer studied—at any rate, not among professional biologists. On the contrary, Darwin remains among them today almost like a living presence, his great organizing idea still functional and indeed ineluctable, his testimony on countless subjects still respected, his originality of mind still admired. Darwin, in short, is indispensable; that is one thing recent biological developments have in common.

Another thing they have in common is their ability to provoke emotional responses and to cause noisy and sometimes violent controversies. In West Virginia, night riders bomb schoolhouses where evolution is taught. In Washington, shouting demonstrators interrupt Edward O. Wilson as he is about to address the American Association for the Advancement of Science, and douse him with water. Everywhere, scientists and social scientists dispute fervently with each other: Wilson's critics attack his ideas as akin to the social Darwinism which, they say, "provided an important basis for the enactment of sterilization laws and restrictive immigration laws by the United States . . . and also for the eugenics policies which led to the establishment of gas chambers in Nazi Germany."[35] And Wilson answers hotly, "I resent this ugly, irresponsible, and totally false accusation."[36] Ethological theories of aggression are sharply rejected by many anthropologists, paleontologists, and others who hold that human beings have as much cooperation as competition in their evolutionary inheritance. The notion of genetically determined and race-linked intelligence levels is indignantly repudiated by those who maintain that there is neither evidence for such ideas nor, given their potential for social damage, sufficient reason even to pursue them.

Darwin's theory began in controversy, and its various offspring survive in controversy because the issues involved go to our deepest conceptions of ourselves, to our pride in our origins, to our sense of our present dignity, to our hopes for the future. Many people find it difficult to accept facts which do not patently flatter their self-esteem or theories which strike them as socially retrograde. Violence aside, all of that is understandable, and perhaps, in the long run, healthy, the ferment of ideas out of which better ideas may arise. In the short run, too, the persistent controversy suggests not only hot tempers or bad manners but also welcome evidence of moral commitment and intellectual freedom.

And yet, despite the rising level of discord, despite the remarkable discoveries, the laboratory breakthroughs, and the daring speculations, one recognizes in many of the new bottles some very old wine. Criticizing Wilson's theories, Stephen Jay Gould asserts: "The issue is not universal biology vs. human uniqueness, but biological potentiality vs. biological determinism."[37] It is, in other words, the issue that has for decades been debated as heredity versus environment, or nature versus nurture (and, for that matter, much the same issue that was once argued as free will versus determinism). The stakes are the same as they have always been: on the one hand, the hope for a better understanding of human nature; on the other hand, the risk of blaming what are really social shortcomings on imagined innate human defects. That the argument is an old one, however, neither diminishes its relevance nor blunts its emotive force.

Each of the biological controversies of the 1970s has a long history. The quarrel between ethologists and anthropologists over the competitive or cooperative nature of human behavior has its logical and biological roots in the Victorian era, in the divergent views of Herbert Spencer and Peter Kropotkin, among others. The current hostility between "creation research" religionists and biological scientists goes back in a virtually unbroken line to the first outraged reviews of the *Origin of Species*, written by clergymen. The more these things change, the more their emotional potential remains the same.

But disputes between moralists on the one hand and scientists on the other are rather less interesting than the fact that scientists are so often conscious moralists themselves. Perhaps the experience of the atomic physicists in World War II deters other scientists from viewing their own work as existing in a social vacuum. Whatever the cause, biological scientists do have explicit ethical concerns, and they frequently discuss these concerns in the course of their scientific work. Robert Sinsheimer, a biologist who is now chancellor of the University of California, Santa Cruz, has cautioned his colleagues about the potential hazards of gene splicing, for instance. He warns that, although truth is the goal of science,

> truth is necessary but not sufficient, that scientific inquiry, the revealer of truth, needs to be coupled with wisdom if our object is to advance the human condition. . . . Our thrusts of inquiry should not too far exceed our perception of their consequence.[38]

"Truth . . . coupled with wisdom," Sinsheimer says; without wisdom, our knowledge could be dangerous. But there are no college courses in wisdom, not even in graduate school, no seminars in good judgment, not even a freshman course in introductory common sense. These qualities are taken, negatively, to be unteachable, or sometimes positively, as obliging corollaries of advanced training. So ethical problems surface in all directions, of sufficient urgency to raise tempers, and hands, not only among the bombers of schoolhouses but even in the august assemblage of the American Association for the Advancement of Science; and everywhere it is assumed that ethical decisions are required and that wise choices are available—and yet there is no agreement at all on how such choices are to be made.

But if wisdom itself is elusive, it may be useful to identify two distinct categories of contemporary dispute, and for each of them to try to distinguish the stronger arguments from the weaker. In the process of making such distinctions, we may find it possible to sketch out patterns of attitudes appropriate to each of the categories.

VII

In one category of contemporary dispute, the venturesome but disturbing speculations of some scientists are pitted against the strongly held scientific and ideological convictions of other scientists. One such case that has troubled biologists and social scientists for several years is the controversy about sociobiologists' claims of genetically influenced human behavior. The sociobiologists are more consciously and explicitly ethical theorists than are most other scientists. Edward O. Wilson begins his book on sociobiology with an essay called "The Morality of the Gene," and in the first paragraph he leads us through the following close argument:

> Camus said that the only serious philosophical question is suicide. That is wrong even in the strict sense intended. The biologist, who is con-

cerned with questions of physiology and evolutionary history, realizes that self-knowledge is constrained and shaped by the emotional control centers in the hypothalamus and limbic system of the brain. These centers flood our consciousness with all the emotions—hate, love, guilt, fear, and others—that are consulted by ethical philosophers who wish to intuit the standards of good and evil. What, we are then compelled to ask, made the hypothalamus and limbic system? They evolved by natural selection. That simple biological statement must be pursued to explain ethics and ethical philosophers, if not epistemology and epistemologists, at all depths.[39]

Teasing out the strands of that compact statement, one recognizes that Wilson is using the words "philosophical," "consciousness," and "knowledge" so as to emphasize their rational or objective implications. These, he says, are complemented and complicated by signals in the form of emotions, which must be taken seriously as information about, and modifiers of, the total human experience. However, these signals are not rational or objective; they are consulted, Wilson says, in order to "intuit" the "standards of good and evil." Furthermore, the signals themselves have been bred into specific locations in the human brain in much the same way the nesting or honeycomb-building instincts are bred into birds and bees: by the incessant Darwinian process of natural selection.

If we have followed this reasoning, we have been led a long way from what we normally consider rationality; this is exactly where Wilson wants us. He is now ready to propose how, according to his theory, our genetically programmed emotions "tax the conscious mind with ambivalences" in order to stimulate activities that will promote not personal satisfaction or social well-being, but rather, long-term genetic success.

That, again, is a new way of putting an old theory of ethics; Darwin himself anticipated it in *The Descent of Man*, where he proposed that "the moral nature of man has reached its present standard, partly through the advancement of his reasoning powers and consequently of a just public opinion, but especially from his sympathies having been rendered more tender and widely diffused through the effects of habit, example, instruction, and reflection. It is not improbable that after long practice virtuous tendencies may be inherited."[40] But Wilson's formulation is not "merely" a new way of putting an old hypothesis; it is also the beginning of a serious attempt to establish a systematic investigation of genetic factors in ethical behavior. Dissenting biologists assert that in this, as in most other matters relating to human beings, the sociobiologists have yet to establish their hypotheses on a basis of convincing empirical data. Furthermore, critics like Stephen Jay Gould believe that to argue for a genetic role in human behavior could have the unfortunate side effect of reinforcing existing social arrangements, thus undermining efforts at social reform. Morally significant human activities are not genetically or otherwise predetermined in any specific way, Gould maintains, since our range of potential behavior, whatever our genetic endowment, is still vast. Richard Leakey agrees: "Very few behavioral patterns are built into the human brain," he writes; "it is built in such a way as to maximize *behavioral* adaptability. Within reasonable biological limits, humans, it is fair to say, could adapt to living in almost limitless numbers of ways. Indeed, this flexibility is manifest in the rich pattern of cultures expressed throughout the world."[41]

Sociobiologists willingly agree that people are capable of diverse behavior; but their new explorations of the sources of that behavior are fortified by the fact that for at least a generation now, geneticists have recognized that traits are usually not determined exclusively by the genes or by the environment. Rather, one must ask of the variance in any trait, in a given population and environment, what proportion is due to genetic differences, what proportion is due to environmental differences, and what proportion is due to covariance and interaction. Wilson argues that the behavioral evidence he has compiled, together with the general presence of genetically based variation in human and other animal traits of all kinds, make it unlikely that there is no genetically based variance in general human traits such as aggression or intelligence. Of course it is also unlikely that there would be no environmental influences on these traits. The existence of strong environmental effects on a trait is, after all, compatible with strong genetic differentiation among individuals in a particular environment.

Sociobiologists are working on the assumption that the prolongation of this controversy is due to a deficiency of reliable data. As their research goes on, it will be seen whether they will be able satisfactorily to distinguish and quantify the various factors in trait variation and thus, presumably, to resolve the issue.[42] Critics of sociobiology, however, do not believe that nature-nurture problems

131

can ever be resolved as they are now formulated, partly because the very terms of the argument are defective. What exactly is a trait, they ask. Is aggression, territoriality, or dominance a "thing" upon which selection can act? If genes act differently in different environments, where is the pure "thing" that expresses the amount of a behavioral character that is due to genes? Such fundamental doubts about the sociobiologists' whole enterprise make any early resolution of this controversy seem unlikely.

VIII

In a second category of evolutionary dispute, the freedom of scientific investigation itself is being directly called into question because of its potential hazards. The unknown risks involved in recombinant DNA research, or gene splicing, have caused politicians, public-interest groups, and scientists themselves to urge caution in proceeding with the research. In 1978 a government highcontainment laboratory was opened, in which the potential dangers of gene splicing were to be assessed. There were pickets on hand at the opening of the laboratory, denouncing the planned research on the grounds that it was the first step toward genetic manipulation of humans.

Ominous as that possibility is, however, there are two other kinds of problems associated with genetic engineering which are more immediately threatening: the medical problem and the evolutionary problem. The medical problem arises from the possibility that gene splicing may produce new types of organisms that are dangerous to current forms of life (including humans) and are not containable in laboratories. That would be a considerable worry in any case, but it is intensified by the fact that the organism of choice for gene splicing is *Escherichia coli*, a bacterium which inhabits the intestinal tracts of humans and other vertebrates. That we ourselves are the hosts of this organism would make it seem a poor choice for genetic manipulation; nevertheless, it remains the organism of choice because it is comparatively well studied. To wait until some other organism were as well understood as *E. coli* would require some years; and biological researchers are understandably impatient at any such delay.

Some scientists have been reassured by reports at a 1977 conference in Falmouth, Massachusetts, that a genetically enfeebled strain of *E. coli*, called K_{12}, is a safer host than had been thought: that even deliberate attempts to convert it into an epidemic pathogen have not worked, and that therefore an accidental conversion would be unlikely. Other scientists find this position unconvincing, pointing out that there was no consensus on this subject at the Falmouth conference. Even the enfeebled organisms, they argue, may be able to transmit their reconstructed plasmids to viable ones. Despite reassurances, then, the potential for danger remains a real risk, in the opinion of some scientists.

In addition to the social and medical risks of gene splicing, there is what must be called an evolutionary risk. Robert Sinsheimer insists that it is "extraordinarily anthropocentric" to emphasize the threats to human health in gene splicing, rather than the evolutionary threat to our environment. For one cannot responsibly undertake a basic restructuring of the materials of life without considering this question: can abrupt, irreversible, and self-replicating biological inventions fail to disturb our environmental balance? It may seem advantageous in the abstract to create new varieties or species which would produce insulin (as is already being done), or manufacture growth hormones, or fix nitrogen. But can such processes be entrusted to novel, self-propagating species whose biological interest would be to increase and multiply? Any answer to that question must begin with, and return to, a consideration of Darwin's fundamental changing of our way of understanding nature and our place in it. Representative of the pre-Darwinian view is William Whewell, a clergyman and one of the most eminent scientific methodologists of his day, writing in 1833:

> If there be, in the administration of the universe, intelligence and benevolence, superintendence and foresight, grounds for love and hope, such qualities may be expected to appear in the constitution and combination of those fundamental regulations by which the course of nature is brought about, and made to be what it is.[43]

That is to say, the characteristics of the Godhead (intelligence, benevolence, and so on) are known by divine revelation; in a world directly created and superintended by an immanent deity, then, these same qualities must be built into the natural laws which govern us. Whatever is, is right because divine omnipotence has so willed it.

Now consider the philosophical difference in Darwin's total reversal of these assumptions. Having looked at nature closely, ignoring theological postulates, he concluded the *Origin of Species* with this penultimate sentence:

> Thus, from the war of nature, from famine and death, the most exalted object which we are capable of conceiving, namely, the production of the higher animals, directly follows.[44]

In turning the book of Genesis topsy-turvy, this new understanding committed us to a world in which there is no biological superintendence or special creation, only adaption for survival. In the long run, then, in Darwinian terms, whatever is, is "right" not because of divine intervention, not because animals and plants are "beautifully designed" for their environments; but because, without successful adaptation to the demands of a given environment, a biological species simply could not be there at all.

So it is that any move, intentional or unintentional, which alters our environment in a significant way, may be a threat to the adaptations that have evolved in humans and other species over vast reaches of time. We are only beginning to realize to what extent even seemingly minor human interventions in our biosphere have already complicated our chances for survival: chlorofluorocarbons in the atmosphere; oil and pesticides in the sea; tobacco smoke in the human lung; vinyl chloride in the liver; saccharine in our coffee, nitrites in our meat; and Mirex, Kepone, dieldrin, DES, PCB, PBB, DDT, and so on. There are some sixty thousand chemicals now in active industrial use, and we optimistically assume that most of them are not dangerous to human life or to the environment. However, the constantly growing list of pathogenic ones must make us a little skeptical of those who reassure us of the safety of new technologies.

If even relatively crude and external environmental changes have a substantial impact on our lives, can we suppose that the abrupt introduction of new forms of life will always be harmless? Gene splicing, Robert Sinsheimer says, would "introduce quantum jumps into the evolutionary process," with unpredictable results. Those who defend recombinant DNA research argue that existing organisms are so well adapted to their evolutionary niches that novel organisms will almost certainly be less well adapted and hence will not survive. Most mutations have always been harmful, because they disturb an organism's finely tuned development orchestration. Furthermore, they point out, gene-splicing "experiments" have been proceeding in nature for billions of years; the vast majority of new combinations have no doubt been tried, and the useful mutations have been found and adapted. Consequently, essentially all mutations are now selected against, and this would apply as much to laboratory changes as to random ones.

This argument, in the judgment of Sinsheimer and others, takes a very static view of evolution, one which assumes that nature has already tried virtually all of the possibilities; and they see no compelling reason to make such an assumption. Erwin Chargaff, professor emeritus of biochemistry at Columbia University, adds this strong cautionary note: "We are dealing here much more with an ethical problem than with one in public health. . . . Have we the right to counteract, irreversibly, the evolutionary wisdom of millions of years . . . ?" If we proceed with this "irreversible attack on the biosphere," he adds, "the future will curse us for it."[45] That, as Chargaff sees it, is the disturbing conclusion from the basic Darwinian principle that we are what our environment has made of us over a very long period of time.

Why, then, is DNA research proceeding? That seems a fair question, and a fair answer must include the fact that most of the scientists directly involved are convinced that the dangers are negligible. Searching everywhere for the truth about nature, they are of course eager to seek in this very promising direction. Besides that purely scientific reason for doing DNA research, many biologists also foresee practical applications of great value for humanity. David Baltimore, a Nobel laureate from the Massachusetts Institute of Technology, has testified that "DNA research is our best hope for understanding diseases like cancer, heart disease, and malfunctions of the immune system."[46] And gene splicing might be used to develop bacteria which could produce hormones, antibiotics, and other valuable proteins for medicine and industry. Such hopes constitute respectable motives for proceeding with DNA research, and, the researchers believe, justify what they take to be the very slight risks involved.

The problems raised by Sinsheimer, Chargaff, and other scientists have not disappeared, however, despite the optimism and good intentions of the DNA researchers; and it has long since become ap-

135

parent that the terms of this category of dispute are different from the preceding category. There, the issue was serious but comparatively abstract; the social implications may seem ominous, but they are presumably open to resolution by further data and by informed public debate, and the debates themselves are protected both by explicit constitutional guarantees and by the principle of academic freedom.

In the gene-splicing dispute, however, we are on different ground, neither abstract nor perhaps even subject to correction. What is at risk is the possibility of a dangerous and irreversible evolutionary shift. People everywhere (as well as other animals, and even plants) have a life-or-death stake in it. Threatened with potential danger, ordinary citizens have a right to expect that scientists would pursue this research in accordance with the scruples of their more cautious colleagues. Chargaff has proposed that there be congressional action to take the following steps:

> (I) a complete prohibition of the use of bacterial hosts that are indigenous to man; (II) the creation of an authority, truly representative of the population of this country, that would support and license research on less objectionable hosts and procedures; (III) all forms of "genetic engineering" remaining a federal monopoly; (IV) all research eventually being carried out in one place, such as Fort Detrick.[47]

Scientists, however, are not being as cautious as that. Research is now going ahead in scores of laboratories, and already there have been violations of the National Institutes of Health safety guidelines, at Harvard and at the University of California, San Francisco, as well as reports of ignoring the guidelines in industrial laboratories. Industry is not at present required by law to adhere to the NIH guidelines, and potential hazards are multiplied by their current and prospective volume-oriented production of self-replicating organisms.

If there is a serious accident as a result of using *E. coli* in all this research, how, Nicholas Wade asks, will historians explain to future generations the continued use of this laboratory organism? The answer, Wade writes, would have to be:

> Prohibition of *E. coli* . . . would have delayed gene-splicing research for . . . several years . . . Researchers were unwilling to accept a major delay for what seemed to most to be a purely speculative risk . . . Research and the pursuit of knowledge being fundamental values of indus-

trialized societies, the majority of the public was favorably disposed to accept the scientists' arguments.[48]

IX

We are always moralists, Dr. Johnson said, but only occasionally mathematicians. It is sometimes assumed that science, strictly speaking, has no ethics, that the gap between what is and what ought to be is broad and unbridgeable. But our ethics, whatever its source, can hardly emerge from a vacuum of knowledge; in fact our knowledge often tempers our ethical inclinations. Scientific knowledge has at the bare minimum a selective ethical function, identifying false issues which we can reasonably ignore: imagined astrological influences on our ethical decisions, for instance. Science offers us the opportunity of basing our ethical choices on factual data and true relationships, rather than on misconceptions or superstitions; that must be considered a valuable service.

Beyond that selective function, biological information has often been directly used (and misused) to support various types of ethical thinking. Unscrupulous people have sometimes appealed to spurious readings of scientific data in order to bulwark their arguments; that was what happened to Darwinism when Nazis perverted it in an attempt to legitimize their racist ideology. More characteristically, though, the growth of scientific knowledge has tended to have socially progressive implications. Factual knowledge of the physical world has, on the whole, been a better basis for human understanding, human solidarity, and human sympathy than were folklore or superstition. The old myth-supported notions of tribal and racial supremacy have been at least partly superseded, among educated persons, by the biological knowledge that we are one people, one species, in one world.

Finally, the scientific temper of mind is itself of service to moralists, showing itself as sometimes supplementary to, and sometimes superior to, those more primitive feelings that Edward O. Wilson says have typically been consulted to "intuit" ethical standards. Konrad Lorenz, working with assumptions similar to Wilson's, writes:

> The scientist who considers himself absolutely "objective" and believes that he can free himself from the compulsion of the "merely" subjective should try—only in imagination, of course—to kill in succession a let-

137

tuce, a fly, a frog, a guinea pig, a cat, a dog, and finally a chimpanzee. He will then be aware how increasingly difficult murder becomes as the victim's level of organization rises. The degree of inhibition against killing each one of these beings is a very precise measure for the considerably different values that we cannot help attributing to lower and higher forms of life.[49]

We "cannot help" this feeling, Lorenz believes. He obviously is not thinking about the American Rifle Association or the whaling fleets or the G.I.'s at My Lai, Vietnam. The fact is that the toleration, even the enjoyment, of killing "higher forms of life" must of necessity emerge from those same "emotional control centers" in the brain that Wilson appeals to as sources of ethical standards. One problem with this sociobiological and ethological theory of ethics is that it seems to operate on the assumption that if you have an "emotional" or "intuitive" sense of right and wrong, you will choose what is right. Ethical philosophers, however, have almost always thought otherwise. We cannot, in fact, trust emotion as an unassisted ethical guide; Hitler was as passionate as Jesus.

So the objectivity that Lorenz finds morally inconsequential (and, in his brief critique of Kant, a bit ludicrous) may have something to offer to ethics, after all. It is the "objective" scientists, these days, who are in the vanguard of ethical thought: who are, for instance, enlarging our understanding of the capacities of the higher mammals and of our moral responsibilities with respect to them. The fascinating work of Jane van Lawick-Goodall with chimpanzee societies in Africa has broadened our knowledge of primate behavior and, in the process, has illuminated the kinship of humans and the higher animals. Human beings, proud of the role of *Homo faber*, the creative animal, the toolmaker, now have to share this role with the clever chimps, who, Jane Goodall tells us, can "manipulate objects to a wide variety of purpose," and "can use an object spontaneously to solve a brand-new problem that without the use of a tool would prove insoluble."[50] The revolutionary laboratory work begun by Beatrice and Allen Gardner[51] has indicated that chimpanzees even have a distinct sense of self, thus belying the old and rather arrogant belief that human beings are unique among animals in their awareness of selfhood. No wonder, then, that scientists are now beginning to ask, quite seriously, as Carl Sagan does, questions like this: "If chimpanzees have consciousness, if they are capable of abstractions, do they not have what until now has been described as 'human rights'? How smart does a chimpanzee have to be before killing him [or her] constitutes murder?"[52]

There are no more absolute values in ethics than in anything else, but there are relative values in the various existing ethical systems; and one could make a persuasive case that those systems that are not only the most altruistic but also sensitive to the broadest constituencies, are, by virtue of those qualities, superior to the others. Richard Dawkins writes, "If I say that I am more interested in preventing the slaughter of large whales than I am in improving housing conditions for people, I am likely to shock some of my friends." And he adds, "Whether the ethic of 'speciesism,' to use Richard Ryder's term, can be put on a logical footing any more sound than that of 'racism,' I do not know. What I do know is that it has no proper basis in evolutionary biology."[53] With a growing recognition among biologists of the ugly and self-defeating aspects of "speciesism," we may have reason to foresee a future consensus that a narrowly species-centered ethics is inadequate, not so much to our emotions (which have almost always failed us in this matter) as to our reason, now under instruction by new biological perceptions.

In the truly well-balanced human being (that will o' the wisp of utopian thought) reason and emotion would be always in harmony, indeed in symbiotic function. In the meantime, it is reassuring to discover that biologists, engaged in "objective" research, so often become passionate about their work, and about the world it affects. Our perception of truth, it appears, sometimes causes, and sometimes is served by, moral fervor.

None of this would be so evident or so pertinent to our lives if biology were not a science so thoroughly unified by the principle of evolution as to afford philosophical perspectives of its own; and that unification, of course, we owe to Charles Darwin. In 1834, a year after William Whewell wrote the words quoted above, about the divine "administration of the universe," the polymath Samuel Taylor Coleridge died, believing, despite Whewell's comforting words, that the science of zoology was in danger of falling apart because of its huge mass of uncoordinated factual information. That was just four years before Darwin picked up Malthus's *Essay on the Principle of Population* and was inspired with the great organizing principle that would for the first time make a mature and coherent science of biology. Evolution by natural selection continues to serve biologists in their professional work and to inspire them to earnest pondering about our place in the universe: some of the wisest thinkers writing about the human condition today are biologists. That their ethical conclusions are diverse should not trouble us; the opposite would in fact be disturbing. It goes almost without saying that, while the physical world may be better understood by virtue of a unifying principle, the moral complexities of life will never be accounted for by simplistic propositions. "The moral faculties," Darwin wrote in *The Descent of Man*, "are generally and justly esteemed as of higher value than the intellectual powers. But we should bear in mind that the activity of the mind in vividly recalling past impressions is one of the fundamental though secondary bases of conscience. This affords the strongest argument for educating and stimulating in all possible ways the intellectual faculties of every human being."[54]

X

Anatole France once began a literary lecture by announcing: "Ladies and gentlemen, I have come here to talk to you about myself, apropos of Shakespeare, Molière, and so on." Adventuring with Darwin for more than thirty years has left me feeling rather like that. Darwinism, evolution by natural selection, is the proper objective study of biologists. But Darwinisticism (as Morse Peckham has called it), the evolution of opinions, philosophies, and world-views under the influence of Darwinism, is the hazardous privilege of everyone else; and, properly hedged about with logical caution, it can be a risky but potentially rewarding influence on our thinking.

Part of the risk is in that emotional commitment I discussed earlier. Although Darwinism can be studied objectively, it often impinges upon emotionally charged areas of our experience, and therefore sometimes arouses hostility. Having published my ideas about Darwin on many occasions, I have received my share of anonymous hate mail, ranging from the politely disturbed ("You sound intelligent, informed, and smug") to the patently deranged ("I hope the good Lord damns you to hell for all eternity . . ."). I am not eager to ally myself with such ill-considered attitudinizing, and yet paradoxically I too value my emotional involvement with Darwinism. My kind of involvement is a very complicated matter: it is a focusing, an intellectual and emotional shaping, of virtually everything I have ever learned and experienced. Consequently, because I have spent my whole life as a poet, I find that I have for years been writing poems which I now retrospectively refer to as "the Darwin poems," and which I plan eventually to publish as a separate volume. Having adventured along so personally in this essay, I hope it will now seem appropriate to end by appending one of those poems, as an example of the emotional shaping that I am talking about. Clearly the following poem could not have been written without the shaping force of evolution in my consciousness, and perhaps in my subconscious mind as well. It represents one of the ways Darwin and Darwinism have shaped my perceptions of my own past and my sense of where, at this point, I have arrived.

THE VOYAGE HOME

> *The social instincts . . . naturally lead*
> *to the golden rule.*
> *Darwin,* The Descent of Man

1

Holding her steady, into the pitch and roll,
in raw midwestern hands ten thousand tons
of winter wheat for the fall of Rome,
still swallowing the hunger of the war:
the binnacle glows like an open fire,
east-southeast and steady,
Anderssen, the Viking mate,
belaboring me for contraband,
my little book of Einstein, that
"Commie Jew." (So much for the social instincts,
pacifism, humanism, the frail
and noble causes.) I speak my piece
for western civ: light bends . . .
stars warp . . . mass converts . . .

"Pipe dreams," says the Dane, "pipe dreams."
"Well, mate, remember,
those Jewish dreams made nightmares
out of Hiroshima, and
blew us out of uniform, alive."
He stomps down off the bridge; some day
he'll fire me off his rusty
liberty: I read too much.
The ocean tugs and wrestles with
ten thousand deadweight tons
of charity, trembling on
degrees and minutes. Anderssen
steams back in with coffee, to
contest the stars with Einstein, full ahead.
We haven't come to Darwin.

2

Freezing on the flying bridge,
staring at the night for nothing,
running lights of freighters lost
in a blur of blowing snow,
we hold on through the midnight watch,
waiting out the bells.
With Einstein in our wake, the tricks
are easier: liberty
churns on, ten knots an hour,
toward Rome. One starry night
we ride at last with Darwin on
the *Beagle*: endless ocean, sea
sickness, revelations
of Toxodon and Megalonyx—a voyage
old as the Eocene, the watery death
of Genesis. The going
gets rough again, the threat of all those bones
churning the heavy swells: Anderssen,
a true believer, skeptical,
and Darwin trapped in a savage earthquake,
the heave of coastal strata conjuring
the wreck of England, lofty houses gone,
government in chaos,
violence and pillage through the land,
and afterward,

fossils gleaming white along
the raw ridges.
"Limeys." Anderssen puts his benediction
to empire: "Stupid Limeys." After that
we breathe a bit and watch the stars and tell
sad stories of the death of tribes, the bones,
the countless bones: we talk about
the war, we talk about
extinction.

3

Okinawa, Iwo Jima:
slouching toward Tokyo, the only good Jap
is a dead Jap.
We must get the bomb, Einstein writes
to F.D.R., waking from
the dreams of peace, the noble causes:
get it first, before
the Nazis do. (The only good Nazi
is an extinct Nazi.)
At the death of Hiroshima, all day long
we celebrate extinction, chugalugging
free beer down at the PX, teen-
age kids in khaki puking pints
of three-point-two in honor
of the fire: no more island-hopping now
to the murderous heart of empire.
Later, in the luxury of peace,
the bad dreams come. "Certainly,"
Darwin broods, "no fact
in the long history of the world
is so startling as the wide and repeated
extermination
of its inhabitants."

4

Off somewhere to starboard, the Canaries,
Palma, Tenerife: sunrise
backlights the rugged peaks, as Darwin,
twenty-two years old
and never having set a foot
on any soil but England's, gazes at

the clouds along the foothills.
Longitudes ease westward; it's
my birthday: twenty-two years old
as Tenerife falls into the sunset,
I'm as greedy for the old world
as Darwin for the new, Bahia, Desire,
the palms and crimson flowers
of the Mediterranean, clear water
dancing with mines. Ahead of us
a tanker burns; the war
will never end.

5

"You talk a lot," says the melancholy Dane.
"You sure you're not Jewish yourself?
You got a funny name."
"Well, mate, I'm pure Celtic on one side,
pure Orphan on the other: therefore half
of anything at all—Jewish, Danish,
what you will: a problem, isn't it,
for Hitler, say, or the Klan,
or even Gregor Mendel, sweating out the summer
in his pea patch?"
The fact is, I know those ancestors
floating through my sleep:
an animal that breathed water,
had a great swimming tail,
an imperfect skull, undoubtedly
hermaphrodite . . . I slide
through all the oceans with these kin,
salt water pulsing in my veins,
and aeons follow me into the trees:
a hairy, tailed quadruped,
arboreal in its habits, scales
slipping off my flanks, the angle of my spine
thrust upward, brain
bulging the skull until
I ride the *Beagle*
down the eastern trades to earthquake,
to naked cannibals munching red meat
and Spanish grandees with seven names
crushing the fingers of slaves.

144

Who are my fathers? mothers? who
will I ever father?
I will sire the one in my rubber sea-boots, who
has sailed the seas and come
to the bones of Megatherium.
From the war of nature, from famine and death,
we stand at last creators
of ourselves: "The greatest
human satisfaction," Darwin muses, "is derived
from following the social instincts." Well,
the thing I want to father
is the rarest, most difficult thing
in any nature: I want to be,
knee-deep in these rivers of innocent blood,
a decent animal.

6

Landfall: Yankee liberty discharges
calories on the docks, where kids
with fingers formed by hairy
quadrupeds cross
mumbo jumbo on their chests
and rub small signs for hope
and charity.
Liberty, sucked empty of its
social instincts, follows the *Beagle*
down the empty avenues of water
to amber waves of grain, to feed
the children of our fathers' wars,
new generations of orphans, lives
our quaint old-fashioned bombs
had not quite ended.

7

Alone
on the fantail
I hear the grind of rigging, and
Darwin is beside me, leaning on the rail,
watching the wake go phosphorescent.
We've been out five years, have seen
the coral islands, the dark skins
of Tahiti; I have questions.

145

"Darwin," I whisper, "tell me now,
have you entered into the springs of the sea,
or have you walked in search of the depth?
Did you give the gorgeous wings to peacocks,
or feathers to the ostrich?
Have you given the horse his strength
and clothed his neck with thunder?
Who has put wisdom in the inward parts,
and given understanding to the heart?
Answer me."
The breeze is making eddies in the mist,
and out of those small whirlwinds come the words:
"I have walked along the bottom of the sea
wrenched into the clouds at Valparaiso;
I have seen the birth of islands and
the build of continents; I
know the rise and fall of mountain ranges,
I understand the wings of pigeons,
peacock feathers, finches; my mind creates
general laws out of large
collections of facts."
The rigging sighs a little: God
is slipping away without
saying goodbye, goodbye to Jewish dreams.
"But the activities of the mind,"
Darwin murmurs, "are one of the bases of conscience."
Astern the pious Spaniards go on praying
and crushing the fingers of slaves; somewhere
the Mylodon wanders away,
out of the animal kingdom and
into the empire of death.
For five billion years
we have seen the past, and
it works.

8

So this is the final convoy
of the social instincts: the next
time missiles fly to Rome,
they will carry Einstein's dream of fire,
and afterward there will be no need
for liberties, hope, or charity.

Now we ride the oceans of
imagination, all horizon
and no port. Darwin
will soon be home, his five-year
voyage on this little brig
all over; but when will I
be home, when will I arrive
at that special creation: a decent animal?
The land is failing the horizons, and
we only know to take the wheel
and test the ancient strength of human struggle,
remembering that we ourselves, the wonder
and glory of the universe, bear
in our lordly bones the indelible stamp
of our lowly
origin.

NOTES

1. Parts of this essay are adapted from The Norton Critical Edition, *Darwin* (New York, 1970; revised, 1979). "The Voyage Home" originally appeared in *Poetry,* © 1981.

2. Richard Dawkins, *The Selfish Gene* (New York, 1977), p. 5.

3. See "Darwin, Pater, and a Crisis in Criticism" in Philip Appleman, William Madden, and Michael Wolff, eds., *1859: Entering an Age of Crisis* (Bloomington, Ind.: 1959).

4. *Darwin's Notebooks on Transmutation of Species*, ed. Sir Gavin de Beer (London, 1960), First Notebook, p. 232.

5. Andrew Carnegie, *The Empire of Business* (London, 1902), p. 67.

6. Quoted in Matthew Josephson, *The Robber Barons* (New York, 1934), p. 299.

7. Edward S. Corwin, "The Impact of the Idea of Evolution on the American Political and Constitutional Tradition," in Stow Persons, ed., *Evolutionary Thought in America* (New Haven, 1950), p. 186.

8. Thomas Nixon Carver, quoted in Richard Hofstadter, *Social Darwinism in American Thought* (Boston, 1955), p. 40.

9. Hofstadter, p. 40.

10. See Maurice R. Davis, ed., *Sumner Today* (New Haven, 1940), p. 92, and Hofstadter, p. 58.

11. Quoted in Robert E. L. Faris, "Evolution and American Sociology" in Persons, p. 163.

12. James J. Hill, quoted in Hofstadter, p. 45.

13. Josephson, p. 420.

14. Andrew Carnegie, *Problems of Today* (New York, 1933), p. 125.

15. Quoted in Hofstadter, p. 201.

16. Quoted in Hofstadter, p. 79.

17. Richard Tawney, *Religion and the Rise of Capitalism* (New York, 1926), p. 247.

18. Peter Kropotkin, *Mutual Aid* (London, 1902), pp. vii–ix.

19. Kropotkin, pp. xiii–xiv.

20. Julian Huxley and T. H. Huxley, *Touchstone for Ethics* (New York and London, 1947), p. 92.

21. Huxley, *Touchstone for Ethics*, p. 91.

22. Joseph Wood Krutch, *The Modern Temper* (New York, 1929), pp. 12, 136–37.

23. John Herman Randall, Jr., "The Changing Impact of Darwin on Philosophy," *Journal of the History of Ideas,* 22 (1961), 458–59.

24. Richard E. Leakey and Roger Lewin, *Origins* (New York, 1977), p. 32.

25. Nicholas Wade, *The Ultimate Experiment: Man-Made Evolution* (New York, 1977), p. 1.

26. Wade, *The Ultimate Experiment,* pp. 15, 108–9.

27. George Stade, "K. Lorenz and the Dog Beneath the Skin," *The Hudson Review,* 26 (1973), 60.

28. Konrad Lorenz, *On Aggression* (New York, 1966), p. 20.

29. Edward O. Wilson, "Human Decency Is Animal," *New York Times Magazine,* October 12, 1975, p. 39.

30. Edward O. Wilson, *Sociobiology* (Cambridge, Mass., 1975), p. 4.

31. Wilson, *Sociobiology,* p. 63.

32. John C. Loehlin, Gardner Lindzey, and J. N. Spuhler, *Race Differences in Intelligence* (San Francisco, 1975), p. 3.

33. Carl Sagan, *The Dragons of Eden* (New York, 1977), Chapter 5.

34. "A Statement Affirming Evolution as a Principle of Science," *The Humanist,* 37 (1977), 4.

35. *New York Review of Books,* November 13, 1975, p. 43.

36. *New York Review of Books,* December 11, 1975, p. 60.

37. Stephen Jay Gould, *Ever Since Darwin* (New York, 1977), p. 252.

38. Wade, *The Ultimate Experiment,* p. 107.

39. Wilson, *Sociobiology,* p. 3.

40. Charles Darwin, *The Descent of Man,* Chapter 21.

41. Leakey and Lewin, *Origins,* p. 245.

42. Here and elsewhere in this discussion I am indebted to Professor Craig E. Nelson of the Department of Biology at Indiana University for helpful suggestions. He is not, of course, responsible for the personal opinions expressed in this essay.

43. William Whewell, *Astronomy and General Physics Considered with Reference to Natural Theology* (London, 1833), pp. 4–5.

44. Charles Darwin, *The Origin of Species,* Chapter 15.

45. Wade, *The Ultimate Experiment,* pp. 104–5.

46. Wade, *The Ultimate Experiment,* p. 115.

47. Erwin Chargaff, "On the Dangers of Genetic Meddling," *Science,* 192 (1976), 938.

48. Wade, *The Ultimate Experiment,* p. 84.

49. Lorenz, *On Aggression,* p. 218.

50. Jane Van Lawick-Goodall, *In the Shadow of Man* (Boston, 1971), p. 240.

51. For a useful survey of the language-learning abilities of chimpanzees, see Carl Sagan, *The Dragons of Eden* (New York, 1977).

52. Sagan, *The Dragons of Eden*, p. 120.

53. Dawkins, *The Selfish Gene*, pp. 10–11.

54. Darwin, *The Descent of Man*, Chapter 21.

ON READING JOHN RUSKIN

FRANCIS G. TOWNSEND

I first made the acquaintance of John Ruskin in January, 1946, about a month after I had been honorably discharged from the United States Marine Corps. Ruth and I had chosen Ohio State because we had heard of its general strength in nineteenth-century literature. On the first day of class at my new institution, I found myself in a Victorian seminar conducted by one Charles Frederick Harrold, who was a stranger to me. The first day he gave a long lecture, in which he outlined all of Victorian literature, and told the five of us that from then on we would read books and report to one another in class.

Inspired by the tremendous knowledge of Professor Harrold, I went home to our basement apartment in downtown Columbus, a block from the Public Library, and that afternoon checked out a book by one of the writers Harrold had mentioned, Thomas Carlyle. It was a book called *Sartor Resartus*, which I had heard of. That night I read it, and the next day in the seminar Harrold asked what books we had been reading. I spoke up and said I had read *Sartor Resartus* the night before, so he asked me to report on it. I held forth for an hour on the subject with the help of occasional questions from Harrold. At the end he asked what edition I had used. With sublime ignorance I said it was some old text, dated about 1905, and edited by no one in particular. Harrold assimilated this information, said I had made a good report, and neither of us ever talked about the incident again.

In that first week another student, Jack Heidi, began reporting on the life and work of John Ruskin, who was connected in some way with Cook and Wedderburn. I was mildly interested and since I had decided to sample his works anyway, I went to the library and checked out the first Ruskin book which was handy, an odd collection of twenty-five letters to a working man, entitled *Time and Tide.* It was one of the wildest, most undisciplined books I had ever read, and yet it was this first reading that led to my lifelong connection with Ruskin.

On this first acquaintance with Ruskin I was not nearly so impressed by him as a writer as I was by the others we were studying in Harrold's seminar. Arnold was far more artistic; *Culture and Anarchy,* on first reading, seemed far superior to anything Ruskin ever managed. Newman's prose was far more sensitive, and Carlyle, initially at least, was more stimulating, but my fascination with Ruskin grew. As a prose stylist he was an unparalleled virtuoso. He had a magnificent power to go straight to the heart of the issue, unrivalled, as I believe now, by any nineteenth-century critic, and an incredible way of losing the train of his own argument and descending from the sublime to the ridiculous from one page to the next. Even his folly was fascinating.

Why did this strange, sometimes deranged, writer make such an impression on me in January, 1946? I had been born during World War I, had been a child during the Roaring Twenties, and had grown to manhood in the Great Depression. By rights I should have been a member of the Democratic party, like nearly everyone around me, because from 1929 to 1939 no one in my family managed to hold any job for more than about two years. We survived in the way of the poor, circa 1933, by pooling the resources of two or more interrelated families, two or three members of which might be working at any one time. We were never quite sure of who owed what to whom. Now in those ten years, to the best of my recollection, the total amount of financial aid my family got from the government was ridiculously small, perhaps as much as four hundred dollars. It was fairly clear, however, that the adherents of the Pendergast machine in Missouri were feeling little pain.

When I emerged from World War II, my faithful Penelope and I were plunged into the most striking of the postwar anomalies, which we found no one was particularly interested in, except the GIs who were working for college degrees in cities like Columbus, Ohio. The people who had not been called up for service during the preceding years had lived in rent-controlled apartments; the veterans returning from places like the South Pacific, flush with cash saved during the years spent on islands where spending was impossible, descended by the thousands on Columbus and tried to find places to live. The landlord who owned a rent-controlled apartment could do nothing, unless he also owned a dilapidated building, in which case he could slap a coat of paint on the outside, tack up a plywood partition or two on the inside, install a second-hand privy and stove, and charge whatever he pleased, because according to the rationale he was bringing new rental units into the market.

Thus in the winter and spring of 1946, graduate students at Ohio State faced the economic problem of A and B: if you went into A's apartment and it was clean and nicely furnished, with French doors between the parlor and the dining areas, a foyer, and a tiled bathroom with tub, sink, and stool, you could safely estimate the rent at $35.00 a month; if you went into B's apartment and found a dirt-encrusted floor, wallpaper hanging from the walls, water stains on the ceiling, and a bath on the next floor up, you were reasonably sure the rent was between $45.00 and $65.00 a month, depending on the benevolence of the landlord. The reason was rent control. It was infuriating to spend money on high rent and find other people with far better quarters for a fraction of the rent, simply because they had been there the preceding two or three years while you had been otherwise occupied. The explanation, of course, was that you had to look out for the poor people: if you took off rent controls, their rents might go up. To be sure, the rents had gone up, right through the ceiling, but that was beside the point, whatever the point was—to help the poor, I suppose, as rent controls preserved the good life in the South Bronx and Manhattan.

Here was a case of flagrant, palpable injustice which anyone could see. All that was needed was a pair of eyes. No intelligence was required, nor any subtle analysis, only a pair of eyes, yet people did not see it. I did not know what to call this perversity, but the advancement of knowledge has given us blessed folk of the late twentieth century a word for it. My friends had perceptions; they knew what they wanted to see and were expected to see, and they saw it. If I pointed out the obvious inequities involved, they answered, "But we can't have increases in rent!" They simply could not see that there had already been monumental increases, even when the fact was right before their eyes.

The rest of the price controls imposed by the government during World War II were equally well intentioned and led to equally anomalous ends. Just before the war I had worked for the F. W. Woolworth Company as an assistant manager. In those days Woolworth stocked nearly everything that could be sold for a dollar or less, and in 1940 almost everything in the American home except fixtures and furnishings could be acquired for that price, from hardware, dry goods, bathroom sundries, and assorted picture frames (each with a glossy photo of a movie star), to Hershey's Arcadia (ten-pound slabs of milk chocolate broken into fragments before your eyes with a wooden mallet and a chisel, and sold at twenty cents a pound). Few archeologists of the future will know the size and shape of a ruby iridescent cuspidor in 1940, much less the price, but in addition to those bits of information I also knew the cost and selling prices of more than ten thousand items of daily use in the United States, if you count sizes and colors separately.

In the South Pacific, 1943–1945, I read the overseas edition of *Time* and followed with interest the debate over the effect of price controls. The pundits of the left pointed with pride to the government statistics, showing how well the line had been held: the pundits of the right viewed with alarm governmental interference with freedom of the marketplace. In June, 1945, I came back from overseas and took the first opportunity to wander down the aisles of a nearby Woolworth store and check retail prices. What had happened was obvious. A sizable number of the best-selling items had disappeared; in some cases there was a substitution, almost the same but modified ever so slightly and priced about fifty per cent more, a price which represented, one supposes, the value of the new brand name. The facade of price control concealed an inflation of roughly fifty per cent.

But my friends, who were nearly all good liberals of the New Deal variety, had all arrived independently at identical conclusions. They knew that price controls were good for the poor and they did not want to be bothered by evidence, which always confuses the issue. Between rent controls and price controls I lost respect for the liberal Establishment. Since I had already been disillusioned with the business mentality—after all, I was a child of the Great Depression—I was neither left nor right, and then I read *Time and Tide.* These twenty-five letters addressed to Thomas Dixon struck my mood in the winter of 1946. Things that I was to read shortly thereafter confirmed me in my esteem for Ruskin. "For, indeed, I am myself a communist of the old school—reddest of the red;"[1] and a little later, "I am, and my father was before me, a violent Tory of the old school;—Walter Scott's school, that is to say, and Homer's."[2] Here, in John Ruskin, was the exemplar of Wordsworth's "eye that cannot choose but see." He was impervious to the weight of opinion, informed or otherwise, in the society around him. He was not a reed shaken by the wind. Neither the intellectual world nor professional opinion nor social prejudice could move him. He was impervious to the demands of fashion; he refused to be, in one of his marvelous phrases, a respectable architectural man-milliner.[3] Matthew Arnold warned us of the difficulty of thinking for ourselves when everyone around us is talking like a steam engine, but Arnold was not immune to this particular disease. Ruskin could see, and he could not turn away from his vision. This fidelity to the evidence of the eye, this devotion to the obvious has, in recent times, been one of the marks of distinction that have established Ruskin's continuing value as a writer of critical prose.

It is fascinating to watch him in action. As an illustration of why Ruskin is so provocative, why it is easy to refute him, and why in the long run he defies refutation, consider his letter to the *Daily Telegraph,* Christmas Eve, 1868, in which he poses a problem.[4] Citizen A of Town X takes a train to Town Y to take business away from Citizen B, while at the same time Citizen B of Town Y takes a train to Town X to take business away from Citizen A. Is the national wealth increased thereby? Of course any economist can justify the activity with talk about diversifying products, establishing prices in the marketplace, the mechanics of distribution, and so forth. Ruskin was not so naive about such matters as he sometimes liked to pretend; he knew the conventional arguments. But after all the arguments have been made, there is still a question to be answered. Does it really make sense? To which, in a world of essences and absolutes, the only conceivable answer is no.

The trouble is, Ruskin was living in Victorian England and his foes were Gradgrind and McChoakumchild who lived in a different kind of world, or perhaps the same world with a different set of absolutes. And in 1946 the trouble with me was that I had no idea whatsoever of the kind of economist Ruskin was fighting against, and my only guide was R. H. Wilenski, who knew Marx and Keynes, presumably, but almost nothing about the economic orthodoxy of 1860. I was in the same position as an English graduate student in 1980 who brings to reading *Unto This Last* and *Munera Pulveris* all the rich background of an elementary Economics course, or even less.

Such a student faces the same kind of problem reading Milton on the subject of archangels, if, like most graduate students nowadays, she has scant faith in archangels, but she can avoid serious difficulty by thinking of Raphael in Eden as a charming Cupid come to dinner at Dido's court. Since she believes in neither Cupid nor Raphael, she can accept both as pleasant fictions. She faces a similar problem with a novelist like Hardy, whose handling of moral issues is as questionable today as it ever was, but Hardy was using a genre which, to employ Newman's phrase, does not run immediately into argument. Critical prose does just that: it is a literature of confrontation. There is little mediation between the writer's mind and the reader's; in fact, the more nearly perfect the prose, the sharper the clash. When a Victorian critic like Ruskin confronts issues which are within the province of a modern social science, the immediate reaction of a modern student is to discount everything he says, thus reducing Ruskin's possible literary significance to a bag of rhetorical devices. Why bother with somebody who is out of date?

I sought to answer the question by accepting Wilenski's estimate of Ruskin as an economist, namely that he had made important contributions to modern thought on the subject; thus the substance of what he said would have permanent value, at least as a historical document. Very early in my study of Ruskin, therefore, I found it necessary to read Adam Smith, David Ricardo, Parson Thomas Malthus, John Stuart Mill, and lesser lights like Henry Fawcett. Certainly Ruskin was unjust to them; I would agree with John T. Fain that at times Ruskin deliberately misrepresented them. Even more damaging to my opinion of his importance was my dawning realization that to any historian of economic thought it is fairly obvious that the men he opposed contributed to the advancement of the science, and he did not.

Yet, paradoxically, it is they who have gone out of style, and not Ruskin. He was not writing about Economics as they understood the term: he was establishing the limits of Economics as a science. As he said in *Munera Pulveris,* "Political Economy is neither an art nor a science; but a system of conduct and legislature, founded on the sciences, directing the arts, and impossible, except under certain conditions of moral culture."[5]

In my opinion, there is a single idea which undergirds everything he wrote on the subject. In any society, given a certain amount of money, people will always spend it one way or another. The problem is that the choices men make when they do spend will determine the quality of the society. There is no way an economy can avoid making moral choices, for instance, whether to produce grapes or grapeshot, to use one of Ruskin's examples.[6] In the case of a building, to have or have not is a relatively simple question to answer. But when we have it, will it be a monstrosity, like a false Gothic ("send down a gross of angels from Kensington") in the nineteenth century, or, in the twentieth, a childish arrangement of steel and glass blocks signifying nothing? Ultimately the decision of the capitalist or the commissar is of little moment compared with the decision of the Beaux Arts Committee. In Ruskin there is a deadly insistence on pursuing every issue back to its roots in Western culture. Sin resides in the will, in the free choice between opposed courses. *Mores,* the manners and the customs of the nation, are the record of its past choices. Taste is the only morality.[7]

Yet as I reread *Time and Tide* more than thirty years later, I wonder how my interest survived the perplexity anyone would feel on first looking into Ruskin. Of the "twenty-five letters addressed to a working man of Sunderland on the laws of work," the first three are on the subject. The fourth letter, however, expresses his reaction to the national budget and its relative expenditures on the arts and on preparations for war, a slight digression, perhaps, except that it is followed by a fifth letter, in which he tells about the pantomime at Covent Garden, *Ali Baba and the Forty Thieves.*

The forty thieves were girls. The forty thieves had forty companions, who were girls. The forty thieves and their forty companions were in some way mixed up with about four hundred and forty fairies, who were girls. There was an Oxford and Cambridge boat-race, in which the Oxford and Cambridge men were girls. There was a transformation scene, with a forest, in which the flowers were girls, and a chandelier, in which the lamps were girls, and a great rainbow which was all of girls.[8]

In all this nonsense Ruskin found only one saving grace. Mr. W. H. Payne and Mr. Frederick Payne came on stage costumed as the fore and hind parts of a donkey, and performed a pleasant little dance with an innocent little girl of eight or nine, who danced with a natural ease and charm which put the rest of the show to shame. In all the audience only Ruskin applauded.

> Presently, after this, came on the forty thieves, who, as I told you, were girls; and, there being no thieving to be presently done, and time hanging heavy on their hands, arms, and legs, the forty-thief girls proceeded to light forty cigars. Whereupon the British public gave them a round of applause. Whereupon I fell a thinking; and saw little more of the piece, except as an ugly and disturbing dream.

Indeed disturbing, but now certainly Ruskin will pick up the thread of his argument. Unfortunately the sixth letter is about the Japanese jugglers whom Ruskin had paid to see on Thursday night, just before the Friday night when he saw the pantomime *Ali Baba.* The Japanese jugglers explode into a dithyramb on such disparate themes as Balzac's *Contes Drôlatiques,* the illustrations of M. Gustave Doré, Evangelicals and the Bible with animadversions on the authorship thereof, the function of dancing in Exodus, Judges, and Jeremiah, together with the Cancan in the Paris of Napoleon III, and lastly, Satanism in the nineteenth century, this in Letter XI, curiously entitled "The Golden Bough."

It was absurd, and I loved it, but in those days we had to be orderly about these things, and so I accepted Wilenski's way of distinguishing between the Jekyll and Hyde in Ruskin. My aim was to make straight the ways of the lord in *Fors Clavigera* and elsewhere. Before I could get to that point, however, it was necessary to know something about *Modern Painters,* which seemed to have been his principal work before 1860.

Here in these five volumes the confusion was worse confounded, because to all outward appearance the book was thoroughly rational and organized down to the last detail, yet when I had finished the five volumes I did not know what they had said. Like a well-trained lad of the twentieth century I consulted the best commentary so that I would know what to think. The best at the time was Henry Ladd's *The Victorian Morality of Art,*[9] a systematic, orderly, rational analysis of the esthetics of a man who was none of these. A graduate student pricks up his ears when he comes upon the term *imagination:* he knows good fodder by instinct. Ruskin must have been writing about imagination; a sizable part of the second volume is devoted to an analysis of it. There are three forms of it—associative, penetrative, and contemplative, each with its own proper function. He also wrote about Truth and Beauty, exhaustively, to say the least. Ladd traced the ramifications of these terms in the British esthetics of the eighteenth and nineteenth centuries, and did it about as well as it could be done at the time. I tried without very much success to keep the terms separate in my mind, but I still could make no sense of the argument of *Modern Painters.*

In the meantime, however, my Penelope noticed a change in me. I had never cared particularly about the visible world around me, but now I observed the shapes of the clouds and their colors and the way a rain cloud drew a veil of mist across the Illinois prairie. I watched how the marigolds grew beside our beloved crackerbox house, and knew the thrill of catching the first hint of green as the grass broke the soil of what we fondly hoped would be a lovely lawn. In the darkness of a late October night, when a light rain was falling, we went out into the side yard and planted "our stick," a sycamore tree. Every day we made the grand tour of our estate and followed every change in the vegetation, as winter gave way to spring, and one year to the next. The last time we were in Champaign we went back; the sycamore shaded that side of the house.

After reading the first volume of *Modern Painters,* Charlotte Brontë said that Ruskin had given her a "new sense": ". . . this book seems to give me eyes."[10] Nothing more profound has ever been said of him, not by Marcel Proust, not by Lord Kenneth Clark. Ruskin forces us to attend to the world outside ourselves. One who has the patience to read *Modern Painters* is never quite the same afterward; it is impossible to read even the first volume without seeing the world and J. M. W. Turner in a different light.

To learn to look on nature with a wise passiveness is no mean achievement, especially when there are so many quondam artists who explore nature as if they were on a scavenger hunt for usable symbols, a common occupation in the middle of our century. I remember a television drama with high aspirations, a life of Billy the Kid, in which Billy comes to the bailiwick of Pat Garrett, has a drink in the saloon, strides to the swinging doors, and peers into the west. "There's a red sun a'settin'," he says. Perhaps it is better to watch the sunset for its own sake. Too many artists are like Wordsworth's philosophers, who prize

> the transcendent universe
> No more than as a mirror that reflects
> The proud Self-love her own intelligence.

But to learn to look at art as Ruskin did is quite another matter. What he had to say about "The Old Shepherd's Chief Mourner" leaves one with mixed emotions, to put it mildly, with a smile certainly, with tears possibly, though not of grief but embarrassment. Yet even here there is something to be learned from Ruskin. In 1950 it was all too easy to dismiss a Victorian painter as an illustrator; who ever heard of putting a literary idea on canvas? Quattrocento and cinquecento painters to be sure, but in their best efforts we can descry an abstract design struggling to break the chains of representation and soar upward into the unsullied purity of contemporary art. Giotto, my masters? Murillo serves his need! As a critic Ruskin had no monopoly on the ridiculous. More recent critics have come to a saner estimate of him, namely, that he was often wrongheaded but seldom trivial.

Thirty years ago the problem with Ruskin was to find a way to read his works intelligently and thus to secure a sympathetic hearing for him. Even at the nadir of his reputation it was obvious to Victorian scholars that some knowledge of him was essential to an understanding of the age, and even a small acquaintance with him is an introduction to some of the finest passages in English prose, like the first half of "The Nature of Gothic," the comparison between Giorgione and Turner in *Modern Painters V*, the approach to St. Mark's in *The Stones of Venice II,* the brief analyses of Milton's "Lycidas" and of Byron's "The Prisoner of Chillon." He has not lacked for distinguished art critics and historians who know and respect his work, like Joan Evans and Lord Kenneth Clark, who began his television series on the Humanities with a quotation from Ruskin. Both concede, however, that despite his brilliant insights, and the marvelously acute observation of external fact on which those insights are based, his books will never again be widely read.[11] The question is, can John Ruskin's books be read as anything more than aperçus? Can they be read as coherent essays? Probably, for the common reader the answer is still no. But for a reader well versed in the nineteenth century that answer no longer holds true, at least for Ruskin's early work, down to 1860, or for his last book, his autobiography *Praeterita,* written in the lucid intervals of his madness, 1885–1889. The middle years, however, still present a problem. Fortunately, however, in the process of learning to read Ruskin's early work and his autobiography better than we could a generation ago, we may have learned a few things about how to study what he wrote in those middle years, 1860–1885.

The Sphinx riddle of the early works was the baffling existence of *Modern Painters,* a major critical essay of roughly the length of *War and Peace,* which set out in 1843 to prove a thesis, namely, that art and art education could be a potent force for the moral improvement of man, and thus of society. Seventeen years later, in 1860, in the fifth and final volume, after innumerable lengthy digressions and in spite of huge gaps in the argument, *Modern Painters* ended by asserting that art is a reflection of society and that the way to improve art is to reform society. Somewhere in the voyage the pilot had shifted course one hundred and eighty degrees.

Until about 1950 conventional criticism was quick to point out the inconsistencies, the lapses, the downright self-contradiction in *Modern Painters.* But it is not a conventional treatise, with an intellectual position neatly staked out, fertilized, and cultivated, ending with all the plants in neat little rows, and it cannot be read intelligently as such. Instead it must be read as the exploration of a proposition, to which in the end a negative answer is given. Once *Modern Painters* is seen, not as the defense of an intellectual position, but as the record of an intellectual process, criticism of its inconsistency seems irrelevant.

As for the gaps in the argument, the most obvious and the most important coincides with the gap between the second and third volumes. *Modern Painters I* was published in 1843, *Modern Painters II* in 1846, *Modern Painters III* not until 1856, after a ten-year interval. In 1846 Ruskin was still in the first flush of success, confident of his ability and his thesis. By 1856 he had known defeat, and he had radically altered his thesis, for reasons unexplained in the text of *Modern Painters*, but understandable when we know what he was doing between 1846 and 1856.

Seeking an answer to his main question—namely, whether or not the arts could be an effective instrument of moral improvement— he had turned to architecture, the most social of the arts because the most closely connected with the basic facts of human existence, and he had recorded his research in two architectural treatises, *The Seven Lamps of Architecture*, 1849, and *The Stones of Venice* in three volumes, the first in 1851 and the second and third in 1853. In them his original position was abandoned and his new position established. In a sense the two architectural treatises constitute a footnote to *Modern Painters*, the longest footnote in literary history, and absolutely indispensable to the reading of the main text, since the treatises are the turning point of the whole argument. These three books, which comprise Volumes *III* to *XI* of the Library Edition, should be read as a unit.[12]

I suggested this reading of *Modern Painters* in 1951. Admittedly it was oversimplified and my use of evidence was highly selective, but it has served its purpose, most recently in Robert Hewiston's *John Ruskin: The Argument of the Eye,*[13] which pieces out my impoverished frieze, and adds a vizor and a term. It is now clear that Ruskin must be read with due regard for chronology. Listen to Jay Fellows, a scholar whose critical approach is psychological: "Although my instincts are to view a body of literature—Ruskin's more than most—in its 'collective aspect,' as if, removed from serial progression, it were alive, autonomous, all portions occurring simultaneously, I have attempted, though with few references to dates, to proceed with what I hope to be a tactful regard to sequence, beginning close to the beginning, ending at the end, . . ." He adopted this procedure because in Ruskin's case it becomes "perhaps necessary." The result was *The Failing Distance: The Autobiographical Impulse in John Ruskin,*[14] the most controversial study of Ruskin in almost fifty years.

Some of Fellows' interpretations are questionable, but he does tell us much about Ruskin's autobiography. Since 1972 when James Olney wrote the first full-length, truly scholarly study of this genre,[15] the idea that the autobiographic impulse lies near the source of creative activity has gained increasing acceptance, it seems to me. The experience of any human being is unique, in the absolute sense of that word, since an individual's precise genetic heritage and environmental experience are never duplicated. The urge to express oneself is almost universal: it is also impossible to satisfy. The best anyone can do is to create a metaphor acceptable as an expression of his/her life as it really was.

Fellows argues that in John Ruskin the autobiographical impulse was extraordinarily insistent almost from the beginning, for what reason is not clear. Fellows speculates that possibly Ruskin had a fear of introspection, a typically Victorian literary reaction to the excesses of Romantic subjectivism, or that possibly he suffered from a fear of his own emptiness, of the deep uncertainty which he compensated for by an ugly habit of dogmatic assertion. He was forever seeking a window with a view of vast distances, forever avoiding a mirror which would force him to confront himself. And just as he sought distance in space, so he sought remoteness in time, preferring the future and the past over the present. He could use his eyes, no one better, but close contact, touching, was perilous. Consider the startling clarity of two images he selected to express his childhood. In one image he is a child, seated behind a table in an alcove, reading and writing, looking out into the fullness of the drawing-room, observing the life of his parents—he has no life of his own, except for his eyes. In the other image he is a child, alone in a room, with nothing to occupy his mind but the pattern in the carpet, which he studies avidly. From what we know of the external facts of his life, he was not really that lonely, but from what we know of his inner life, his loneliness must have been terrifying. What emerges from these two images is the portrait of a child isolated from his kind, unable to find himself, acted upon, not acting, a *voyeur* of life, not a participant in it.

Hence the necessity to create a self. All through his life John Ruskin was writing his autobiography in various forms. At times it took the shape of his diaries and notebooks, addressed to a later self who would employ the observations in his research or, perchance, in an autobiography. This is an escape from the present to the future. At times it took the shape of a history of his own thought, disguised as an analysis of art, of economics, of cultural phenomena, or whatever came to hand. The most obvious is the history of the landscape feeling in *Modern Painters III,* in which he used his own experience as representative of the European mind. This is an escape from the present to the past.

And then as he goes through middle age the distance closes in on him, the future vanishes, and he is forced to live in the here and now. These are the years when his work reflects the tensions that tear him apart. There is no longer any escape, and in the collection of letters known as *Fors Clavigera* he must confront the oppressive evils in the foreground, immediately before his eyes, and finally, himself. He begins to compose fragments of an autobiography—loose, disjointed, like pieces of a puzzle. Then a man who had dominated his youth begins to fascinate him; the letters keep returning to this figure. Fitted together, these bits resemble an incomplete portrait of Sir Walter Scott. Were they experiments in the creation of an *alter ego*?

The confrontation ended in Ruskin's first mental breakdown. When he recovered enough to work, he had to be very careful to control what he called "his daily maddening rage,"[16] and in his last years of effective life he turned to the composition of *Praeterita,* but now he was no longer an old man indulging his emotions. He was an artist creating a character, a fictional person in the past, safely removed in distance and time. Cook and Wedderburn, Ruskin's editors, tried as a matter of policy to interpret *Praeterita* as the literal truth:[17] it seems reasonably clear that the John Ruskin of *Praeterita* never existed.[18] The real John Ruskin was not that lonely, nor was he that ineffectual. As Fellows says, *Praeterita* is a book by an old man about a young man whom he dislikes; it is more biography than autobiography.[19]

Fellows' interpretation is highly speculative, but it has already borne fruit. Elizabeth Helsinger calls *Praeterita* "strangely self-destructive," and notes that it has no principles of inclusion. It is apparently formless, like the young protagonist, whom the old writer compares to a number of formless animals, a tadpole, for example, or an insect with a chrysalid stage, such as a caterpillar. In Helsinger's words: "*Praeterita* is hardly adequate as personal history or apology. It is an apparently perverse undertaking, almost a sabotage of the self."

Helsinger sees it as a rejection of conventional autobiography. In a conventional autobiography there is a progression along a definite track, with events given order and precedence by their part in the

163

metamorphosis of the child into the man. Instead, in *Praeterita* there is a series of views, paintings if you wish, in which a place is summoned up with all of the attendant emotions associated with it during a lifetime. The surface arrangement is deceptively chronological, while the real arrangement is that of a portfolio of Turner engravings. The chapter headings are the titles of pictures, which are metaphors of Ruskin's existence.

Here, as in *Modern Painters*, the problem for the reader is that the composition is so massive that one has to move far away from the picture in order to see it. Close up it seems chaotic although beautiful in detail. There is a complicating factor: *Praeterita* is incomplete. The last paragraph, which is probably the most powerful paragraph that Ruskin ever wrote, is also his last moment of conscious life. What he intended to write is clear because we have his prospectus for the work, which was to consist of three volumes, each in turn consisting of twelve chapters. The last two chapters were to echo the opening two. The very last chapter was to be entitled "Calais Pier," where Ruskin first left the enclosure of his life in England and ventured into the world of Western civilization, or, seen in another irrational way, the place of embarkation for a journey into a new life. In the middle of the second volume, in the fifth, sixth, and seventh chapters, he wrote in his marvelously haphazard way about Geneva, and about Lucca, the Campo Santo in Pisa, and Florence, which those expert in such matters might mistake for the Protestant and Catholic centers of Western Europe.[20]

There is more in Elizabeth Helsinger's article but that is enough to show its bent. To it I have added a few thoughts of my own about the "Calais Pier" and the Campo Santo, without, I hope, distorting it. Is it too fanciful? In 1969, eight years before Helsinger's article, Pierre Fontaney analyzed in detail one of the most famous purple passages in all of Ruskin's work, the description of the Rhone at Geneva, in that fifth chapter of the second volume of *Praeterita*.[21]

> But the Rhone flows like one lambent jewel;
> its surface is nowhere, its ethereal self
> is everywhere, the iridescent rush and
> translucent strength of it blue to the
> shore, and radiant to the depth. . . .
> No wasting away of the fallen foam, no

pause for gathering of power, no helpless
ebb of discouraged recoil; but alike
through bright day and lulling night, the
never pausing-plunge, and never-fading
flash, and never-hushing whisper, and,
while the sun was up, the ever-answering
glow of unearthly aquamarine, ultramarine,
violet-blue, gentian-blue, peacock-blue,
river-of-paradise blue, glass of a painted
window melted in the sun, and the witch
of the Alps flinging the spun tresses of
it for ever from her snow.

Ruskin proceeds to infuse a spirit into the Rhone, as if the
fluminal deities had returned, and the river is personified in a magnificent pathetic fallacy extended to almost inordinate length,
which returns at last to the jewel simile with which the whole passage began, ". . . and the dear old decrepit town as safe in the embracing sweep of it as if it were set in a brooch of sapphire."

The passage is an example of his consummate mastery of prose
style, but also of his characteristic failure to subordinate his rhetorical powers to the whole composition, or so it seems. Although the
passage is brilliant, it is a digression. It has attracted the attention
of Joan Evans, Lord Kenneth Clark, and John D. Rosenberg, none
of whom, however, adequately accounts for its peculiar incandes-
cence.[22] Pierre Fontaney sets the passage in the whole context of
Ruskin's description of the approach to Geneva, in this fifth chapter
entitled "The Simplon." The features Ruskin chooses to describe
"may be identified with a small number of archetypal motifs.
These motifs recur under different forms, appearing first in a readily
identifiable guise and then in a more cryptic fashion." The images
have a personal significance; he uses them often in his works. Eventually, according to Fontaney, the motifs and the images converge.

Geneva is the city at the center of the world, with the mountain
rising beyond it, the *axis mundi*. The old city is a paradise, a
"bird's nest," a place of security. The path to it must have its ritual
obstacle, so Ruskin does not follow the highroad across the moat—
he takes the precarious suspension bridge which can accommodate
only a few people at a time, the Bridge Perilous. And then, of
course, there must be a trial before the hero can unlock the mys-

165

tery. He must choose an article of jewelry which is what he really most desires. He goes to the shop of Mr. Bautte, the jeweler, passing through a "narrow arched door," a "secluded alley," a "monastic courtyard," ascending a "winding stair," and coming at last to a "green door." And now, having made his journey to the Underworld, he faces the moment of trial, presided over by a clerk, or "Ruling power," as Ruskin calls him. The hero makes his choice, steps outside, and before him lies the Rhone, like a jewel, its blue the color of the sky, the sea, the virgin, and the peacock; and the river dances "as if Perdita were looking on to learn." Shades of the underworld and Winnington!

Having analyzed the passage in detail, Fontaney pronounced it a subtle and complex set of variations on a few archetypal themes. Fontaney concluded, however:

> There is no doubt that Ruskin was not aware of the imaginative structure of these pages as I have reconstructed it, and that he did not know that his relaxed, rambling narrative ran in the time-honoured grooves of ancient motifs and myths.

In other words, Ruskin, of all people, did not know enough about mythology to have planned such an intricate effect in English prose. Who could have thought the old man had so much blood in him?

Ruskin happened to comment on this problematical passage in a letter to one of his female correspondents: ". . . I've written a nice little bit of *Praeterita* before I went out, trying to describe the Rhone at Geneva."[23] His tone suggests that although he was pleased by his day's work, he did not take it seriously, so Fontaney may be right in arguing that the passage was unconscious, or then again he may be wrong, because Ruskin could be playful about such matters. Criticizing Ruskin is like playing with Montaigne's cat.

From these successful studies of Ruskin's early work and of his autobiography we have learned what traps to avoid and what strategies to pursue in reading the works of his middle years. There is a Ruskin who is deceptive because his organization is too massive to be readily comprehensible, a sort of macro-Ruskin. I have pointed out why it is hard to grasp the overall pattern of *Modern Painters* and *Praeterita*. To give another example, there is the matter of the epiphanies in *Praeterita*. Most autobiographies trace the development of a child into an important, powerful personality; and of course in such a book there is a place where a single incident unifies the protagonist's experience and gives it meaning and direction, like the epiphany vouchsafed a certain Irishman at the beach, in the persons of certain bathers sacred and profane. Helsinger points out that Ruskin describes in his letters and diaries no less than seven religious conversions, and in his autobiography he experiences eight moments of esthetic revelation: "... these passages span a period of seventeen years and refer to eight different occasions on which Ruskin says his 'true,' ... 'best,' ... or 'new' life began."[24] For example, describing his first view of the Alps, 1833, he says:

> ... I went down that evening from the garden-terrace at Schaffhausen with my destiny fixed in all of it that was to be sacred and useful. To that terrace, and the shore of the Lake of Geneva, my heart and faith return to this day, in every impulse that is yet nobly alive in them, and every thought that has in it help or peace. (*Works, XXXV*, p. 116)

For a second example, in 1835 at the Col de la Faucille, he received what he called the "confirming sequel" of his first view of the Alps.

> But the Col de la Faucille, on that day of 1835, opened to me in distinct vision the Holy Land of my future work and true home in this world. My eyes had been opened, and my heart with them, to see and to possess royally such a kingdom! (*Works, XXXV*, p. 167)

For a third example, in May, 1842, at Norwood he discovered that if he drew ivy as he saw it, his drawing was better composed than if he had consciously worked at it. Later in 1842 at Fontainebleau, he drew an aspen tree outlined against a blue sky, and saw that the lines were composed "by finer laws than any known of men." (*Works, XXXV*, p. 314)

> The woods, which I had only looked on as wilderness, fulfilled I then saw, in their beauty, the same laws which guided the clouds, divided the light, and balanced the wave. "He hath made everything beautiful, in his time," became for me thenceforward the interpretation of the bond between the human mind and all visible things; and I returned along the wood-road feeling that it had led me far;—Farther than ever fancy had reached, or theodolite measured. (*Works, XXXV*, p. 315)

For a final example, on first visiting Lucca in 1845, he was overwhelmed by the tomb of Ilaria de Caretto.

> . . . here suddenly, in the sleeping Ilaria, was the perfectness of these, expressed with harmonies of line which I saw in an instant were under the same laws as the river wave, and the aspen branch, and the stars' rising and setting; but treated with a modesty and severity which read the laws of nature by the light of virtue. (*Works, XXXV*, p. 349)

To say the least, one epiphany is understandable, but eight seems careless of him, except that they stress the essential timelessness of his life, the failure of the young man to change and develop, and the way the old man scorned him for it. But then again, there is a logical sequence in these four examples, from the inanimate to the animate to the human, each order in turn submitting to the laws of nature, and owing its beauty to that submission. There is progress, just as there is in the amorphous animals to which Ruskin compared himself, from the tadpole to the frog, from the caterpillar to the butterfly; nevertheless through all its changes the animal retains its identity.

But just when we begin to expect patterns everywhere in Ruskin, we discover that there is another Ruskin who is highly deceptive because, like a wayward freshman, he cannot follow an outline but must continually deliver asides to his audience, a sort of micro-Ruskin. Jay Fellows points out that in Ruskin's middle years all tenses are condensed into one, where everything is present to his mind, and his prose becomes parenthetical. Parentheses appear within sentences, as sentences within paragraphs, as paragraphs within chapters.[25] His passages become reflections of everything in his mind at the moment without regard to time or sequential logic. They are solipsistic, but then solipsism has not met with unmixed condemnation recently. And at times, just when we are forced to admit that a digression is a digression, we begin to notice that considered in isolation from its context it is superb. Lord Kenneth Clark observes that the apparent digressions in Ruskin should be read with special care.[26]

Everyone who has studied Shakespeare for a number of years has had the experience of reading a play which on first acquaintance seems confusing, but which after repeated readings has a clear outline, marred by occasional digressions. Then one day we know in a flash the reason for a digression and its relation to the whole. We come to assume that in Shakespeare everything contributes to the total effect,—but wait; there is still Peter's scene with the musicians in *Romeo and Juliet,* and perhaps Borachio speaks for Shakespeare when he says, "I tell this tale vilely," as indeed he does. The experience of reading Ruskin has the same puzzling quality.

In addition to the macro-Ruskin and the micro-Ruskin there are other obstacles to the reading of Ruskin, but these are more easily set aside. It is a mistake to search for conformity between Ruskin and social science. Carlyle spoke derisively about determining moral issues by a count of heads; it would be a mistake to expect Ruskin to put much stock in behavioral criteria arrived at by questionnaires, any more than Moses or Mohammed would. His interests lay in other directions, where quantification goes galumphing into infinity. The money supply is not ultimately important: how people choose to spend the supply of money is the real question. A nation which engages in titanic efforts to clutter its threshold with garbage will indeed generate impressive statistics, mostly worthless.

It is a mistake to be distracted by Ruskin's preoccupation with St. George's Guild. It is not just graduate students who are misled by it: the impracticality of it is occasionally cited as indicative of the general incompetence of Ruskin as a thinker. To suggest that to Ruskin St. George's Guild was not very important catches even serious scholars by surprise. There is nothing novel about the suggestion; his editors, Cook and Wedderburn, advanced it in their introduction to *Fors Clavigera.* They felt that what he wrote about St. George's Guild should be read as utopian literature, a happy thought since both Thomas More and John Ruskin were celestial idealists with hard heads for business.[27] After all, one of the most interesting tributes to Ruskin came from a Liverpool journal which, after observing his lucrative operations in the publishing field with his protegé George Allen, pronounced him "a great tradesman."[28] Ruskin felt a kinship with Jonathan Swift; does anyone criticize Swift for implying that horses are smarter than people? St. George's Guild was Ruskin's equivalent of Houyhnhmmland.

It is a mistake to be disconcerted by Ruskin's self-contradictions. To think in terms of polarities was characteristic of Ruskin from the beginning. For him, to think of one side of a proposition led him to think of the other; thesis begot antithesis and self-contradiction became a way of life, until the only consistency in his work lies in its anticipated inconsistency.[29] In Ruskin's words, "the more I

169

see of useful truths, the more I find that, like human beings, they are eminently biped; . . .''[30] The dominant opposition in his entire literary output is between good and evil. In his early work it appears as light and dark, in the works of his middle years as life and death, in his apocalyptic moments as heaven and hell, in one guise or another, as for example St. George's Guild and the goddess Britannia of the Marketplace.

But despite all that we have learned about reading John Ruskin, the works of his middle years, 1860–1885, are still puzzles. That they have great merits no one doubts; these, however, all too often lie buried in a context which cannot sustain interest. That is why there are so many selections from Ruskin, by John D. Rosenberg, by Joan Evans, by Lord Kenneth Clark, by Harold Bloom, by Robert L. Herbert.[31] They are impressed by Ruskin, but they feel that his virtues must be disengaged from his vices. It would seem, however, that his vices and his virtues are well-nigh inseparable. Our gains have come from exploring the complex and highly deceptive patterns in his essays.

Let us turn one last time to that little-known book published in 1867, *Time and Tide,* where for me it all began. Why do the Japanese jugglers appear in Letter VI and how can the ensuing explosion of diverse subjects be fitted into any recognizable pattern?

The subject of *Time and Tide* is the laws of work, and the first three letters are logical and orderly. The digressions begin in Letter IV, because Ruskin has been reading the account in the *Pall Mall Gazette* of the doings of the House of Commons, including the projected budget for the Army and Navy (25 millions) and for "science and art" (164 thousands). It is a matter of choice and the values of the nation are clear.

After that instructive comparison Ruskin returns in Letter V to the laws of work, specifically to how much constitutes a "modest competence." Certainly the worker is entitled to a small sum for entertainment, but that raises an interesting question, and with a bound Ruskin is off on a false scent, describing his night at the pantomime *Ali Baba.* When the British workers pay for entertainment, this, or worse, is what they buy, a splendid story burlesqued by a bevy of cigar-smoking girls. Then in Letter VI enter the Japanese jugglers.

> Sir Toby Belch. O, ay, make up that! He is now
> at a cold scent . . .
> Fabian. Did not I say he would work
> it out? The cur is excellent
> at faults.

Their manual dexterity is marvelous, but one of them wears masks which in the Japanese fashion are well made but "inventively frightful," suggesting as they do mankind's kinship with the lower animals. At the beginning of Letter VII, *Time and Tide* simply falls apart. The second paragraph consists of a single sentence which would be embarrassing in a freshman theme.

> I had intended to return to those Japanese jugglers, after a visit to a theatre in Paris; but I had better, perhaps, at once tell you the piece of the performance which, in connection with the scene in the English pantomime, bears most on matters in hand.

In the next paragraph he describes a dance by a girl of about thirteen, whose motions were a series of contractions and jerks, like those of a puppet. Watching her, he thinks of Exodus 15:20. "And Miriam, the prophetess, the sister of Aaron, took a timbrel in her hand, and all the women went out after her with timbrels and with dances." And with that Ruskin's mind leaps to Paris.

> Not at once, however, to the theatre, but to a bookseller's shop, No. 4, Rue Voltaire, where, in the year 1858, was published the fifth edition of Balzac's *Contes Drôlatiques,* illustrated by 425 designs by Gustave Doré.

Ruskin is like the Homeric hero who leaped on his horse and fled in all directions. Transitions are supposed to signal a logical progress, not a digression, except that in this case the digression is worth the confusion. Balzac's text is full of blasphemies, and the illustrations revel in "loathsome and monstrous aspects of death and sin," reaching a climax in a picture of a man cut in half by a downward sweep of the sword, with full anatomical detail. The letter ends with a swift return to the British public and the way it chooses to spend its money. Just then the Evangelicals were buying a new edition of *The Holy Bible, with Illustrations by Gustav Doré,* in cheap monthly parts.

All of which supposedly leads to Letter VIII, entitled "The Four Possible Theories Respecting the Authorship of the Bible," which does not sound like a law of work, but wait: perhaps there is method in his madness.

> Celia. How prove you that in the great heap
> of your knowledge?
> Rosalind. Ay, marry, now unmuzzle your wisdom.

In this particular letter he feels it necessary to justify his use of the Bible as a moral authority, because he, as well as much of his audience, no longer believes it is the inspired word of God. His position is much the same as Matthew Arnold's in 1867. The Bible represents the best moral judgment that western civilization has been capable of arriving at, that judgment which is best supported by the experience of men and nations. What the Bible condemns is what has proved destructive to men and nations.

By now we know for sure only that what follows will be surprising. Letter IX is headed "The Use of Music and Dancing under the Jewish Theocracy, Compared with Their Use by the Modern French." The ancient notion of singing and dancing as a prayer of thanksgiving for man's deliverance from evil has yielded to the new dispensation, such as in Geneva, once a center of Christianity, where the Sabbath is now a time for drunken brawling to the rhythm of horse pistols fired aimlessly into the air, or in Paris, where the supreme choreographic expression of the nineteenth century is the Cancan, which is not exactly what Miriam performed. Ruskin's use of the touchstone method is gargantuan.

The dance theme was introduced in Letter V with the girl who danced with the donkey. It was continued in Letter VII with the puppet-girl whose dance consisted mostly of contractions and jerks. Her dance set Ruskin to thinking of Miriam the prophetess, sister of Aaron, and what dancing meant then and now (Letter IX). That this is the structure of the five letters is clear from the transitional passages, but the bewildering profusion of images, together with the ad hoc remarks which they generate, tends to obscure the line of the argument.

If such is the structure of Ruskin's sermon, then we should expect what follows to be the homilist's interpretation and his exhortation. This time we are not disappointed. Letter X is headed "The

172

Meaning and Actual Operation of Satanic or Demoniacal Influence." Ruskin believes in Satan, though not in "the gramnivorous form of him, with horn and tail," but rather as that force, whether within or without, that reduces the powers and the virtues of men to whatever "corruption is possible to them." The Satanic Power rides with us on our way, as the Fiend rode behind Albert Dürer's Knight, but that is not to be feared so much as the state of mind in which we do not know the Fiend when we see him, just as men live in modern society without recognizing its power to corrupt. Letter XI tells us how to recognize the Adversary: he is the Lord of Lies and the Lord of Pain. Ruskin concludes by admitting that he has been led away from his subject, the laws of work, to which he will return in Letter XII, and he does, although not for long.

So this long section of *Time and Tide,* Letters IV through XI, is not a series of digressions. It is rather one enormous digression, nearly one-third of the whole book, ostensibly organized around the dance theme, but actually a complex arrangement of juxtapositions on a larger theme, the corruption of modern society. The whole digression is triggered by the annual appropriations for war and for science and art, and what this budget tells about the nation. "By their fruits ye shall know them."

Here in embryo are the later works of John Ruskin, both the ideas and the rhetoric. Here, within a few pages, Ruskin has brought together as wildly unlikely a set of elements as can easily be imagined, and yes, in a way it is about the laws of work, as the subtitle promised. Yet something is wrong. Therefore, since brevity is the soul of wit, perhaps here, as elsewhere in Ruskin's work, our verdict must be brief: "Your noble son is mad." Let us remember, however, that he who pronounced that judgment was not himself a paragon of wisdom.

NOTES

1. *Fors Clavigera,* Vol. XXVII of *The Complete Works of John Ruskin,* ed. Sir E. T. Cook and Alexander Wedderburn (London: George Allen, 1903-12, 39 vols.), p. 116; hereafter cited as *Works.*
2. *Praeterita I,* Works, XXXV, p. 1.
3. *The Crown of Wild Olive, Works,* XVIII, p. 434.
4. *Works,* XVII, p. 544.

5. *Works,* XVII, p. 147.

6. *Unto This Last, Works,* XVII, p. 104.

7. See *The Crown of Wild Olive, Works,* XVIII, p. 434.

8. References to *Time and Tide* (*Works,* XVII) are by letter number.

9. Henry Ladd, *The Victorian Morality of Art: An Analysis of Ruskin's Esthetic* (New York: R. Long & R. R. Smith, 1932).

10. Quoted from the introduction to *Modern Painters I, Works,* III, p. xxxix. She was describing her reactions in a letter to W. S. Williams, of Smith, Elder & Co.

11. Joan Evans, ed., *The Lamp of Beauty: Writings on Art by John Ruskin* (London: Phaidon Press, 1959), p. 7; Lord Kenneth Clark, ed., *Ruskin Today* (London: John Murray, 1964), p. xvii.

12. See the introduction to *The Stones of Venice II, Works, X,* pp. xlvi–xlviii.

13. Robert Hewison, *John Ruskin: The Argument of the Eye* (Princeton, N.J.: Princeton Univ. Press, 1977).

14. Jay Fellows, *The Failing Distance: The Autobiographical Impulse in John Ruskin* (Baltimore: The Johns Hopkins Univ. Press, 1975), p. viii.

15. James Olney, *Metaphors of Self: The Meaning of Autobiography* (Princeton, N.J.: Princeton Univ. Press, 1972).

16. See Gaylord C. LeRoy, "John Ruskin: An Interpretation of His 'Daily Maddening Rage,' " *Modern Language Quarterly* 10 (March, 1949): 81–88.

17. Helen Gill Viljoen, *Ruskin's Scottish Heritage: A Prelude* (Urbana: Univ. of Illinois Press, 1956), pp. 17–19.

18. Fellows, p. 12.

19. Fellows, p. xii.

20. The preceding three paragraphs are based on Elizabeth K. Helsinger, "Ruskin and the Poets: Alterations in Autobiography," *Modern Philology* 74 (November, 1976): 142–70.

21. Pierre Fontaney, "Ruskin and Paradise Regained," *Victorian Studies* 12 (March, 1969): 347–56.

22. Clark, pp. 40–42; Joan Evans, *John Ruskin* (London: Cape, 1954), p. 100; John D. Rosenberg, *The Darkening Glass: A Portrait of Ruskin's Genius* (London: Routledge, Kegan Paul, 1963), p. 223.

23. *Works,* XXXVII, p. 564.

24. Helsinger, p. 163.

25. Fellows, Chapter IV.

26. "We should read Ruskin for the very quality of his mind, which, when abused, makes him unreadable." Clark, p. xx.

27. *Works,* XXVII, pp. lvii–lviii.

28.. See note 3, Works, *XXVII,* p. lxxxv.

29. Fellows, p. 4.

30. *Works,* V, p. 169.

31. Harold L. Bloom, ed., *The Literary Criticism of John Ruskin* (New York: Doubleday, 1965); Robert L. Herbert, ed., *The Art Criticism of John Ruskin* (New York: Doubleday, 1964).

THE EPITOME OF
MATTHEW ARNOLD

R. H. SUPER

A complete edition of an author's works has not entirely succeeded if it does not bring about some re-estimate of the hierarchy of the works, some reconsideration of which pieces do indeed best represent the author to the present generation and speak most meaningfully to us. In fairness it must be said that some recent selections from Arnold's prose do get away somewhat from the traditional choices; it would also be silly to attempt to belittle such favorite essays as "The Function of Criticism at the Present Time," "The Study of Poetry," or *Culture and Anarchy* (though of the last work I must protest against any inclination to prune off the concluding portion). Nevertheless, the exclusive attention to the old favorites has in many instances done injury to Arnold's character for flexibility and perceptiveness, in part at least by focusing on some familiar catchwords like "criticism of life," "the best that has been thought and said," "Hebraism and Hellenism," "Barbarians, Philistines, and Populace," to the point where even serious discussions of him sometimes appear to be built upon the catchwords only, and not upon the works from which they come.

It is tempting, therefore, to try one's hand at making a new selection of Arnold's prose, a selection based on a necessarily close reading of everything he wrote for publication, and made without prejudice, made disinterestedly. Such a selection as I envisage would give a more comprehensive view of Arnold's range than any now extant, and at the same time it would show the remarkable homogeneity of his thinking upon all subjects—literary, religious, educational and social. It would also be made up almost entirely from the writings of his last dozen years (1876–1888). The works of the sixties won such attention when they first appeared that they still dominate one's thinking, but there is a tentative, an exploratory character about them (sometimes concealed under a kind of self-assurance that offends many readers). After his long engagement with religious questions in the early seventies, he went back, at about age fifty-four, over the whole range of his interests, touching upon now one, now another, with a maturity and comprehensiveness that his earlier work did not show. *God and the Bible* was, in fact, his last "book"; everything he published subsequently was in the form of collections of occasional essays and lectures, their miscellaneous nature amply illustrated by such titles as *Last Essays on Church and Religion, Mixed Essays, Irish Essays and Others,* and *Discourses in America.* These are the collections from which I shall draw, and to them I will add the last essay he published, "Civilisation in the United States."

I

As he wrote the Preface to *Last Essays,* he imagined that he was about to return "to devote to literature, more strictly so-called, what remains to me of life and strength and leisure" (VIII, 148).[1] It was not to be quite so clear-cut and simple, partly because he could not avoid the fatal attraction to current politics. Nevertheless, in keeping with his new resolve, he published in the *Quarterly Review* for January, 1877, almost simultaneously with the writing of the Preface to *Last Essays,* a discussion of the work of four critics upon Milton—Macaulay, Addison, Johnson, and Scherer—which was intended to re-examine and re-affirm his own standards of literary criticism, to be an essay on critical method, and implicitly to set a program for his future work. The title he gave it, "A French Critic on Milton," suggests a limitation and a kind of second-handedness that has done the essay a great disservice.

Arnold begins with a witty account of Macaulay's first great literary triumph, the *Edinburgh Review* essay on Milton in August, 1825. Arnold had met Macaulay in the early 1850s, presumably at Lord Lansdowne's house in Berkeley Square; from the outset the rhetoric of "the great apostle of the Philistines" (III, 210) provoked in Arnold only the malicious impulse to prick its bubble, and so he does here. But his aim is not mere ridicule: it is to show how profoundly unsatisfying is criticism which, by its very flashiness, takes the eye of the reader away from its object and attracts it rather to the critic. It is our business, says Arnold, "to learn the real truth about the important men, and things, and books, which interest the human mind," in order to acquire "a stock of sound ideas, in which the mind will habitually move, and which alone can give to our judgments security and solidity" (VIII, 170).

This same "positivism of the modern reader" rejects a purely conventional judgment like Addison's, which tells us that *Paradise Lost* "is looked upon by the best judges as the greatest production, or at least the noblest work of genius, in our language" (VIII, 171). "The truth is, Addison's criticism rests on certain conventions: namely, that incidents of a certain class *must* awaken keen interest; that sentiments of a certain kind *must* raise melting passions; that language of a certain strain, and an action with certain qualifications, *must* render a poem attractive and effective" (VIII, 172). But a reader's pleasure is not built upon syllogisms; if in fact he takes no pleasure in the work, Addison's essay will not help him find any springs of delight whatsoever.

Two critics of Milton there are, however, who *do* look at the object as in itself it really is (Arnold does not use that expression in this essay), Dr. Johnson and Edmond Scherer, the latter a contemporary French Swiss critic who, in this later period, occupies for Arnold somewhat the place Sainte-Beuve had occupied earlier. Johnson's "Life of Milton" gives us "the straightforward remarks . . . of a very acute and robust mind. . . . But Johnson's mind . . . was at many points bounded, at many points warped. He was neither sufficiently disinterested, nor sufficiently flexible, nor sufficiently receptive, to be a satisfying critic of a poet like Milton." His verdict upon "Lycidas"—"Surely no man could have fancied that he read 'Lycidas' with pleasure had he not known the author!"—was a "terrible sentence for revealing the deficiencies of the critic who utters it" (VIII, 174). Scherer, in contrast, is without bias; Milton in no way commands or offends his prejudices. And at the same time, he is a critic of sufficient learning to avoid the errors of ignorance: "Well-informed, intelligent, disinterested, open-minded, sympathetic, . . . he knows thoroughly the language and literature of England, Italy, Germany, as well as of France" (VIII, 174). And so Arnold illustrates for us by convincing example how Scherer's critique leads his readers to what is indeed a right judgment upon his subject. Even Scherer, however, has the fault of a theorist: he sings the praises of "the method of historical criticism—that great and famous power in the present day" which is to supplant mere "personal sensation." It is "the old story of 'the man and the *milieu.*'" "The advice to study the character of an author and the circumstances in which he has lived, in order to account to oneself for his work, is excellent. But it is a perilous doctrine, that from such a study the right understanding of his work will 'spontaneously issue.' In a mind qualified in a certain manner it will—not in all minds. And it will be that mind's 'personal sensation.' . . . Let us not confound the method with the result intended by the method—right judgments. The critic who rightly appreciates a great man or a great work, and who can tell us faithfully—life being short, and art long, and false information very plentiful—what we may expect from their study and what they can do for us; he is the critic we want, by whatever methods, intuitive or historical, he may have managed to get his knowledge" (VIII, 175-76). Such a critic Scherer is, despite his affirmation of a false or misguided theory. And his ultimate sense of Milton's value rests upon what Arnold agrees is Milton's "true distinction as a poet, his 'unfailing level of style.'" "Shakspeare himself, divine as are his gifts, has not, of the marks of the master, this one: perfect sureness of hand in his style," says Arnold, recurring to a position he had stated as early as the 1853 "Preface." "Alone of English poets, alone in English art, Milton has it; he is our great artist in style, our one first-rate master in the grand style" (VIII, 182-83). Satisfying as all this is, Arnold cannot help turning a glance once more toward Johnson for the touch of human sympathy in his description of Milton as an old man—a warmth of emotion that moves us more than even the best criticism can do (VIII, 182). And it was no wonder that not long afterward, Arnold published his selection from Johnson's *Lives of the Poets.*

A year later (January, 1878) a companion piece was published in the *Quarterly,* "A French Critic on Goethe." Again the critic was Scherer, and again the essay has been neglected, no doubt because it, too, seems from its title to be second-hand. It is far from that: it is a statement of critical principles by one of England's finest critics, applied to the work of a fellow practitioner of the art, and the object of the criticism is one of the greatest writers of his time, one on whom Arnold all his life set a high value. Again, though less prominently, there were the unsatisfactory examples—Carlyle, Herman Grimm. When the latter calls Goethe "the greatest poet of all times and of all peoples," he "is looking at the necessities, as to literary glory, of the new German empire" (VIII, 254-55). In a sentence, the nationalist motive for literary evaluation is dismissed, and we teachers of American literature may be warned against being too indiscriminate. Carlyle, like Arnold's contemporary G. H. Lewes, was rather the propagandist for Goethe than the critic. Arnold remembers with gratitude his debt to Carlyle for attracting attention in a direction where attention was deserved, but in the last analysis he finds the praise undiscriminating; so too is Lewes's. "On looking back at Carlyle, one sees how much of *engouement* there was in his criticism of Goethe, and how little of it will stand. That is the thing—to write what will *stand*. Johnson, with all his limitations, will be found to *stand* a great deal better than Carlyle," Arnold wrote to his sister while he was working on this essay. The publicist takes refuge in enthusiastic and meaningless rhetoric ("bright, genial, glorious creations, comparable to any to be found in the long galleries of art!"); the true critic must be held to the standard Aristotle set in the *Nicomachean Ethics*—he must judge things "as the judicious would determine" (VIII, 264). "Admiration is salutary and formative, true; but things admirable are sown wide, and are to be gathered here and gathered there, not all in one place; and until we have gathered them wherever they are to be found, we have not known the true salutariness and formativeness of admiration" (VIII, 255).

In a single paragraph Arnold runs through the kinds of faults to which the critic is liable—a concentrated and more comprehensive statement than anything in "The Study of Poetry," which was written, after all, for a less sophisticated audience. "Many and diverse must be the judgments passed upon every great poet, upon every considerable writer. There is the judgment of enthusiasm and admiration, which proceeds from ardent youth, easily fired, eager to find a hero and to worship him. There is the judgment of gratitude and sympathy, which proceeds from those who find in an author what helps them, what they want, and who rate him at a very high value accordingly. There is the judgment of ignorance, the judgment of incompatibility, the judgment of envy and jealousy. Finally, there is the systematic judgment, and this judgment is the most worthless of all. The sharp scrutiny of envy and jealousy may bring real faults to light. The judgments of incompatibility and ignorance are instructive, whether they reveal necessary clefts of separation between the experiences of different sorts of people, or reveal simply the narrowness and bounded view of those who judge. But the systematic judgment is altogether unprofitable. Its author has not really his eye upon the professed object of his criticism at all, but upon something else which he wants to prove by means of that object. He neither really tells us, therefore, anything about the object, nor anything about his own ignorance of the object. He never fairly looks at it, he is looking at something else. Perhaps if he looked at it straight and full, looked at it simply, he might be able to pass a good judgment on it. As it is, all he tells us is that he is no genuine critic, but a man with a system, an advocate" (VIII, 254–55). To this list we must add one other kind of failing, the delight in searching out and expounding, as an end in itself, the private world of symbolism the poet may throw out at us. There is here, Arnold tells us, a "sound and admirable rule of criticism": "Let us ask how a poet's work accords, not with any one's fancies and crotchets, but 'with human nature and the nature of things at large, with the universal principles of poetic beauty as they stand written in the hearts and imaginations of all men' [Arnold here quotes Carlyle], and we shall have the surest rejection of symbol, hieroglyphic, and mystification in poetry. We shall have the surest condemnation of works like . . . the second part of *Faust*" (VIII, 274). I shall leave it for others to consider the implications of this paragraph for contemporary academic criticism.

In preparing two lectures on the eighteenth-century Bishop Joseph Butler, Arnold seized upon an expression of the Bishop's which thenceforth became a catchword of literary, as well as theological, criticism for him: "Things and actions are what they are, and the consequences of them will be what they will be; why then should we desire to be deceived?" (VIII, 12). And so he is able to conclude: "It is by no means as the greatest of poets that Goethe deserves the pride and praise of his German countrymen. It is as the clearest, the largest, the most helpful thinker of modern times. . . . Goethe is the greatest poet of modern times, not because he is one of the half-dozen human beings who in the history of our race have shown the most signal gift for poetry, but because, having a very considerable gift for poetry, he was at the same time, in the width, depth, and richness of his criticism of life, by far our greatest modern man. . . . His preciousness and importance as a clear and profound modern spirit, as a master-critic of modern life, must communicate a worth of their own to his poetry, and may well make it erroneously seem to have a positive value and perfectness as poetry, more than it has. . . . Nevertheless, poetical defects, where they are present, subsist, and are what they are. And the same with defects of character. Time and attention bring them to light; and when they are brought to light, it is not good for us, it is obstructing and retarding, to refuse to see them'' (VIII, 274–75). This, then, is the function of criticism.

When one seeks an example of Arnold's practical criticism at its best, one will no doubt be influenced by irrelevant matters as well as solid critical judgments. Arnold knew and loved both Wordsworth and the Wordsworth country so well that it is hard to resist the essay he prefaced to his 1879 selection from Wordsworth's poetry. But a more nearly complete exemplar of the method Arnold has been setting forth is the lecture on ''Emerson,'' and in addition there is more of Arnold in it. He saturated himself in the works of Emerson immediately before and during his voyage to America to lecture in the autumn of 1883, only a little more than a year after Emerson's death, and he wrote the lecture (on stationery he had pilfered from the writing-salon of the Cunarder) at odd moments during the first month of his tour of America. The lecture copy was printed for him by the Harvard University printers, proofs were corrected on the train journey between Princeton and Yale, and the lecture was delivered for the first time in Chickering Hall, Boston, on December 1. He had hoped to be able ''to slip away from New York and see Concord, and the grave where Emerson is buried, and Boston Bay, all by myself, and then to write my lecture with this local impression fresh upon me,'' he wrote to his sister; to do this, alas, was not possible, but when some dozen days after the first delivery of the lecture he was entertained by the Emerson family in Concord, he was not disappointed: ''very pleasing country—gentle hills, and New England homesteads, and elm-bordered roads (such elms!), and the quiet river flowing through it."

Seldom is Arnold more engaging than in his description of the intellectual influences he had felt at Oxford in his youth, those of Newman, Carlyle, and Goethe, and then Emerson, whom he had actually met at that time in the company of Clough (though he does not mention Clough in the lecture). "It is not always pleasant to ask oneself questions about the friends of one's youth; they cannot always well support it. Carlyle, for instance, in my judgment, cannot well support such a return upon him. Yet we should make the return; we should part with our illusions, we should know the truth. . . . I set myself, therefore, resolutely to come at a real estimate of Emerson, and with a leaning even to strictness rather than to indulgence. That is the safer course. Time has no indulgence; any veils of illusion which we may have left around an object because we loved it, Time is sure to strip away" (X, 168). Coming to the aid of Time, then, Arnold proceeds to strip away the illusions. To the Americans, saturated with Emerson's poetry and thinking of it with affection, it might indeed seem that his work has taken its place with the great poetry of the language. But that is "that personal sort of estimate which, for my part, even in speaking of authors dear to me, I would try to avoid." "In truth, one of the legitimate poets, Emerson, in my opinion, is not. His poetry is interesting, it makes one think; but it is not the poetry of one of the born poets." This, he might have added, despite the strong influence Emerson had upon his own early poetry. "But I regard myself, not as speaking to please Emerson's admirers, not as speaking to please myself; but rather . . . as communing with Time and Nature concerning the productions of this beautiful and rare spirit, and as resigning what of him is by their unalterable decree touched with caducity, in order the better to mark and secure that in him which is immortal" (X, 169).

The same mission leads him to deny Emerson a place among the great writers, the great men of letters, "men like Cicero, Plato, Bacon, Pascal, Swift, Voltaire,—writers with, in the first place, a genius and instinct for style" (X, 171). "It is a curious thing, that quality of style which marks the great writer, the born man of letters. It resides in the whole tissue of his work, and of his work regarded as a composition for literary purposes. Brilliant and powerful passages in a man's writings do not prove his possession of it; it lies in their whole tissue'' (X, 172). Emerson's claim as a philosopher gets even shorter shrift: "He cannot build; his arrangement of philosophical ideas has no progress in it, no evolution; he does not construct a philosophy" (X, 174), and he himself knew it. It would be pleasant, finally, if one could bestow on the author of *English Traits* the praise of being among the great "markers and recorders of the traits of human life,— . . . writers like Montaigne, La Bruyère, Addison," but again, "tried by the highest standards, . . . Emerson's observation has not the disinterested quality of the observation of these masters" (X, 175).

"And now I think I have cleared the ground. I have given up to envious Time as much of Emerson as Time can fairly expect ever to obtain. We have not in Emerson a great poet, a great writer, a great philosophy-maker. His relation to us . . . is a relation of, I think, even superior importance. His relation to us is more like that of the Roman Emperor Marcus Aurelius. . . . He is the friend and aider of those who would live in the spirit" (X, 177). One recognizes here something of the judgment upon Goethe which Arnold had already passed, as "the largest, the most helpful thinker of modern times." It is precisely in his helpfulness to modern man that Emerson sur- passed his friend Carlyle; "Carlyle's perverse attitude towards hap- piness cuts him off from hope. He fiercely attacks the desire for happiness. . . . He is wrong. . . . Tell [man] and show him that he places his happiness wrong, that he seeks for delight where delight will never be really found; then you illumine and further him. But you only confuse him by telling him to cease to desire happiness, and you will not tell him this unless you are already confused your- self" (X, 183). Indeed, in the long run, Carlyle may live more by his correspondence with Emerson than by his literary works, just as "it is in the immense Goethe-literature of letter, journal, and conversa- tion, . . . that the elements for an impression of the truly great, the truly significant Goethe are to be found" (X, 173-74; VIII, 275). Emerson saw things better than his friend. "By his conviction that in the life of the spirit is happiness, and by his hope that this life of the spirit will come more and more to be sanely understood, and to prevail, and to work for happiness,—by this conviction and hope Emerson was great, and he will surely prove in the end to have been right in them" (X, 184-85). "As Wordsworth's poetry is, in my judgment, the most important work done in verse, in our language, during the present century, so Emerson's *Essays* are, I think, the most important work done in prose" (X, 182).

II

Arnold's best-selling book was *Literature and Dogma*, a work which by its title linked the methods of literary criticism with the criticism of theology. It is beautifully written, and more in keeping with the temper of twentieth-century religious thinking than is likely to be acknowledged by those who regret Arnold's venture into the world of theology. But because it is a critique upon a body of writing with which we are all thoroughly familiar, we are likely to be somewhat confused by our own preconceptions. "A Psychological Parallel," an essay Arnold wrote for the *Contemporary Review* in the latter part of 1876, makes clearer than anything else Arnold wrote, precisely how, in his view, the superstitions of the founders of Christianity neither impugned their honesty nor ultimately discredited their insight. It was meant, he declared, to be his concluding essay on religion, an essay in which he would try to resolve the question of how we are to regard St. Paul's undoubted belief in the physical resurrection of Jesus and in his material appearance to his followers on earth after his crucifixion. "Does either the belief of those things by a man of signal truthfulness, judgment, and mental power in St. Paul's circumstances, prove them to have really happened; or does his believing them, in spite of their not having really happened, prove that he cannot have been a man of great truthfulness, judgment, and mental power?" (VIII, 113)

Somewhere Arnold had picked up a curious collection, by this time about forty years old, of type-facsimile reprints of seventeenth-century tracts upon witchcraft, from which he drew an account of the trial and execution of two old widows of Lowestoft at Bury St. Edmunds in 1664. The judge was Sir Matthew Hale—learned, humane, sweet of temper; one of the witnesses, who affirmed that he had no doubt whatsoever that the victims had been bewitched, was Sir Thomas Browne, held up in our own day as a pioneer of modern science. "Now, the inference to be drawn from this trial is not by any means that Hale was 'an imbecile or credulous enthusiast.' The whole history of his life and doings disproves it. But the belief in witchcraft was in the very atmosphere which Hale breathed, as the belief in miracle was in the very atmosphere which St. Paul breathed. What the trial shows us is, that a man of veracity, judgment, and mental power, may have his mind thoroughly governed, on certain subjects, by a foregone conclusion as to what is likely and credible" (VIII, 121).

The other part of the main question is illustrated by one of Hale's contemporaries, a fellow of Queens' College, Cambridge, named John Smith, who about fifteen years before the trial Arnold described had preached an annual New Year's Day sermon at Huntingdon against witchcraft and diabolical contracts. Firmly and unequivocally as he expressed his belief in the notion that devils still walked the earth and had communication with men, his true interest is in the spiritual. "When we say the devil is continually busy with us," he said, "I mean not only some apostate spirit as one particular being, but that spirit of apostacy which is lodged in all men's natures. . . . The tyranny of the devil and hell is not so much in some external things as in the qualities and dispositions of men's minds. . . . *All sin and vice is our own creature*" (VIII, 126–27). "Here, in our Cambridge Platonist," Arnold comments, "we have a man who accepts the erroneous belief in witchcraft, professes it publicly, preaches on it; and yet is not only a man of veracity and intelligence, but actually manages to give to the error adopted by him a turn, an aspect, which indicates its erroneousness. Not only is he of help to us generally, in spite of his error; he is of help to us in respect of that very error itself" (VIII, 127). Fifty-two years after the trial at Bury St. Edmunds, the last execution for witchcraft in England took place; another twenty years and the penal statutes against witchcraft were repealed. The spirit of the time had altered completely. But the spiritual value of John Smith's sermons remained untouched.

Jesus, too, constantly makes use of the apocalyptic language of the Old Testament and of the apocryphal Book of Enoch. Arnold never suggests, as he does with St. Paul, that Jesus literally believed that language, though there is probably no reason intellectually why Arnold should not have done so. He does, however, compile about a dozen paragraphs of the sayings of Jesus, drawn from the Gospels (and occasionally slightly altered from the Authorized Version in the interest of clarity) to illustrate how completely Jesus (like St. Paul after him) was concerned with the spiritual renovation of mankind, not with a heavenly life beyond. It is a serious intellectual error in popular Christianity—and the term includes those who subscribe literally to the Thirty-Nine Articles—to adhere to a literal, supernatural interpretation of this language. "The objections to popular Christianity are not moral objections, but intellectual revolt against its demonstrations by miracle and metaphysics. . . . 'Things are what they are, and the consequences of them will be what they will be;' and one inevitable consequence of a thing's want of conformity with truth and fact is, that sooner or later the human mind perceives it. . . . But, meanwhile, the ground-belief of all Christians, whatever account they may give to themselves of its source and sanctions, is in itself an indestructible basis of fellowship. Whoever believes the final triumph of Christianity, the Christianisation of the world, to have all the necessity and grandeur of a natural law, will never lack a bond of profound sympathy with popular religion. Compared with agreement and difference on this point, agreement and difference on other points seem trifling" (VIII, 146). And therefore, though the Articles "present the Creeds as science, exact science; and this, at the present day, very many a man cannot accept," it is easy for such a man "to exaggerate to himself the barrier between himself and popular religion. . . . It is expedient for him rather to think it less great than it is, than more great" (VIII, 133). Let him, then, not secede, not commit the folly of the Comtists in founding a "modern" religion, but work within the Church as "a national society for the promotion of goodness." Many of the prayers and services of the Church will appear to him "the literal, beautiful rendering of what he himself feels and believes. The rest he may rehearse as an approximative rendering of it;—as language *thrown out* by other men, in other times, at immense objects which deeply engaged their affections and awe, and which deeply engage his also; objects concerning which, moreover, adequate statement is impossible. To him, therefore, this approximative part of the prayers and services which he rehearses will be poetry. It is a great error to think that whatever is thus perceived to be poetry ceases to be available in religion. The noblest races are those which know how to make the most serious use of poetry" (VIII, 132).

The notion of the Church of England as "a great national society for the promotion of what is commonly called *goodness*" (VIII, 65) is the thesis of the address Arnold gave before the London clergy at

Sion College on February 22, 1876. It derived from his very early stand, taken after Coleridge and his own father, that "the Clerisy of the nation, or national Church, in its primary acceptation and original intention, comprehended the learned of all denominations, the sages and professors of the law and jurisprudence, of medicine and physiology, of music, of military and civil architecture, of the physical sciences, with the mathematical as the common organ of the preceding; in short, all the so-called liberal arts and sciences, the possession and application of which constitute the civilization of a country, as well as the theological,"² a passage Arnold alluded to in his very first theological essay, "The Bishop and the Philosopher" (January, 1863; III, 51). The concept of the Church as a society devoted to education and matters of the intellect was gradually fading throughout the nineteenth century as first the Dissenters, then secular groups, then the State, took on a greater share of the responsibility for the schools and the universities, and even Oxford and Cambridge were obliged to admit non-subscribers to the Thirty-Nine Articles; still, throughout the century the surest way to a bishopric was through a mastership in a school or a fellowship at the university, and two of Dr. Arnold's successors at Rugby became archbishops of Canterbury. But the theme of comprehensiveness remained Arnold's thesis in this essay, his final attempt to explain why the author of *Literature and Dogma* remained very firmly within the Church he had seemed to so many to undermine.

With reference to his own writings, he says merely that he is entirely in accord with Bishop Butler that the business of the clergy "is virtue and religion, life and manners, the science of improving the temper and making the heart better" (VIII, 65), but that the present is one of the times in which this function of the Church is endangered by the intellectual offense given to many people "from the predominance of the systems of theologians, and from the want of a new and better construction than theirs to put upon the Bible" (VIII, 66). And so he regards his criticism of dogmatic theology as an attempt to preserve the essence of the Church.

Of the serious threats to the establishment from the outside—Protestant Nonconformity, Roman Catholicism—and from dissident groups within—Sacramentalists, Evangelicals, and Broad Churchmen—none is so great as the estrangement of the working classes, whose ideal is "a future,—a future on earth, not up in the sky,—which shall profoundly change and ameliorate things for them; an immense social progress, nay, a social transformation" (VIII, 71). And notwithstanding the fact that "the superstitious worship of existing social facts, a devoted obsequiousness to the landed and propertied and satisfied classes, does not inhere in the Christian religion," the Church is regarded by the advocates of the workingmen as "the ally of tyranny, the organ of social oppression, the champion of intellectual bondage" (VIII, 71, 73). Even though the best voices of the Church tradition have spoken against inequality and private interest, and despite "the immense labours and sacrifices of the clergy for the improvement of the condition of the popular, the working classes;—for their schools, for instance, and for their physical well-being in countless ways" (VIII, 75-76), it is incumbent upon the Church itself to respond to the ideal of the working classes, to insist on an "immense renovation and transformation of our actual state of things"; it is important that the clergy as a body should sympathize heartily with that ideal. "And this they can best bring themselves to do, . . . by accustoming themselves to see that the ideal is the true original ideal of their religion and of its Founder. . . . If the Church of England is right here, it has, I am persuaded, nothing to fear either from Rome, or from the Protestant Dissenters, or from the secularists. It cannot, I think, stand secure unless it has the sympathy of the popular classes. And it cannot have the sympathy of the popular classes unless it is right on this head. But, if it is right on this head, it may, I feel convinced, flourish and be strong with their sympathy, and with that of the nation in general" (VIII, 78). This is the same Arnold who in his political essays affirmed the responsibility of the nation for the well-being of the poorer classes: "The well-being of the many comes out more and more distinctly, in proportion as time goes on, as the object we must pursue" (VIII, 289).

The arguments of the Dissenters are dismissed with a sentence from Butler: "If goodness is the end, and 'all good men are,' as Butler says, 'equally concerned in promoting that end,' then, as he goes on to conclude, 'to do it more effectually they ought to unite in promoting it' " (VIII, 82). A society for the promotion of goodness is the stronger for being national, and the dogmatic grounds for separation are in our day trivial. "The more the sense of religion grows, and of religion in a large way,—the sense of the beauty and

rest of religion, the sense that its charm lies in its grace and peace,
—the more will the present attitude, objections, and complaints of
the Dissenters indispose men's minds to them" (VIII, 84). "What
the clergy have to aim at, is the character of simple instruments for
the public good. . . . By opening itself to the glow of the old and
true ideal of the Christian Gospel, by fidelity to reason, by placing
the stress of its religion on goodness, by cultivating grace and peace,
[the Church of England] will inspire attachment, to which the attachment which it inspires now, deep though that is, will be as
nothing; it will last, be sure, as long as this nation" (VIII, 85–86).
The rhetoric of the lecture combines exhortation with hope and is
inspired by a genuine, conservative affection for the old as well as a
firm conviction as to the needs of English society in a revolutionary
era.

III

In 1859 Arnold was sent to France, French Switzerland, and
Holland to inquire into the provision for elementary education in
those countries; he published his official report not only as a blue
book but also as a separate volume for a wider public, and to introduce this separate volume he wrote an Introduction (March, 1861)
which is the earliest statement of his concept of a modern society.
In 1879 he republished the Introduction with the title "Democracy,"
as the first of his *Mixed Essays*, so placed because of the centrality
of its ideas to his thinking.[3]

Unlike France, England had undergone no revolution; but, to
quote Burke, "in the silent lapse of events, as material alterations
have been insensibly brought about in the policy and character of
governments and nations, as those which have been marked by the
tumult of public revolutions" (II, 4). Englishmen have a horror of
State-action, a horror which has a firm and valid basis in history,
but there are "reasons for thinking that the circumstances which
once made that jealousy prudent and natural have undergone an essential change," and "in the present altered conjuncture," State-
action is becoming "not only without danger in itself, but the
means of helping us against dangers from another quarter" (II, 4).
England has long been governed by the aristocracy, who governed,
indeed, "in the grand style," but acquiescence in their power no
longer prevails; "the superiority of the upper class over all others is

no longer so great; the willingness of the others to recognise that superiority is no longer so ready. This change has been brought about by natural and inevitable causes, and neither the great nor the multitude are to be blamed for it. . . . Life itself consists, say the philosophers [in this case Spinoza], in the effort *to affirm one's own essence*; meaning by this, to develop one's own existence fully and freely, to have ample light and air, to be neither cramped nor overshadowed. Democracy [i.e., the people] is trying *to affirm its own essence*; to live, to enjoy, to possess the world, as aristocracy has tried, and successfully tried, before it'' (II, 6-7). And to this end, democracy requires, not political freedom, which an Englishman boasts that he already has, but social freedom, equality.

"Can it be denied, that to live in a society of equals tends in general to make a man's spirits expand, and his faculties work easily and actively; while, to live in a society of superiors, although it may occasionally be a very good discipline, yet in general tends to tame the spirits and to make the play of the faculties less secure and active?'' (II, 8) In France, the revolutionary doctrine of equality "has undoubtedly given to the lower classes, to the body of the common people, a self-respect, an enlargement of spirit, a consciousness of counting for something in their country's action, which has raised them in the scale of humanity'' (II, 9). It was France that best sensed the spirit of the time. "The growing power in Europe is democracy; and France has organised democracy with a certain indisputable grandeur and success. The ideas of 1789 were working everywhere in the eighteenth century; but it was because in France the State adopted them that the French Revolution became an historic epoch for the world, and France the lode-star of Continental democracy'' (II, 10-11).

In England the lower classes have been slower to assert their power, partly because of the excellences of the English aristocracy and partly because of the virtues of the common people, who have an innate deference and at the same time an innate ability to act independently rather than collectively. With the inevitable disappearance of the aristocratic dominance, however, and the growth of democracy, either England will become *Americanised*, or she must turn to the action of the State as a buttress against individualism rampant. At present, the aristocracy has found a most peculiar ally in its opposition to the intervention of the State, the Protestant

Dissenters of the middle class, who have the memory and example of long years of discrimination against them on the part of the State. "Not only did the whole repudiate the physician, but also those who were sick. For it is evident, that the action of a diligent, an impartial, and a national government, while it can do little to better the condition, already fortunate enough, of the highest and richest class of its people, can really do much, by institution and regulation, to better that of the middle and lower classes. The State can bestow certain broad collective benefits, which are indeed not much if compared with the advantages already possessed by individual grandeur, but which are rich and valuable if compared with the make-shifts of mediocrity and poverty" (II, 21).

By its nature, the essay is directed most especially against the opposition of the Dissenters to State control of education; they have, in Arnold's view, every reason to be discontented rather with the private education they have thus far provided for themselves. "By giving to schools for these classes a public character, [the State] can bring the instruction in them under a criticism which the stock of knowledge and judgment in our middle classes is not of itself at present able to supply" (II, 22). The Dissenters have been a great force in maintaining liberty of conscience against persecution. "It is a very great thing to be able to think as you like; but, after all, an important question remains: *what* you think. . . . In modern epochs the part of a high reason, of ideas, acquires constantly increasing importance in the conduct of the world's affairs. A fine culture is the complement of a high reason, and it is in the conjunction of both with character, with energy, that the ideal for men and nations is to be placed. . . . Culture without character is, no doubt, something frivolous, vain, and weak; but character without culture is, on the other hand, something raw, blind, and dangerous" (II, 24). If, then, the middle classes continue in their isolation from the collective action of the State, they will not the less become the rulers of the nation; "but they will certainly *Americanise* it. They will rule it by their energy, but they will deteriorate it by their low ideals and want of culture" (II, 25).

Arnold concludes with observations that, not surprisingly, anticipate much of *Culture and Anarchy*. There is first his definition of the State, which he ascribes to Burke: "The State is properly . . . *the nation in its collective and corporate character*" (II, 26). To

191

those who point with dismay at the character of the people's representatives, Arnold replies, first, that these representatives are themselves made better through their responsibility; "their position itself, . . . if they are men of only average honesty and capacity, tends to give them a fitness for acting on behalf of the nation superior to that of other men of equal honesty and capacity who are not in the same position" (II, 27). And second, he says that it is the responsibility of the democracy to see that its representatives are not inferior. "Hesitating, blundering, unintelligent, inefficacious, the action of the State may be; but, such as it is, it is the collective action of the nation itself, and the nation is responsible for it" (II, 28). "One irresistible force, . . . *the modern spirit*" determines that change will come, and it is through collective action that we can best meet the demands of change (II, 29). Arnold's notion of the forces of history in the post-revolutionary era is more fully set forth in this essay than anywhere else.

It is not surprising, then, that the same volume of *Mixed Essays* should contain Arnold's fullest discussion of one of the catchwords of the French Revolution, "Equality," a lecture he delivered at the Royal Institution on February 8, 1878. If parts of *Culture and Anarchy* (1867–1869) have seemed to many people to savor of intellectual elitism, "Democracy" and "Equality," separated in time by seventeen years and straddling therefore the date of that work, show the persistence of the popular ideal for society in Arnold's thinking.

Arnold bases his argument, not, as the French were inclined to do, upon a doctrine of "natural rights," but on the Englishman's ground of expediency and on the sound awareness that "rights" are created—and taken away—by law. He focuses on a single portion of the law, the law of inheritance, to show how in England it creates monstrous inequalities unknown to most of the Continent. "Property is created and maintained by law. It would disappear in that state of private war and scramble which legal society supersedes. Legal society creates, for the common good, the right of property; and for the common good that right is by legal society limitable. That property should exist, and that it should be held with a sense of security and with a power of disposal, may be taken . . . as a settled matter of expediency. With these conditions a good deal of inequality is inevitable. But that the power of disposal should

192

be practically *unlimited*, that the inequality should be *enormous*, or that the degree of inequality admitted at one time should be admitted *always*,—this is by no means so certain" (VIII, 285).

The aim of every society ought to be "a high standard of civilisation" (VIII, 284), not merely among the wealthy and the aristocratic, but at every level. "An individual or a class, concentrating their efforts upon their own well-being exclusively, do but beget troubles both for others and for themselves also. No individual life can be truly prosperous, passed, as Obermann says, in the midst of men who suffer. . . . To the noble soul, it cannot be happy; to the ignoble, it cannot be secure. Socialistic and communistic schemes have generally, however, a fatal defect; they are content with too low and material a standard of well-being. That instinct of perfection, which is the master-power in humanity, always rebels at this, and frustrates the work" (VIII, 289-90). Now "civilisation is the humanisation of man in society," and "to be humanised is to make progress towards . . . our true and full humanity," "an advance, not along one line only, but several" (VIII, 286). Some nations have advanced along one line, others along other lines (here are our old friends "Hellenism" and "Hebraism"): "The power of intellect and science, the power of beauty, the power of social life and manners,—these are what Greece so felt, and fixed, and may stand for. They are great elements in our humanisation. The power of conduct is another great element; and this was so felt and fixed by Israel that we can never with justice refuse to permit Israel, in spite of all his shortcomings, to stand for it" (VIII, 287). To become fully civilized, we must move along all these lines. It might be said that the Italians excel, even among their lowest classes, in a sense for beauty; the Germans, in a sense for intellect and science; the English, in a sense for morality; and the French, in a sense for social intercourse and manners (VIII, 287-88). Moreover, "a community having humane manners is a community of equals, and in such a community great social inequalities have really no meaning, while they are at the same time a menace and an embarrassment to perfect ease of social intercourse" (VIII, 289).

British inequality, to tell the truth, "materialises our upper class, vulgarises our middle class, brutalises our lower. . . . What the middle class sees is that splendid piece of materialism, the aristocratic class, with a wealth and luxury utterly out of their reach, with a standard of social life and manners, the offspring of that wealth and luxury, seeming utterly out of their reach also. And thus they are thrown back upon themselves—upon a defective type of religion, a narrow range of intellect and knowledge, a stunted sense of beauty, a low standard of manners. And the lower class see before them the aristocratic class, and its civilisation, such as it is, even infinitely more out of *their* reach than out of that of the middle class; while the life of the middle class, with its unlovely types of religion, thought, beauty, and manners, has naturally, in general, no great attraction for them either.[4] And so they too are thrown back upon themselves; upon their beer, their gin, and their *fun"* (VIII, 302). England's two political parties represent the middle and the upper classes, and yet "one of the great obstacles to our civilisation is . . . British nonconformity, another main obstacle to our civilisation is British aristocracy!" (VIII, 304). There will be no immediate change among the politicians; "the matter is at present one for the thoughts of those who think. It is a thing to be turned over in the minds of those who, on the one hand, have the spirit of scientific inquirers, bent on seeing things as they really are; and, on the other hand, the spirit of friends of the humane life, lovers of perfection." Let them reflect upon the way in which the English laws of property and bequest affect the civilization of the English people, and let them, as Menander said, "Choose equality" (VIII, 305).

It would have taken a truly prophetic vision, in the heyday of Gladstone, to foresee the almost complete demise of the Liberal party that we have witnessed in the present century, and Arnold did not have that gift; nevertheless, he called himself "a Liberal of the future" (IX, 138), in contrast to the Liberals of his own day who were almost as blind as the Tories, and who "do not see how the world is really going" (IX, 151). "The Future of Liberalism" (July, 1880) was meant to be "the last of my publications about politics and social matters" (of course it was not), and hence aimed at a final summary of his views; it is *Culture and Anarchy* abridged and matured, and the catchwords are now those he invented in his more recent essays such as "Equality."

Liberalism, says Arnold, appeals to one of the great needs of humanity, the need for expansion, and it serves that need through its commitment to liberty and to trade. The extension of the franchise has been good, and Arnold urges its further extension to the agricultural laborers (an extension that came along almost immediately). There is no natural right in a man to the possession of a vote, "but if experience has established any one thing in this world, it has established this: that it is well for any great class and description of men in society to be able to say for itself what it wants, and not to have other classes, the so-called educated and intelligent classes, acting for it as its proctors, and supposed to understand its wants and to provide for them. They do not really understand its wants, they do not really provide for them" (IX, 140). And because Liberalism appeals to the instinct in man for expansion, it will ultimately prevail; politics is progressive, and "instinctively, however slowly, the human spirit struggles towards the light; and the adoptions and rejections of its agents by the multitude [i.e., the swingings of the pendulum between Liberal and Conservative governments] are never wholly blind and capricious, but have a meaning" (IX, 141).

Unfortunately, the Liberal politicians have lost sight of the true end of politics. Their devotion to free trade has produced the "hellholes" of the industrial towns and the middle-class ugliness of North London. They have waged their campaigns upon trivialities like marriage to a deceased wife's sister, the right to churchyard burials on the part of Dissenters, and local option with respect to the consumption of porter and gin. "The true and noble science of politics is even the very chief of the sciences," says Arnold in an Aristotelian tone, "because it deals with [the question, how to live,] for the benefit of man not as an isolated creature, but in that state 'without which,' as Burke says, 'man could not by any possibility arrive at the perfection of which his nature is capable,'—for the benefit of man in society" (IX, 141). It is incumbent upon the Liberals, then, to keep an eye firmly upon the full range of human perfection. They have done something with the provision of elementary education for the masses. "But elementary education goes so little way" (IX, 153). Let the Liberals attend to the needs of the people for knowledge, for beauty, for social life and manners—and let them attend especially to the needs of the industrial poor, whom indeed their free-trade doctrine has created.[5] And above all let them understand that the needs of man "include equality as well as political liberty and free trade. . . . When Liberal statesmen have learned to care for all these together, and to go on unto perfection or true civilisation, then at last they will be professing and practising the true and noble science of politics and the true and noble science of economics, instead of, as now, semblances only of these sciences, or at best fragments of them. And then will come at last the extinction or the conversion of the Tories, the restitution of all things, the reign of the Liberal saints" (IX, 159–60). Until then, England will be governed alternately by two groups, not of true politicians, but of political opportunists.

It would not be true to assert that the Liberal of Arnold's future was the Labourite of our present; nevertheless, a hundred years after Arnold's essay we can see that the State in Britain has indeed moved far in the direction he was predicting, with tuition-free university education, death duties that break up the huge estates, green belts and clean air, and the attempt to provide decent housing for all.

IV

Arnold was very conscious, as he wrote the essays we have been looking at, of the way in which they were interlinked and, as he thought, all served the same end. He prefaced the *Last Essays on Church and Religion* with the assertion that he was now closing his "series of . . . attempts to deal directly with questions concerning religion and the Church. Indirectly such questions must often, in all serious literary work, present themselves; but in this volume I make them my direct object for the last time. . . . And in returning to . . . literature, . . . I am returning, after all, to a field where work of the most important kind has now to be done, though indirectly, for religion" (VIII, 148). By the time he collected *Mixed Essays*, he was saying: "Whoever seriously occupies himself with literature will soon perceive its vital connection with other agencies. . . . Literature is . . . a powerful agency for benefiting the world and for civilising it. . . . But it cannot do all. In other words, literature is a part of civilisation; it is not the whole. . . . Civilisation is the humanisation of man in society" (VIII, 370). When, therefore, he undertook to debate with his friend T. H. Huxley on the relative worth of literary and scientific studies, he wove his argument out of propositions he had developed in his political and social essays, as well as his literary ones.

"Literature and Science" was the most popular of Arnold's

American lectures. He had actually composed and delivered it as Rede Lecture at the University of Cambridge on June 14, 1882, a year before he committed himself to his American lecture tour, and it was published on both sides of the Atlantic at that time. It expressed, he told his sister, "in general my doctrine on Studies as well as I can frame it," and despite its prior publication it was so much in demand as a lecture in this country that he delivered it twenty-nine times, sometimes on successive nights, and got thoroughly sick of it before he was done. (He delivered "Numbers" and "Emerson" eighteen times each.) Though its immediate occasion was an amiable attack on literary studies by Huxley, its thesis grew out of Arnold's study of higher education on the Continent in 1865; he concluded his report on that study (1868) with these words: "The ideal of a general, liberal training is, to carry us to a knowledge of ourselves and the world. We are called to this knowledge by special aptitudes which are born with us; the grand thing in teaching is to have faith that some aptitudes of this kind everyone has. This one's special aptitudes are for knowing men,—the study of the humanities; that one's special aptitudes are for knowing the world,—the study of nature. The circle of knowledge comprehends both, and we should all have some notion, at any rate, of the whole circle of knowledge. The rejection of the humanities by the realists, the rejection of the study of nature by the humanists, are alike ignorant" (IV, 300). His reflections on the appropriate balance between humanistic subjects and scientific ones developed in his annual reports as inspector of schools during the next decade; in his General Report for 1876 he wrote: "To have the power of using, which is the thing wished, these data of natural science, a man must, in general, have first been in some measure *moralised*; and for moralising him it will be found not easy, I think, to dispense with those old agents, letters, poetry, religion. So let not our teachers be led to imagine, whatever they may hear and see of the call for natural science, that their literary cultivation is unimportant. The fruitful use of natural science itself depends, in a very great degree, on having effected in the whole man, by means of letters, a rise in what the political economists call *the standard of life*." The lecture itself, a witty reply to Huxley's rather heavy-handed attack, is so well known as to need no summary. In it Arnold commits himself to a kind of "great books" reading list in which he probably had no great conviction—"All knowledge that reaches us through books is literature. . . . Euclid's *Elements* and Newton's *Principia* are thus literature" (X, 58)—though almost immediately he seems to be talking of studying, not the scientists themselves, but "what has been done by" them (X, 59), or the history of science. (It might be added, however, that he quotes the Latin of the *Principia* in both his notebooks and his published works.) The distinction between what he calls "instrument-knowledges" (X, 63) and the kind of knowledge which will "establish a relation between the new conceptions, and our instinct for beauty, our instinct for conduct" (X, 66)—as the humane letters will do—has an unquestionable validity. He ends with a denial that the alternatives are mutually exclusive and that modern technical advances threaten the older studies. "The more that men's minds are cleared, the more that the results of science are frankly accepted, the more that poetry and eloquence come to be received and studied as what in truth they really are,—the criticism of life by gifted men, alive and active with extraordinary power at an unusual number of points;—so much the more will the value of humane letters, and of art also, which is an utterance having a like kind of power with theirs, be felt and acknowledged, and their place in education be secured" (X, 68-69). "The majority of men will always require humane letters; and so much the more, as they have the more and the greater results of science to relate to the need in man for conduct, and to the need in him for beauty" (X, 73). No better work can be chosen to represent Arnold's life-long interest in his father's profession and his own, and so indeed he intended it.

V

Arnold paid two visits to the United States—his strenuous lecture tour of 1883-1884 which took him as far west as the Mississippi and as far south as Richmond, Virginia, and his more comfortable visit to his daughter (who by this time had married an American) and to a few friends in the summer of 1886. He had already written twice about life in America, once before his first visit and once after it; now, after his return from the second visit, he determined to fulfill certain lecturing obligations in the provinces (at Hull, Bradford, and Bristol) with a discourse on what he described to a friend as "a very ticklish subject," "Life in America." When he published the lecture as "Civilisation in the United States" (April, 1888) his title linked it to the social essays he had previously published, for it must be recalled that he had made much of the proposition that "civilisation is the humanisation of man in society" (XI, 352). To his English critics it seemed (as I think it does to Americans now) "full of telling phrases, delicate humour, and delightful English," "bright, lively, luminous," full of "Matthewarnoldism"; to G. W. Smalley, London correspondent for *The New York Tribune*, it was the most deplorable thing he had ever read. It was the last essay Arnold published; on the day of his death he wrote: "Smalley has written a letter [to the *Tribune*] full of shriekings and cursings about my innocent article; the Americans will get their notion of it from that, and I shall never be able to enter America again." The essay is an exercise in the practical application of Arnold's ideas about man in society.

The United States, he said, by virtue of having been constituted in the modern age, has established a set of political institutions which "compl[y] well with the form and pressure of those circumstances and conditions which a modern age presents" (XI, 351). And so too with its solution of the social problem: "The people of the United States [are] a community singularly free from the distinction of classes, singularly homogeneous; . . . the division between rich and poor [is] consequently less profound there than in countries where the distinction of classes accentuates that division. . . . The United States, politically and socially, are a country living prosperously in a natural modern condition" (XI, 351). The ordinary man in America has a far more comfortable life than the ordinary man in England: public transportation is better and cheaper, plain food better and less expensive than in England. Even some luxuries, like ice cream, oysters, and good fruit, are inexpensive. The practical working of social equality shows itself most notably in the "charm in American women—a charm which you find in almost all of them, wherever you go. It is the charm of a natural manner, a manner not self-conscious, artificial, and constrained. It may not be a beautiful manner always, but it is almost always a natural manner, a free and happy manner; and this gives pleasure. Here we have, undoubtedly, a note of civilisation, and an evidence, at the same time, of the good effect of equality upon social life and manners" (XI, 356).

But the ultimate requirement of civilization is that it be *interesting*, and here the Americans fall short. "The great sources of the *interesting* are distinction and beauty: that which is elevated, and that which is beautiful" (XI, 358). Of public architecture they have nothing good; the Americans are (Arnold persists in believing) merely the English middle-class Puritans transplanted, and "if we in England were without the cathedrals, parish churches, and castles of the catholic and feudal age, and without the houses of the Elizabethan age, but had only the towns and buildings which the rise of our middle class has created in the modern age, we should be in much the same case as the Americans" (XI, 359). "In truth everything is against distinction in America, and against the sense of elevation to be gained through admiring and respecting it. The glorification of 'the average man,' who is quite a religion with statesmen and publicists there, is against it. The addiction to 'the funny man,' who is a national misfortune there, is against it. Above all, the newspapers are against it" (XI, 360–61). (On his first visit to the United States, Arnold had almost forcibly to be brought to an introduction with Mark Twain, whom he had taken for one of these professional "funny men.")

The most notable example of the failure of the Americans in civilization is their newspapers, and here Arnold most amusingly recounts some of the things that had been printed about him during his lecture tour. To be sure, his model was not the worst but the best of the English newspapers, *The Times*; but what was one to think of the best of the American newspapers when *The New York Times* wrote of the editor of *The New York Tribune*: "Mr. Whitelaw Reid is personally a sneak and in his newspaper an habitual liar"?

What is worst of all, the Americans admit to no sense of any imperfection in their lives. Instead of facing their defects and striving to remedy them, instead of using their undoubted advantages to make further improvements, they publicly glorify themselves as "the greatest nation upon earth." "Ours is the elect nation for the age to come. We are the chosen people," says one of their authors (XI, 366). And this tone is simply accepted. "There are plenty of cultivated, judicious, delightful individuals there. They are our hope and America's hope; it is through their means that improvement must come. They know perfectly well how false and hollow the boastful stuff talked is; but they let the storm of self-laudation rage, and say nothing" (XI, 366–67). Most important of all, the example of America is the image of what England may well become: "To us, too, the future of the United States is of incalculable importance. . . . As our country becomes more democratic, the malady here may no longer be that we have an upper class materialised, a middle class vulgarised, and a lower class brutalised. But the predominance of the common and ignoble, born of the predominance of the average man, is a malady too. . . . That, of true human nature, distinction and beauty are needs, that a civilisation is insufficient where these needs are not satisfied, faulty where they are thwarted, is an instruction of which we, as well as the Americans, may greatly require to take fast hold, and not to let go" (XI, 368). He has recurred to the fear expressed nearly thirty years earlier, in "Democracy," that in its progress toward the modern era, England may succumb to the danger of being "Americanised."

These ten essays, then, I should propose as the ones which best illustrate the whole range of Arnold's thought, and show also the extent to which his ideas on all subjects are essentially of a piece. It is perhaps worth noticing that half of them are lectures: very much of Arnold's best work was first delivered from the public platform, from the Oxford lectures on poetry down. His persistent subject is the adaptation of human life (especially, of course, in England) to the world moulded out of the ideas of the French Revolution, the "modern" world. Not a rigorous theorist and with no inclination to mould a society according to a theoretical concept, he was nevertheless a shrewd observer of "the way the world was going," a pragmatist who first of all insisted that "things and actions are what they are, and the consequences of them will be what they will be; why then should we desire to be deceived?" (VIII, 12) And he was one who then refused to let the view of things as they really are be narrowed to a view of a single, materialistic aspect of them.

NOTES

1. Parenthetical references are to my edition of *The Complete Prose Works of Matthew Arnold* (Ann Arbor: University of Michigan Press, 1960–77). 11 vols.

2. Coleridge, *On the Constitution of Church and State, Complete Works,* ed. W. G. T. Shedd (New York, 1853), VI, 53.

3. When this early essay is placed, as here, in the midst of so many later essays, the reader may sense Arnold's remarkable growth in stylistic felicity as he matured.

4. Arnold's duties as inspector of schools for many years excluded those schools conducted by the Church of England, and it became habitual with him to equate "middle class" with religious Nonconformity.

5. In regard to Ireland, moreover, all the Liberal vices are intensified, both their timidity in the face of vast inequalities of wealth and power and their deference to British middle-class (largely Nonconformist) prejudices (IX, 159).

PATER REDIVIVUS

GERALD MONSMAN

"I believe that the worst page of prose Pater wrote is better than the best that anybody else ever wrote," George Moore exuberantly confessed to Edmund Gosse. And earlier, at the outbreak of the First World War, Moore had written to Gosse upon rereading Walter Pater's first novel: "I feel I must write to you for I have just finished 'Marius the Epicurean' and the occasion is the greatest that can happen in any life worth talking about. You are thinking I fear of what is happening in Flanders but I beg you to dismiss these futilities that will settle themselves for better or worse from your mind and consider the really important thing—the great English prose work has been written and perfectly written and you and I would do well to lay aside our pens." Moore's effusiveness easily could have been written off by Gosse as only an Irishman's hyperbole, and certainly in the following half century criticism rarely did more than invoke the purple of the Mona Lisa passage as an illustration of nineteenth-century rhetoric or cite the hard, gemlike flame of the Conclusion to *The Renaissance* as evidence of Pater's hedonistic decadence. But recently J. Hillis Miller has remarked that "Walter Pater is, along with Coleridge, Arnold, and Ruskin, one of the four greatest English literary critics of the nineteenth century. He is also, of the four, the most influential in the twentieth century and the most alive today, although often his influence can be found on writers who deny or are ignorant of what they owe to him. Pater is effective today as a precursor of what is most vital in contemporary criticism." And Harold Bloom has declared: "More than Swinburne,

203

Morris, Rossetti, he became the father of Anglo-American Aestheticism, and subsequently the direct precursor of a Modernism that
vainly attempted to be Post-Romantic. I venture the prophecy that
he will prove also to be the valued precursor of a Post-Modernism
still fated to be another Last Romanticism."

Such a revaluation is based on a growing recognition of Pater's
very special place in the transition from the idealism of the nineteenth century to the radical empiricism of the twentieth. Unlike
Enlightenment rationalists, who were inclined to locate meaning in
a transcendent or absolutist system of valuation, the romantics
and, increasingly, the Victorians typically wavered between a commitment to the traditional idea of a time-transcending, eternally
complete Absolute and a fascination with the notion of a gradually
self-realizing World-Spirit. No such counterplay marks Pater's
thought; he represents the most thorough instance of the Victorian
tendency to find the productive force for the creation of values,
ideals, and purposes solely within the temporal process itself. To
understand the distance that Pater has traveled away from the romantics of the early decades of his century and toward the post-
modernists of our time, one might notice how in the poetry of Keats,
for example, the aesthetic object had been grounded in a timeless,
directly present Platonic reality that underwrites its signification:

> When old age shall this generation waste,
> Thou shalt remain, in midst of other woe
> Than ours, a friend to man, to whom thou say'st,
> "Beauty is truth, truth beauty,"—that is all
> Ye know on earth, and all ye need to know.

For Keats, the urn remains eternally present in ideal perfection generation after generation by virtue of its direct correspondence to a
primordial "truth" that engenders all mortal beauty. In Pater's
thought, however, no absolute reality ever can be present in any direct way; dissolved within the play of language itself, "being" is
always decentered, always in movement away from the present
toward the past and the future. Objects, over and above "the solidity with which language invests them" by suggesting fixed referents,
have no extralinguistic reality accessible to the mind of man:

> Analysis . . . assures us that those impressions of the individual mind to
> which, for each one of us, experience dwindles down, are in perpetual

flight; that each of them is limited by time, . . . all that is actual in it being a single moment, gone while we try to apprehend it, of which it may
ever be more truly said that it has ceased to be than that it is. To such a
tremulous wisp constantly re-forming itself on the stream, to a single
sharp impression, with a sense in it, a relic more or less fleeting, of such
moments gone by, what is real in our life fines itself down.

(*Renaissance*, 235–36)

Pater, more than any other Victorian writer—more than Thackeray
or Dickens or George Eliot or Trollope or, even, Hardy—was consciously aware that if art and language do not correspond directly
to any primordial reality outside their own linguistic borders, then
they must perforce create their own reality. By challenging the mimetic assumptions of Victorian fiction—that language directly represents reality—Pater's writing initiated a major ideological split,
pointing the way toward the new twentieth-century recognition that
the conventions upon which narration depends are openly artificial
and that fiction cannot mirror any reality outside its own verbal
compass.

Having lived with Pater, so to speak, for some fifteen years now
(I'm almost beginning to feel like one of those maiden sisters of
his), my "experience" has convinced me that his prose becomes
most problematic (and, hence, interesting) precisely at that point
where narrative conventions and the language of critical discourse
turn back upon the writing author to create a poetics of the self. In
this, there is a kind of inevitability. If it is not possible to use words
to get outside the limits of language, then the writer's text can only
choose to examine and reenact the scene of its own writing. Pater's
inability to approach himself directly—an inability, let me add,
grounded no less in an ontological impossibility than in a personal
reticence—dictates that his life-story will be unlike that of Augustine,
Gibbon, Rousseau, or Newman. His autobiographical prose has
more in common with such fictionalized autobiographies as James
Joyce's *Portrait of the Artist as a Young Man*, Samuel Butler's *The
Way of All Flesh*, Charles Dickens's *David Copperfield*, or, most
nearly, Thomas Carlyle's *Sartor Resartus*. But none of these, unless
it be *Sartor Resartus*, suggests as powerfully as Pater's portraits—
the "imaginary portrait" is his particular name for this fictionalized
or fantasized autobiography—the tortured effort, so characteristic
of our own century, to come to terms with that elusive and frag-

mentary being the autobiographer calls "I." I am speaking here not merely of the way in which an author masks elements of his own experience in a fictional work, a commonplace occurrence. What Pater's art does is to insist upon a purgative and transforming *interchange* between the author's experience and that of the fictional character. Each in turn *becomes* the other. Neither the author's life nor that of his hero is understood to be a self-contained existence; neither is the origin of the other, that to which the one can be referred as explanation of the other. This interjection of the authorial personality into the imaginary or historical past causes reality and fantasy to engage in a perpetual interplay in which each state turns back upon the other. Such a destabilized, open-ended interplay, refusing to define either the plot-line or the authorial level of inscription as the ground-situation, emerges also, somewhat later, in the music and painting of the last decade of the nineteenth and the early decades of the twentieth centuries. In Debussy's *L'après-midi d'un faune*, Schoenberg's *Verklärte Nacht*, or Stravinsky's *Petrushka,* or in works by Ives, Stockhausen, and others; or in such paintings as Mondrian's *Composition in White and Black* or Picasso's *Demoiselles d'Avignon,* there is an evident breakdown of mimetic assumptions and an avoidance of all determinate categories, such as a clearly signaled symphonic end.

In the history of critical commentary on *Marius the Epicurean*, there has been, owing largely to a failure to grasp this open-ended set of relationships between Pater's literary sources, his imaginary creations, and his own authorial stance, a substantial amount of insistence upon the failure of the novel to achieve a structural or thematic coherence. Henry James, for example, grumbled to a friend that the work fell apart in the middle—"that the first volume of *Marius* was given over to paganism, and a large part of the second to an equal admiration of Christianity, and that it was not possible to admire opposites equally." And T. S. Eliot's famous critique was the most unsympathetic of all. Having cast doubts on Pater's mental ability, Eliot then proceeded to call *Marius* "incoherent; its method is a number of fresh starts; its contents is a hodge-podge of the learning of the classical don, the impressions of the sensitive holiday visitor to Italy, and a prolonged flirtation with the liturgy." The editor of Pater's letters found a more subtle incoherence in Pater's "imperfect fusion of 'vision' and 'design.'" Noting that

Pater spoke of the finishing of *Marius* as a "duty," Lawrence Evans sensed a discrepancy between those dutiful intentions of portraying a humanistic religion within the pre-Nicene Church and the presence of certain ironies and ambiguities constituting "an undertow that works against the apparent progression to the threshold of assent." In the later chapters dealing with the death of Marius, "Pater's control has slipped," he said; Marius, although aware of the vision of the ideal community, is excluded from it owing to Pater's conflicting and unreconciled impulses. And as for *Gaston de Latour*, the second volume in the projected trilogy that had begun with *Marius*, early reviewers, while noting that an unfinished novel by its fragmentary nature lacks unity, exhibited an equal skepticism that it would have achieved any semblance of cohesion. They found Pater indecisive, indefinite, his characters nebulous and undefined: "We do not think that Pater ever had a definite conception of just what should be the development of the character, the opinion, in the work he had undertaken." Had these critics not explicitly or implicitly *faulted* Pater's strategy of undercutting determinate meanings but, rather, *applauded* his texts for deconstructing themselves, they would have grasped his pervasive intention and been well on the way toward appreciating the astonishing richness of his achievement.

But Pater's contemporaries tended to suppose that a novelist (like an autobiographer) had failed when he presented a character who did not behave, in whatever degree of complexity, in certain consistent ways. However profound the intricacies of his psyche may have been, somehow or other an ultimate consistency was expected; and when a writer failed to provide what was expected—for example, that culminating conversion rather than Marius' wavering before Christian faith—there was a tendency to feel that he had failed. This was owing to the combined influence upon many nineteenth-century writers and readers of psychological notions of the coherence of the self and the tradition of a teleological contour of narration. This bias toward a valorized reading of the text, allowing a retrospective summing up of meaning, derived most immediately from the convention of the familiar narrator of the eighteenth- and nineteenth-century novel, who was in total mastery of the story he related, creating order out of disorder. Indeed, long before the genre of the novel appeared, Augustine's *Confessions* had provided, in following the Pauline model of burying the old man and putting on the new, an autobiographical model for the univocal interpretation of a life. In that moment of Augustinian conversion, the totally incoherent debris of history and of psychological experience burned away to produce for the self a transcendental meaning certified by a divine authority. (In this light, Marius's wavering might be seen as a kind of ironic deconstruction of Augustine's one decisive turn toward God.) But by the time of Rousseau, certainly, this convention of a coherent meaning for the persona had been called into question. Rousseau drew on autobiographical conventions, but he also sought to create a new convention of the semi-fictional "I"-narrator who challenged the notion that any person one reads about, whether fictional or real, has to have a certain kind of coherence. One of Rousseau's conceptions of autobiography was that the self did *not* cohere in certain expected ways. Pater, indeed, had studied the *Confessions* of Rousseau carefully and in the Conclusion to *The Renaissance* makes an extended reference to him. There, also, Pater challenges this assumption of the coherent self, labeling it a mirage: "That clear, perpetual outline of face and limb is but . . . a design in a web, the actual threads of which pass out beyond it. . . . Or, if we begin with the inward world of thought and feeling . . . it is with . . . the passage and dissolution of impressions, images, sensations, that analysis leaves off—that continual vanishing away, that strange, perpetual weaving and unweaving of ourselves" (234, 236). If Rousseau had been willing to sacrifice the coherent center of self to those intricacies that baffle, Pater as a young writer—profoundly indebted also to the Gallic skepticism of Montaigne, Pascal, and Sainte-Beuve—even more emphatically failed to find a conventionally fictional unity-of-being within his quotidian experience.

Yet autobiography, like other literary and creative acts, is an act of ordering to the end of understanding; and either the act of mind and the act of organization are imported from fiction and its convention of "character" or that sense of coherence must be generated by the act of composition itself. Pater's recognition that the categories of space, time, matter, identity, causation, and memory are tentative, incomplete, arbitrary, and relative, dictates a unique kind of prose that swallows up veridical reality. Hence his meaning can emerge only from close attention to his writing *as* writing, from those relationships between inner and outer levels of narration and composition. (I will provide in the third section an in-depth discussion of this centered on a specific work by Pater.) Pater's radically new prose mode constituted an anticipation of that sweeping change in the intellectual milieu that ushered in such literary works as those by Borges, Beckett, Nabokov, Robbe-Grillet, Leiris, and Barth and that witnessed the "deconstruction of metaphysics" by such recent writers as Roland Barthes, Jacques Derrida, Gilles Deleuze, Emmanuel Levinas, Paul de Man and others. What in contemporary fiction is perceived to be an obsolete attempt to imitate actions directly through conventional devices of cause and effect, plot, characterization, principles of authorial selection and arrangement based on mimetic assumptions, has been discarded in favor of a new emphasis upon defining the point of view involved in the act of artistic creation; that is, upon the activities of reading and composition as themselves the subjects of fiction. Though the purpose of these contemporary writers is the subversion of traditional literary forms by according verbal constructions a greater significance and reality than any extralinguistic phenomena, it is done to create a more viable fictional form, a more credible picture of a newly complicated twentieth-century reality. Without a conventional story to tell, the contemporary author turns back upon a blow-by-blow account of the processes and problems of the imagination and reason, moving his own artistic self-consciousness to the foreground of the novel. Thus rather than attempting a veridical illusion of life, these modern works affirm the autonomy of their artifice—artifice being, indeed, their meaning—and the various narrative devices that call attention to the fictiveness of the work are strategies for replacing an elusive outer reality with a self-sustaining imaginative reality. Those interlocking stories and speakers within stories and speakers, those interminable narratives the drama of which lies forever in the next frame out—all represent strategies to defer final meaning, to postpone the discovery that there is no absolute ground of reality within quotidian experience, no fixed and necessary actualities. Apropos of *Gaston's* unfinished state, I am tempted to note that the absence of a tidy ending that would give a definitive contour to Gaston's life—an absence so painful to the Victorian sensibility—seems appropriately to thematize the frankly problematic and modern cast of all of Pater's work in which every ending is turned back upon its beginning.

Set beside the other prose writers of Victoria's age—Carlyle, Macaulay, Mill, Ruskin, Arnold, Newman, Darwin, Huxley, Wilde, Butler—Pater is perhaps the least prolific. He is to Victorian prose what Gerard Manley Hopkins, his pupil and friend, is to Victorian poetry: a writer whose every word seems painfully wrung from a recalcitrant language. But despite the "classical smallness" of the body of Pater's writings—the bulk of his correspondence is possibly one-hundredth that of Carlyle's—only the Pater specialist can be assumed to possess a familiarity with any of his work beyond the anthology selections. Thus the "expert" reader for an essay which I published recently in *Victorian Studies* balked at cursory references to several of Pater's shorter imaginary portraits (there are only eight of these completed fictional works in all): "The allusions here (and elsewhere) to relatively minor works, without identifying them by name, or giving their dates, suggests strongly that the author of this paper is writing, whether he knows it or not, for the specialist only." Still, in the wake of the upward revaluation of Pater's reputation the situation is not quite what it was some years ago when, for all one's colleagues knew of him, Pater might as well have been a medieval Persian poet. Fortunate neither in his disciples nor in his biographers, Pater became in academic circles the victim of that impressionistic criticism of art for art's sake that he himself seemed to advocate. Although he was possibly the most personal and self-conscious of all nineteenth-century prose writers, there is also probably no significant writer whose prose lends itself less than that of Pater to a close textual interpretation or explication. Often his precise thought-linkages are masked by a harmonious flow of verbiage that gives the impression of a certain vagueness of outline or intellectual softness. Pater himself encouraged this assumption by such statements as his assertion that since "all art constantly aspires towards the condition of music," the perfection of style "often appears to depend, in part, on a certain suppression or vagueness of mere subject, so that the meaning reaches us through ways not distinctly traceable by the understanding" and language "seems to pass for a moment into an actual strain of music" (135, 137–38).

Oscar Wilde in the *Decay of Lying* has Gilbert, his persona, speak of Pater's style as "far more like a piece of mosaic than a passage of music." Pater's paradoxically elusive, yet markedly personal, style has indeed a static, pictorial quality. J. M. Gray, as appropriate for the curator of the Scottish National Portrait Gallery, compared Pater's style, as afterwards Thomas Wright did also, to the art of Sir Lawrence Alma-Tadema in its carefully controlled and highly wrought details of historical or classical themes. Gray considered Pater's description of the feast in honor of Apuleius to be "a very Tadema in its perfection of finish, in its legitimate and artist-like use of archaeological knowledge for the purposes of mere present beauty; a Tadema, too, in its delighted preoccupation with the lovely details of precious objects of still-life, with the 'togas of altogether lost hue and texture,' the 'crystal cups darkened with old wine,' and the 'dusky fires of the rare twelve-petalled roses.' "

Calculated, finished to perfection, Pater's art is the heir of the Pre-Raphaelites's "truth to nature," their sensitivity to colors, to contrasts of light and shade, and their turning of abstracts into concrete images, "loading every rift with ore" to quote the Keatsian antecedent to the Pre-Raphaelites. If the poetry, paintings, and designs of Rossetti, Burne-Jones, and Morris anticipate Pater's blending of a sensuous mode with a consciousness of art-as-craftsmanship, Burne-Jones in particular, as a Pre-Raphaelite with classical tendencies, might, more possibly even than Alma-Tadema, provide a painterly analogue for Pater's descriptions—a Burne-Jones displaying just a hint also of that decadent decor that Gustave Moreau combined with an almost pedantic quality of academic research. Samuel Butler, who wondered "What is art that it should have a sake?" sniffed that Pater's style was "like the face of some old woman who has been to Madame Rachel and had herself enamelled. The bloom is nothing but powder and paint and the odour is cherry-blossom."

No one, I think, would deny that Pater's style can be highly colored—and not only the notorious "purpurei panni" of *The Renaissance*. (In Pater's diction, rhythms, and tendency to identify empathetically with his subjects, the influence of Swinburne also is here present, surely.) But following *The Renaissance* and the "honeyed effeminacy" of the 1878 "Child in the House," a noticeable chilling of its psychic intensity occurs. The strong emotional and sensuous coloring of the early style gradually yields to an increased gravity, simplicity, and restraint in *Marius* (1885), *Imaginary Portraits* (1887), *Appreciations* (1889), and *Plato and Platonism* (1893). Yet the transition from the color and richness of Pater's early "romantic" style to the restrained and unadorned "classical" simplicity of his later style—to a monochromatic purity of light—is a distinction seemingly less clear-cut when applied to Pater's later imaginative prose than to his critical prose. Whereas the suppression in the second edition of *Appreciations* (1890) of the early essay, "Aesthetic Poetry" (1868), plainly illustrates this shift toward classical simplicity, elements of exotic emotion, including the sensational or sadistic, persisted in combination with colored image and phrase in certain chapters of *Marius* ("Manly Amusement," "The Martyrs"), in "Denys l'Auxerrois" (from *Imaginary Portraits*), in *Gaston de Latour* (1888), in "Emerald Uthwart" (1892), and in "Apollo in Picardy" (1894). Moreover, one would not need to be so hostile as Butler to recognize in Pater's growing restraint and self-curtailed output an elaborately wrought mask. A. C. Benson remarked that Pater's style resembles, in the characters it delineates, "a bas-relief of processional figures," exhibiting itself "in ordered grace and without the heat of action—like a mirror, or like a placid river, it may reflect great actions and varied images of picturesque ruin and romantic suffering without harm to its lucid medium." But even Pater knew that the mirroring instrument might not be so placid or lucid as Benson supposed. "Our knowledge is limited to what we feel," Marius muses, "but can we be sure that things are at all like our feelings? Mere peculiarities in the instruments of our cognition, like the little knots and waves on the surface of a mirror, may distort the matter they seem but to represent" (*Marius*, I: 138). Not without those private distortions characteristic of each individual's experience of the senses, Pater's prose reflects, like the mirror with "little knots and waves on the surface," the sensations and impressions of the physical world around.

Typically, comments on the preciosity, the over-refinement, the artificial or exotic aspects of Pater's style betray an uneasy or subconscious awareness that the natural, physical world has been replaced by an elaborate, formal ordering that only partially disguises a private emotional tension. For Pater, Lady Lisa's smile is always about to dissolve into the scream of Edvard Munch's famous expressionist figure. Some readers who might tolerate a soupçon of Moreau are positively repelled by foreshadowings of Munch. "A passion of which the outlets are sealed, begets a tension of nerve, in which the sensible world comes to one with a reinforced brilliance and relief—all redness is turned into blood, all water into tears. Hence a wild, convulsed sensuousness in the poetry of the middle age, in which the things of nature begin to play a strange delirious part" ("Morris," 303): although Pater is discussing here the schizophrenia of the medieval mind, its failure to escape into the objectivity of nature, the passage is equally descriptive of the . . . surreal? hypnotic? . . . quality with which Pater's own style is tinged, especially in the first dozen years of his writing career. Clearly the psychic turmoil on the unconscious level had, for Pater, its repercussions in a certain stylistic groping through successive stages of composition and revision that often seemed to involve a disproportionate effort for the results obtained, as witness the enormous effort Pater put into revising the third edition of *Marius* (more than six thousand emendations, almost all minute alterations of punctuation, changes of single words, or minor adjustments of phrasing). Pater's description of Plato's method might very well also describe his own compositional style, involving as it did "much labour and scruple, repeated acts of qualification and correction; many readjustments to experience; expansion, by larger lights from it; . . . exclusions and inclusions" (*Plato*, 178). Seemingly, the greater the chaotic randomness within, the more rigid and formal the order imposed from without.

Pater's excessive revisions—he not only revised the studies originally published in periodicals that he intended to include in books, but he often conflated them as well, and afterwards revised the successive issues of each book—show him struggling, not always successfully, to improve his choice of idiom and word form (e.g., uneuphonious recurrence of words) and revising to avoid irrelevant details and solecisims (e.g., exaggerated specificity of image). But despite extensive revisions, Pater's texts often contain a certain irreducible core of factual and grammatical errors as well as rhetorical ambiguities. Zilpha Chandler has enumerated dangling participles, the use of *like* for the conjunction *as*, the use of pronouns with indefinite antecedents, change of subject, change of tense, awkward parentheses, false subordination, indefinite statements (such as *there is* or *there are*), non-structural appendages, sacrifice of sense to sound, and want of correspondency between correlated members. One might observe, speculatively, that this core of errors could indicate a certain psychic static that could not be wholly fine-tuned out of the literary composition. On the interpretive level this psychic static is clearly present in those over-determined passages of self-projection, not just in the early essays on Leonardo and Botticelli, but as late as the 1892 essay on Raphael in which Pater astonishingly misreads a "Mater Dolorosa" as sorrow not over the dead son, "but the grief of a simple household over the mother herself taken early from it" (*Miscellaneous Studies*, 40. Pater is here thinking of the untimely death of his mother that had left him an orphan).

Violet Paget described Pater as "a very simple, amiable man, avowedly afraid of almost everything"—afraid especially, George Moore noted, "of himself." His compulsion to write produced great psychic turmoil, an anxiety he masked by such an elaborate ordering of word and phrase that Max Beerbohm quipped Pater wrote English as if it were a dead language. (George Moore made much the same observation: "In the pages of Pater," he said, "the English language lies in state.") Clearly when Pater's over-control of the emotions and senses gained the upper hand (in passages in *Plato*, for instance), stylistic repose and harmony gave way to the arid and the abstract—a complexity without the energy or heat of immediate sensations and spontaneous emotions. Gosse reports that never had he known a writer "to whom the act of composition was such a travail and an agony as it was to Pater. In his earlier years the labour of lifting the sentences was so terrific that anyone with less fortitude would have entirely abandoned the effort." Typically, Pater painfully built up his sentences out of little squares of paper on which previously he had jotted down quotations, references, or phrases. This obsessive-compulsive passion for discovering some hidden order among these discrete slips—"placed about him, like the pieces of a puzzle" reports Gosse—is reflected also in his obsession with cleansing or purifying his immediate environment, with clean and bright rooms. In contrast to the heaviness and oaken respectability of the other dons' rooms, Pater's at Brasenose

GERALD MONSMAN

was panelled in a sage-green pastel and was furnished in understated
tastefulness; also the drawing-room of the Paters's home in Oxford,
as described by Mary Ward, was decorated with "a sparing allow-
ance of blue plates and pots, . . . a few mirrors, a very few flowers,
chosen and arranged with a simple yet conscious art. I see that
room always with the sun in it, touching the polished surfaces of
wood and brass and china, and bringing out its pure, bright colour."
    To compare Pater's style to a room opened to the light is not to
imply an anticipation of the stripped and plain style of an Albert
Camus or a J. L. Borges, a functionalism deliberately eschewing
any elegance or distinctive effects; Pater's highly wrought prose,
saturated in color and melody, is anything but bare. Rather, the
skillful qualifying and balancing of phrases purges its content of all
narrow assertions and final closures of thought. If the crisp archi-
tectonics and delicate precision of Pater's sentences have been justly
praised for their "light touch," it is also true that his elaborate sentences "are invariably anti-climactic" and often give the effect "of
a natural impulse arrested by second thought into a conscientious
hesitation afraid to drop the subject and conclude." In this, Pater's
prose duplicates the dialectical structure of "the dialogue of the
mind with itself." In contradistinction to the dogmatic treatise
which "*begins* with an axiom or definition," the Platonic dialogue,
"which may be co-extensive with life," says Pater, "does in truth
little more than clear the ground, as we say, or the atmosphere, or
the mental tablet, that one may have a fair chance of knowing, or
seeing, perhaps: it does but put one into a duly receptive attitude
towards such possible truth, discovery, or revelation, as may one
day occupy the ground, the tablet,—shed itself on the purified air"
(*Plato*, 188). One may say that Pater's panic fear of death and the
closure of the grave found relief in an alternate form of selfhood,
an unenclosed prose that by an elaborate process of piling phrases
and qualifications one upon the other counters any movement
toward resolution, continuously reversing the direction of the
thought by its multiplicity of structures. Ultimately, Pater intended
not merely to create an open-ended structure that undercut, frustrated, attenuated, and negated by qualifications and balanced
antitheses any absolute statement, condition, definition, or exacti-
tude, but actually to displace his own identity into that perpetual
reordering of meaning, that endless verbal cycling. This suggests

215

not a longing for ineradicable instability *per se*, but the desire to escape from the solipsistic confines of time and history, consciousness and death through a kind of lexical self-actualization. Viewing the notion of dialectical openness in terms of the root-meaning of the word "style," one may perceive in Pater's thought the working out of a whole interconnected set of ideas. In its original sense, "style" meant a pencil-like instrument used by the ancients to write on waxed tablets, one end pointed for incising the words and one end rounded for smoothing down the tablet so that it could be written on again. One may say that the dialectic process as envisioned by Pater reflects a tension between the inscribing of the wax on the tablet and its smoothing down in order to be reinscribed—a perpetual deconstruction and reconstruction signified by the opposing ends of the stylus. And of the two kinds of smooth tablets, those unwritten on and those which are palimpsestically worn almost to a smoothness, the latter sort reflects the interplay of texts that invariably are engraved previously within the system of discourse: "The thoughts of Plato, like the language he has to use (we find it so again, in turn, with those predecessors of his, when we pass from him to them) are covered with the traces of previous labour and have had their earlier proprietors. . . . In Plato, in spite of his wonderful savour of literary freshness, there is nothing absolutely new: or rather, as in many other very original products of human genius, the seemingly new is old also, a palimpsest" (7-8). To this rich, palimpsestically inscribed tablet, Pater's open-ended syntactical structure precisely corresponds; and Pater well might have been speaking of his own writing when he observed that all knowledge is a kind of flowering of earlier inscriptions: "Ancient, half-obliterated inscriptions on the mental walls, the mental tablet, seeds of knowledge to come, shed by some flower of it long ago, it was in an earlier period of time they had been laid up in him, to blossom again now, so kindly, so firmly!" (66). This palimpsestic motif assumes tablet form at several points in Pater's fiction, as in "the old over-written pavement at the great open door" (*Gaston*, 10) of Saint Hubert's in *Gaston de Latour* or in the elaborately carved desk top at Emerald Uthwart's school. Even the face of Mona Lisa is a kind of over-written tablet on which "all the thoughts and experience of the world have etched" (*Renaissance*, 125) their lust and love, saintliness and sin.

If the waxed tablet corresponds to consciousness—Pater not only has used the phrase "mental tablet," but elsewhere he spoke of "the white paper, the smooth wax, of our ingenuous souls" (*Miscellaneous Studies,* 177)—then inscription of the tablet, the act of composition, represents a loss of innocence or priority through a discovery of belatedness, a movement away from the smooth, unwritten tablet toward the palimpsestic dialectic of "all the thoughts and experience of the world." This process of inscription is suggested metonymically in the contrast of the pagan Winckelmann's "unsinged hands" (*Renaissance,* 222) with the image in "The Child in the House" of the boy Florian, his fingers burned on the sealing wax. This contrast represents the growing self-consciousness characteristic of Western thought from antiquity to the nineteenth century; the inscribing hand now burned by the wax testifies to the pain of that new awareness. And yet, "to burn always with this hard, gemlike flame, to maintain this ecstasy, is success in life" (236). Pater's ambivalence here—Is the absence of an ultimate ground of signification an occasion for pain or for an ecstasy that recognizes the absence of any limitation on the range of possible meanings?—has been seconded in the thought of the French theorizer, Jacques Derrida: "As a quest for that lost or impossible presence of an absent origin, this structuralist motif of broken immediateness encompasses the sad, negative, nostalgic, guilty, Rousseauistic mode of conceiving freeplay, the complementary form of which would be the joyous Nietzschean affirmation of the unfettered elaboration and play of the world, the affirmation of a world of signs—without error, without truth, without origin, which is open to unlimited interpretations." In Derrida's "Nietzschean" sense, writing is, for Pater, a method of establishing an image of himself which is neither finite nor solipsistically isolated. Just as the pen, the stylus, is perpetually cancelling and renewing inscription on the wax of the tablet, so in the text, the style, the conscious mind of man is forever deconstructed and reconstructed. This is why Pater endorses Cicero's description of the death of Plato: "after the manner of a true scholar, 'he died pen in hand' " (*Plato,* 149).

In the solipsistic world of the Conclusion to *The Renaissance,* every impression "is the impression of the individual in his isolation, each mind keeping as a solitary prisoner its own dream of a world" (*Renaissance*, 235); but in art the emotions can find a suitable visionary outlet from the narrow prison of the finite self, and the "fever dream" ("Morris," 302) can be cured. This liberating quality of the aesthetic object is analogous to the relation of the individual to "collective humanity." In his unfinished essay, "Moral Philosophy," Pater wrote that

> all human knowledge is but relative; that is to say that, all man's ideas, and views, the forms in which he mirrors his experience as a whole, or any part of it, are consequences of his position at a particular time and place, each true indeed from its own point of view but false or inadequate at the next point, and all alike mere phases in the mental career of one the very essence of whose life physical and spiritual is mutation itself. A certain *nihilism* even as it is called is latent at least as we have seen, in all modern speculation; from the limited impressions of individual consciousness there seems to exist no open passage to things as they are in themselves, to absolute realities corresponding to those impressions which clear and palpable as they seem may yet be after all but the dreams of one solitary prisoner.

In "custom," in one's sympathy with "all worthy men, living and dead," Pater locates that external authority able to free the individual from his own capricious subjectivity in moral action. "The idea of a sleepless reason which assists and rounds our sleepy intermittent intelligence, in which the eternal . . . ideas of things have a durable, permanent, free, independent existence, lending itself and lifting for a little time our transient, individual intelligence, for us actually translates into that conception of collective humanity."

That the labyrinthine intertextual connections of any literary work should mold the self in the same manner as accumulated social conventions is hardly surprising, for that web of cultural relationships expressive of a collective human reality is precisely what the innumerable interwoven sources of the text reflect. Although the intellectual forms in which the individual "mirrors" his experience are true only relative to his subjective position, the text that "rounds" or orders individual experience can transcend "mutation" and approach that "open passage" leading from the "sleepy" dreamworld of the solitary cell "to things as they are in themselves, to absolute realities"—or at least can glimpse this tantalizingly elusive ground distributed through the mechanics and metaphors of

218

the text's verbal field. Essentially the reflexive text is a palimpsest in which the "knots and waves" of the individual's mirroring senses are corrected by the perceptions of others in a dialectically sustaining, ordering, and enhancing relationship. For Plato, ideas and their words are "substantial things-in-themselves . . . little short of living persons, to be known as persons are made known to each other, by . . . affinities, . . . like to like—these persons constituting together that common, eternal, intellectual world, a sort of divine family or hierarchy, with which the mind of the individual, so far as it is reasonable, or really knows, is in communion or correspondence" (*Plato*, 153). If for Plato words are persons, for Pater persons are words—words at focus "in delicate perspective" (*Marius*, I:154) within the reflexive text. As it is structured, however, Pater's text prohibits the ontological grounding of any *single* level at the expense of another; instead, its reflexive focus becomes a mirroring in which Pater finds that his own image turns back upon the image of his hero and his hero's age—which then, once again, turns back upon the author's life. In this *système décentré,* the ground of meeting between self and other lies somewhere between absence and presence, in that open space filled by the play of signification.

Although reflexiveness is, as I have argued, present generally in Pater's discourse, his imaginary portrait, "A Prince of Court Painters," provides an exemplary yet succinct instance of it. Published only a few months after *Marius*, "Prince" purports to be a fictionalized account of Watteau's life as seen from the perspective of a girl who secretly loves him. Her central problem is an entrapment in that imprisoning "dream of a world," for she fails, finally, to find the "open passage" that art affords. In addition to being a continuation of Pater's primary purpose in *The Renaissance* of exploring the lives and art of notable painters, this portrait of Watteau highlights Pater's tendency to seek inscriptions of himself within the lives and works of others. Just as those Renaissance artists had served as covert projections of Pater's own psychic configurations of perception and response, so here too Pater imports the lineaments of his own life into this critically conceived study of Watteau. As self and other turn back reflexively upon each other, Pater's *personaggi in cerca d'autore* (to echo the title of Luigi Pirandello's masterpiece) seem to step right out of the work—

meaning passes outside the frame as neither reader, author nor character is accorded any ontological differentiation. This transmutation of life into art and art into life had been present in *The Renaissance*, for example, in its dedication to Charles L. Shadwell. In 1864 Pater had modeled the personality type in "Diaphanéité," his earliest extant essay, on his friend Shadwell. Then in the summer of 1865 in the company of Shadwell he traveled for the first time in Italy, particularly to Ravenna, Pisa, and Florence. Interestingly, Shadwell was the name also of a place so near Pater's birthplace as to be identified with it in a number of early descriptions of Pater's life. Now, if one reads the celebration of Shadwell, the person with whom Pater travels, as the fraternal double of the boy born in Shadwell, the place from which Pater travels, then reader and writer — the one to whom the book is dedicated and the one who has written it — have coalesced. Similar patterns of covert meaning are inscribed by Pater in "A Prince of Court Painters."

First, the authorial presence is invoked by the form of a diary in which this portrait is cast. Its subtitle is "Extracts from an Old French Journal"; and although the reader is never told *who* has made these extracts, the obvious inference is that Pater has selected what we read—and do not read. For who else, in order to make an artistic whole, could synthesize those discontinuities of the flux, those multitudinous entries dispersed randomly throughout the journal, each one dated and encapsulated in its momentariness— who but Pater could be the selector of the extracts? At every entry we are reminded that someone other than the imagined original writer of the journal is controlling our perspective. And this editorial presence refuses to hide itself, to accede to an invisibility that allows the reader direct access to the fictional narrator's consciousness. Just as in his review of Octave Feuillet's novel, *La morte*, Pater assumes the role of author under the guise of critic by translating and juxtaposing extracts from the original to create his own English short story from the French novel, so here as author and editor Pater is speaking in two voices at once. And this points to the second way in which the author is personally present in his text: by name. Although the keeper of the journal never names herself, her brother, Jean-Baptiste, whose Christian name she uses, had been in actual fact a pupil of Watteau; and historical records show that this brother indeed did have an elder sister, Marie-Marguerite. That their surname should have been Pater was no coincidence. When Arthur Symons once asked Walter Pater if he were really descended from Jean-Baptiste, Pater whimsically replied, "I think so; I believe so; I always say so." Although Pater probably suspected that such a descent was purely imaginary, he apparently "always" affirmed it as if that would somehow turn it into fact. The delineation of his supposititious ancestors in "Prince" was a kind of lexical invocation of the ennobling, refining influence of an artistic heritage. The mantle which passed from Watteau to Jean-Baptiste, his heir in matters of art, now comes to rest on the shoulders of that other Pater, Walter.

Third, in the rejected Jean-Baptiste, who reestablished a filial relationship with the remote Watteau only upon the latter's death, we have a reflection of Pater's own craving for an absent paternal figure. But also in Marie-Marguerite's relation both to her brother and to Watteau we have an echo of Pater's own life situation. By transposing himself into the feminine role, Pater can express the quiet desperation of a passive and impotent desire to enjoy vicariously a charismatic life and famous career. By projecting himself into both figures, Pater can suggest simultaneously his frustration at being a mere belated imitator of original genius, like Jean-Baptiste, and also his impatience at being condemned, like Marie-Marguerite, to living with the second rate. This subconscious attitude of Pater toward his sisters (in particular toward the talented younger Clara) might seem mean-spirited and egocentric; however, it undoubtedly continues a rivalry that began in childhood when Pater competed for his mother's affection with, in particular, his more handsome and virile elder brother, William. Indeed, Pater's sense of competition with the sibling for the affection of the parent produced a guilt that could be sublimated only by the act of writing. As author, Walter Pater no longer needs to feel inferior or hostile toward his doubles within the family circle; *he* is now the parent and the text is his child. There in the text the frustrations that Pater projects onto Jean-Baptiste and Marie-Marguerite are resolved in the apocalyptic manifestation of their surname—a Pater who becomes himself the original genius as the *pater* of the imaginary portrait.

Fourth, within the text a self-reflexive quality causes reality and fantasy perpetually to turn back upon each other, the one swallowing up the other so that inner and outer levels—imaginary events, historical events, autobiographical events—engage in an interplay that leaves the reader unable to distinguish fact from fiction. Thus, in the entry of October 1717, the heroine is reading the Abbé Prévost's novel, *Manon Lescaut*, and observes that "this is the book those fine ladies in Watteau's 'conversations,' who look so exquisitely pure, lay down on the cushion when the children run up to have their laces righted." But in putting the book the heroine reads into a picture that she sees, the text associates her level of reality with that of the characters in the picture and so hints at the fictitious aspect of her own existence. This novel-within-a-portrait, turning back upon itself as the book the heroine reads, also turns back upon Pater's readers, for *Manon Lescaut* is a book his reader, too, has read. As the reader encounters a text both within and without the work he is reading, both within and without the picture the heroine perceives, a text also both he and the heroine have read even as he now is reading about her life, Pater's reader finds his own identity broken up like light through a prism or multiplied endlessly in the reflected figures within this hall of mirrors. In a footnote to the collected edition of his portraits, Pater calls attention to the anachronistic presence of Prévost's novel in his story: "Possibly written at this date, but almost certainly not printed till many years later." How could a story that we know was so carefully researched have had such an elementary mistake in its chronology? And why, once Pater noticed his error, did he not substitute some other scandalous novel, real or imaginary? As a self-referential way of commenting on his authorial role, the footnote allows Pater to discuss himself as a shaper or misshaper of history. Moreover, calling the reader's attention to such an anachronism served his purpose in blurring the lines between the actual and the imaginary. An actual novel about imaginary characters is introduced in an "imaginary portrait" about an actual person whose life predates the composition of the novel, thus rendering its reality within the plot impossible. It is not necessary to argue that Pater purposely planned this anachronism; rather, not unlike those stylistic or interpretive glitches that betray subconscious tensions, this imperfection arose from a deep and only partially articulated awareness.

Fifth, the recurrent mention of the unfinished portrait of Marie-Marguerite by Watteau becomes not merely a symbol of her unspoken, unconsummated passion for him, but an image also of Pater's relationship to Marie-Marguerite's journal. Just as Jean-Baptiste must complete the portrait of his sister begun by Watteau, so Pater pretends to shape this story of frustrated love out of the inchoate material of her old diary. But by finishing his "imaginary portrait" of Marie-Marguerite, Pater becomes more than just the pedestrian brother who completes the portrait *in* the text; as originator *of* the text, Pater inserts himself as the decentered object of Marie-Marguerite's desire—like Watteau now, an original genius. Whereas Watteau and Mlle Rosalba Carriera are able mutually to complete their artistic embodiments of each other—in Watteau's portrait her name is inscribed within the picture in the same way that Pater puns on the meaning of his name in the text: "She holds a lapful of white roses with her two hands. *Rosa Alba*—himself has inscribed it!"—Marie-Marguerite hides her love from Watteau; and her portrait on the easel undergoes a kind of artistic *coitus interruptus*. Her spasms are those of frustration, anger, jealousy, to be released only in the text: "One puts this and that angry spasm into it, and is delivered from it so" (*Imaginary Portraits,* 39). Never having told her love, she keeps that purity those "fine ladies" in Watteau's pictures yielded up. A loss of virginity—proof enough in those children—is not all that she implies. She suspects unchaste passion—fornication, adultery. This is the point of her reading the story of Manon Lascaut. But Pater knows what to do with those textual spasms, expert that he is at deflowering voluptuous words. If Marie-Marguerite will not take upon herself the knowledge of Manon Lascaut, her dark double, Pater himself will mate her innocence to his experience, accomplishing, as in Leonardo's portrait of Lady Lisa, the necessary fusion of innocence and corruption.

Thus also Blake had married Heaven and Hell; and from his Tyger and Lamb, the two contrary states of the Blakean soul ramify outward to reverberate through the nineteenth century. Pater elaborates this concept of the double in his discussions of such mythic figures as Demeter, Dionysus, Cupid and Psyche, the Dioscuri, and Artemis. Of this last goddess, he remarks that she was both "the assiduous nurse of children, and patroness of the young" and also the divinity "of sudden death" (*Greek Studies,* 168, 170). Even in the myth of the fraternal Dioscuri, Pater discovers a certain ambivalence. He observes that their statues were "carried into battle before the two kings, until it happened that through their secret enmity a certain battle was lost, after which one king only proceeded to the field, and one part only of that token of fraternity, the other remaining at Sparta" (*Plato*, 230). Pater's remastering of Leonardo's Mona Lisa provides the ultimate trope of doubling. This angel-goddess embodies "all the thoughts and experience of the world," and in her smile are both the fostering maternity of Leda and Saint Anne and the sinister eroticism of the murderous lover: "like the vampire, she has been dead many times, and learned the secrets of the grave" (*Renaissance*, 125). Like the vampire lover, the word co-opts the self, tempts it with the collective knowledge hidden within the structures of language, but destroys its possibility for innocence. This, I take it, is what Harold Bloom surmises when he says, "The cycles of civilization, the burden our consciousness bears, render us latecomers but the Lady Lisa perpetually carries the seal of a terrible priority."

The origin of this ambiguous doubling can be traced back at least as far as Pater's days in the Old Mortality Society, in which he had cited the "half-angelic, half-daemonic" (*Miscellaneous Studies*, 253) Charlotte Corday as an example of this dialectical interplay. An Oxford literary society, the Old Mortality—"beyond its contemporaries alike in genius and fame," claimed an early initiate—included such notables in addition to Pater as A. C. Swinburne, J. A. Symonds, T. H. Green, Edward Caird, James Bryce, and Courtenay Ilbert. Ilbert's 1864 election, so he told Gosse, had occurred in "post-Swinburnian days." He "belonged to a late crop of members, to which Pater also belonged"; thus he could not supply the details Gosse sought for his biography of Swinburne. But although Ilbert had joined "in time enough to hear Walter Pater read some of his earliest essays," he unfortunately told Gosse nothing about them. We do know, however, that Pater's first essay for the Old Mortality was "philosophical; Caird described it as a 'hymn of praise to the Absolute,' " and another member later wrote: "I remember it was said of Pater that his speculative imagination seemed to make the lights burn blue." In literature, art, politics, and religion the Society was avowedly "radical," dedicated to social amelioration, liberty of thought, and the ultimate validity of human reason in things secular and sacred. The casual walks and formal essays of the group anticipate the spirit of Pater's aesthetic ideal, "for ever curiously testing new opinions and courting new impressions" (*Renaissance*, 237), as he summed it up in his first book. But S. R. Brooke, although initially flattered to have been elected a member, found the religious views held by the members of the group "very disagreeable in nature, i.e. if any religious views are held at all." Brooke was especially offended by "that belief put prominently forward by W. H. Pater on Feb. 20th, [1864,] 'that a future state is impracticable' " and that "subjective immortality" is all that man can hope for. A few days afterward G. M. Hopkins told H. P. Liddon "about Pater's paper on Fichte's Ideal Student at the Old Mortality Club, in which he denied the Immortality of the Soul."

All of Pater's earliest essays seem to have shared a certain philosophical family resemblance, doubtless attributable to the presence within the Old Mortality of certain characteristic philosophic interests. Fichte was perhaps the first of the German philosophers Pater encountered in his own reading; and, as is clear from his unpublished essay "The History of Philosophy," the skeptical, solipsistic aspect of Fichte's thought—that reality is a dream without a dreamer —must have had a disproportionately stronger impact on the young Pater (*vide* the Conclusion to *The Renaissance*) than the more synthetic elements in Fichte's—or Hegel's or Schiller's—thought. In his explosive February 20 essay, Pater apparently attempted to compel the Positivist idea of subjective immortality to tentative levels of correspondence with Fichtean notions of the self's struggle to transcend limitations. In grappling with this fundamental problem of the grounding of consciousness within the flux, Pater reflects the preoccupations of both Caird and Green as well, who were occupied at this time with a definition of ultimate reality, not as a mere including system, but as an active relater of parts, a unifier of selves. Caird had read to the Society an essay in which he "insisted upon the idea of a Suffering God"; and, in a landmark essay on "Christian Dogma" that obviously addressed central metaphysical issues, Green had described Jesus as a constituent element of the apostle Paul's own consciousness of self. Although Green read his essay on dogma before Pater had been elected to the Old Mortals, such speculation clearly had a direct connection with Pater's own developing theories and set the stage for his efforts to establish some secular ground of meaning for the self.

The philosophical quest that Pater pursued within the Old Mortality for a metaphysical ground within the flux had a personal origin in his acute sense of loss at the deaths of his parents: "Where are the dead?" he cries in a schoolboy poem. "Nowhere," comes his answer. But Pater cannot accept such a harsh, nihilistic vision; and, at the conclusion of his verse, he embraces the traditional comforts of Christianity. Yet neither in Christianity nor, later, in philosophy does Pater achieve an absolute refuge from the threat of annihilation; the most he can do is shore art, as a momentary stay against chaos, against the encroachments of mortality. Thus in the 1873 Conclusion to *The Renaissance* he announces that "while all melts under our feet" (237) aesthetic passion will ground the self's experience of the world. Ironically (or with prescience perhaps?) Pater several times referred to Pascal's terror of "the silence of those infinite spaces" in the very essay upon which he was working when his own death suddenly came. The "abyss" had been ever at Pascal's side, said Pater; from the infinite universe to "the depths of his own nothingness," Pascal recoiled from "*le néant.*" Because of an accident in which he was nearly killed, Pascal came to imagine that gulf as actually real: "As he walked or sat he was apt to perceive a yawning depth beside him: would set stick or chair there to reassure himself." Such "vast unseen hollow places of nature, of humanity, just beneath one's feet or at one's side" (41; *Miscellaneous Studies*, 86, 68, 89, 82) belong also to Pater's basic perception of reality and, at his happiest, inspire in him a vision of the gap as bridged, filled. Thus in the vision at the Temple of Aesculapius, the young Marius is shown "a land of hope, its hollows brimful of a shadow of blue flowers" (*Marius*, I: 40). And later, at the end of the novel as he lies dying, Marius thinks of Cornelius and future generations, "a thought which relieved for him the iron outline of the horizon about him, touching it as if with soft light from beyond; filling the shadowy, hollow places to which he was on his way with the warmth of definite affections" (II: 221).

In the literal sense the only place to which Marius could be on his way is to his grave. Although these "shadowy, hollow places" denote the grave—note that the catacombs so prominent in *Marius* take their name from the Greek, meaning "a hollow"—Pater turns that emptiness against itself to discover in those hollow places wombs of new life. Is there or is there not phallic imagery in

Marius's descent into the catacombs: "An old flower-garden . . . in pensive shade and fiery blossom . . . was bounded towards the west by a low, grass-grown hill. A narrow opening cut in its steep side, like a solid blackness there, admitted Marius and his gleaming leader into a hollow cavern or crypt" (II: 98). This penetration of the hollow restates the earlier image in "The Child in the House" of the aged hawthorn's "crimson fire": "and in dreams all night he loitered along a magic roadway of crimson flowers, which seemed to open ruddily in thick, fresh masses about his feet, and fill softly all the little hollows in the banks on either side" (*Miscellaneous Studies*, 185). Finally, a few years after *Marius*, Pater, describing in *Gaston de Latour* the Cemetery of the Innocents, used the same imagery for a gently ironic purpose: "As if mistaking the jubilant sunshine of this first summer day for the resurrection morning, the occupant of a nameless old stone coffin had tumbled forth. Hanging luxuriantly in the irregularities of the wasted mouldered grey walls, an aubépine of immemorial age flowered above it, filling its hollows with nests of fiery crimson." As motif, the crimson fire of the hawthorn within the hollow has an obvious affinity with the burning of the gemlike flame, an image first employed in "Diaphanéité" to describe the ideal personality: "it is that fine edge of light, where the elements of our moral nature refine themselves to the burning point" (248). Afterward, in his "Winckelmann" essay, Pater echoed this image of the bright star when he wrote that the function of the culture hero is "to define, in a chill and empty atmosphere, the focus where rays, in themselves pale and impotent, unite and begin to burn" (*Renaissance*, 214). Within the abyss, impotence is converted to fire.

"Diaphanéité," read by Pater to the Old Mortality in 1864, introduces this notion of a seminal mode of life within "the vast unseen hollow places of nature, of humanity," for Pater locates his diaphanous hero squarely within this emptiness as the transforming agent: "The world has no sense fine enough for those evanescent shades, which fill up the blanks between contrasted types of character— delicate provision in the organisation of the moral world for the transmission to every part of it of the life quickened at single points!" (*Miscellaneous Studies*, 248). If "the blanks between contrasted types of character" are taken to be that abyss between distinct selves, then the diaphanous hero possesses a degree of Keatsean "negative capability" whereby, lacking a direct presence of his own, he fulfills himself in the sending across or "transmission" (L *trans*− + *mittere* to send) of life from one self to another. At the opening of the essay, Pater cites "saint," "artist," and "speculative thinker" as "some unworldly types of character which the world is able to estimate." Later, as he charts the career of Marius, Pater introduces him to Cornelius, Flavian, and Aurelius as saint, artist, and philosopher. But Marius himself is classifiable as none of these three types, nor as any form *in* the flux (Pater at several points notes that the diaphanous hero "crosses" the mainstream of the world's sense); rather, he is the quintessential expression of that decentered, marginal life *of* the flux, that links, albeit with a typically Paterian break in the gait, the atomistic impressions, "unstable, flickering, inconsistent . . . —that continual vanishing away, that strange, perpetual weaving and unweaving of ourselves" (*Renaissance*, 235–36). In short, the diaphanous hero inhabits the gap of death, filling that open space with the transforming play of life. But in the very act of transformation these "evanescent shades" seem to empty themselves out or to vanish: " 'What,' says Carlyle, of Charlotte Corday, 'What if she had emerged from her secluded stillness, suddenly like a star; cruel-lovely, with half-angelic, half-daemonic splendour; to gleam for a moment, and in a moment be extinguished; to be held in memory, so bright complete was she, through long centuries!' " (*Miscellaneous Studies*, 253). Emerging from a "secluded stillness" not onto some transcendental ground but into the transforming gap between "contrasts" is also what Goethe's "supreme, artistic view of life" did: "Goethe's culture did not remain 'behind the veil': it ever emerged in the practical functions of art, in actual production," doing so not through "the fancied gift of absolute or transcendental knowledge, but by suggesting questions which help one to detect the passion, and strangeness, and dramatic contrasts of life" (*Renaissance,* 230).

Because its decentered grounding gives the diaphanous self only a shadowy reality, Pater's Marius seems initially suspended between waking and sleeping, life and death, being and nonbeing: "Had the Romans a word for *unworldly*? The beautiful word *umbratilis* perhaps comes nearest to it; and, with that precise sense, might describe the spirit in which he prepared himself for the sacerdotal function hereditary in his family" (*Marius*, I: 25). Shadowy or "remaining in the shade" describes the boy's life at White-nights, a world of white things that themselves are " 'ever an after-thought—the doubles, or seconds, of real things, and themselves but half-real, half-material' " (I: 13). This is a state in which the self exists as a belated "after-thought," in which the originating potency of the parent is withheld from it. In an unpublished essay, "Moral Philosophy," Pater says that the authority of humanity is "like the authority of parents idealised." Accordingly, Marius's dead yet still forbidding father—"of whom, remembering but a tall, grave figure above him in early childhood, Marius habitually thought as a *genius* a little cold and severe" (I: 10)—evokes in the hero, who himself desires the originating potency, just this sense of the burden of the past. But because that higher or collective world of language into which old life dies and from which new life springs is a mirror in which the self finds its own image reflected, the hero actually can transcend his belatedness by identifying language as that in which his life consists: "abstract or common notions come to the individual mind through language, . . . into which one's in-dividual experience, little by little, drop by drop, conveys . . . con-tent; and, by the instrumentality of such terms and notions . . . mediating . . . between our individual experience and the common experience of our kind, we come to understand each other, and to assist each other's thoughts, as in a common mental atmosphere." For Pater, as for Plato of whom he speaks, words have become "living persons" who together constitute "that com-mon, eternal, intellectual world, a sort of divine family or hier-archy, with which the mind of the individual . . . is in communion or correspondence" (*Plato*, 151–53). Language mediates the gap between the authority of humanity in the past and the authority of the living self in the present: "That living authority which language needs lies, in truth, in its scholars, who recognising always that every language possesses a genius, a very fastidious genius, of its own, expand at once and purify its very elements, which must needs change along with the changing thoughts of living people" (*Appre-ciations*, 15). Both the "*genius*" of the father, "a little cold and severe," and the "fastidious genius" of language are reimbodied in the author who now affirms his paternal potency through the ex-pansion and purification of language.

Max Muller, for one, had implied something of this specular relation between self and language when he spoke of the words men use as being "like the shadows of things, like the pictures of trees and mountains reflected in the river, like our own images when we look into a mirror." As a structural model both of the sensible world and of the perceiving mind itself, language becomes the means whereby the author bridges the gap of nonbeing—but only by an emptying out of himself or a vanishing into the text. This dialectic between the origin and its repetition, father and son, past and present, never achieves synthesis, but mirrors within the text's play of differences a perpetually decentered reality. The paternal figure is always re-fathered. Thus Marius, "a shadow, handling all things as shadows," finds in Flavian one who will put into him and them "a sudden real and poignant heat" (*Marius*, I: 53). But this recalls the Paterian image of the burned hand, suggesting that Flavian accomplishes his transformation only by a Corday-like self-consuming act. Indeed, for Flavian, whose struggle with language coincides with his death throes, this self-consuming act is akin to Pascal's sufferings, "reinforced in the 'Pensées' by insupportable languor, alternating with supportable pain, as he died little by little through the eight years of their composition" (*Miscellaneous Studies*, 78). And like Plato, Flavian dies almost pen in hand—Marius takes his dictation and guides his hand as the Christ child had guided the hand of the Madonna in Pater's essay on Botticelli. By this act the discord of Flavian's death (not unlike the ghastly strangulation of Winckelmann or a Dionysian rending) is seen to be a mirror version of the higher textual concord, the coming into being of Marius's own literary maturity. Like the cyclic god Dionysus, whose enemies, says Pater, are the "capricious, excessive heats and colds of spring" (*Greek Studies*, 26), Flavian dies of an intense fever that alternates fitfully between heats and colds "in the hot and genial spring-time" (*Marius*, I: 113). This Dionysian cycling between origin and repetition suggests itself already in Flavian's orphanage. His natural father seemingly deceased, his noble but remote patron is all but identified with the textual reality of the sumptuous book that he gives to Flavian. But as author in his own right, Flavian is already replacing this textual father with himself, even as Marius moves in to replace Flavian: his "sharply contracted hand in the hand of Marius" (I: 118).

Although Marius desired to look upon Flavian at death as "a

brother wrongfully condemned to die" (I: 119), a guilty fear inter-
venes similar to that between Marius and his deceased father, producing "alienation" and a "sense of distance between them" (I:
120). As Marie-Marguerite had feared and envied Watteau's experience, so Marius unconsciously fears and envies Flavian's literary
priority. " 'The red rose came first' " (I: 13), quotes Pater, implying that experience always precedes the blank white of the unin-
scribed tabula rasa. Like Lady Lisa or the "half-angelic, half-
daemonic" Corday, Flavian's epitomization "of the whole pagan
world, the depth of its corruption, and its perfection of form" (I:
53), implies that his darkly sensuous, even charnel, experience in-
scribes the visionary purity of Marius's soul. But when Marius
finally discovers an identity with his father, he then can recognize
Cornelius for what he inevitably must be: the son. Dying so that
Cornelius may be enfranchised, as Flavian had to die to free Marius
from his burden of belatedness, Marius discovers that his guilt now
can be transformed to forgiveness of those who unconsciously must
destroy him. Because he himself has become the star, the "hard,
gemlike flame" of the momentarily gleaming, soon-to-be-extin-
guished diaphane, the future generations do not seem to his dying
imagination to live and work in "some inhabited, but distant and
alien, star" (II: 222). He possesses the future because now his life
also will be inscribed by the new "father" who through that inscription comes into being—Walter Pater, the *pater* reborn.

To relate this reflexive ontology to characteristic developments in
the twentieth century, we might contrast Pater's thought fruitfully
with that of an author of metaphysical fantasy whose work in particular Pater seems to anticipate: Jorge Luis Borges. For both Pater
and Borges, "reality" is merely one frame among many within the
structure of artifice; and images of doubling and opposition in their
work signify the absence of any ultimate closure. Thus in Borges's
thought all dialectical opposites perpetually turn back upon each
other—history becomes fiction, fiction history ("The Secret
Miracle"); heroes are traitors, traitors heroes ("Theme of the
Traitor and the Hero"); fathers are sons, sons fathers ("The Cir-
cular Ruins"). In particular the author's role, in what another
writer of fantasy, J. R. R. Tolkien, called "the effoliation and
multiple enrichment of creation," is most cleverly illustrated by

Ts'ui Pên's labyrinthine novel in Borges's story, "The Garden of Forking Paths." Within this fragmentary Chinese novel, every permutation imaginatively possible was meant to be contained: "In all fictional works, each time a man is confronted with several alternatives, he chooses one and eliminates the others; in the fiction of Ts'ui Pên, he chooses—simultaneously—all of them." This idea that selves and things cannot be themselves without also being (or invoking) their dialectical opposites obsesses all of Borges's fiction, poetry, and criticism. Borges boldly applies this paradox even to literary creation, insisting that the author and reader are perpetually changing places: the lesser writer is the greater ("Pierre Menard, Author of the Quixote"), the reader is the author (as in "The Shape of the Sword": "I am all other men, any man is all men, Shakespeare is in some manner the miserable John Vincent Moon"; or from "Tlön, Uqbar, Orbis Teritus": "All men who repeat a line from Shakespeare *are* William Shakespeare"). This dialectical interplay is never stabilized or fixed at any absolute relationship, ultimate category, or final truth about men or things. In this, Borges's sense of the flux, of relativity, is profoundly Paterian, dictating as it does that the various current critical and ideological concepts not be allowed to remain outside the play of differences, limiting but not limited or expanded in turn. Hence images of mirrors, circles, labyrinths, repeating geometrical patterns and so on dominate Borges's reflexive, surreal psycho-physical landscapes.

In "Borges and Myself," a fascinating essay that is a twentieth-century restatement-with-a-difference of "Diaphanéité," Borges ponders this mysteriously decentered relation between his authorial self (the Borges represented in the text) and his quotidian self (Borges the historical man):

> It would be an exaggeration to say that ours is a hostile relationship; I live, I let myself go on living, so that Borges can weave his tales and poems, and this literature is my justification. It is no effort for me to confess that he has achieved some valid pages, but those pages cannot save me, perhaps because what is good belongs to no one, not even to him, but rather to the language and to tradition. Besides, I am fated to perish once and for all, and only some instant of myself will survive in the other man. Little by little, I have been surrendering everything to him. . . . Years ago I tried ridding myself of him. . . . My life is a flight and I lose everything and everything belongs to oblivion, or to him. Which of us is writing this page I don't know.

Like the relation of Pater to his text, complementary and antag-
onistic at the same time, the relation of Borges's public or textual
self to his private self is neither wholly "hostile" nor, since the text
cannot "save" him, wholly tutelary. Like the ceaselessly inter-
changing antinomies of the brothers Dioscuri, text and reader alternate with "enmity" and "fraternity" within cultural history. Thus,
says Borges, what he writes ultimately belongs not merely to the
textual "Borges," but, more generally, "to the language and to tradition." The quotidian self cedes everything to the other "Borges";
but although diminished and outdistanced by his creation, a degree
of knowledge, justification, and elegiac existence for the "I" follows upon that loss: "Spinoza knew that all things long to persist in
their being; the stone eternally wants to be a stone and the tiger a
tiger. I shall remain in Borges, not in myself (if it is true that I am
someone), but I recognize myself less in his books than in many
others or in the laborious strumming of a guitar."

If we return to the image of the burned hand, Pater's understanding of this paradoxically destructive and reconstitutive aspect
of inscription is clearly present at the structural and thematic center
of his *Marius* also: "Scaevola might watch his own hand, consum-
ing, crackling, in the fire, in the person of a culprit, willing to re-
deem his life by an act so delightful to the eyes, the very ears, of a
curious public" (I: 239). By repeating the hand-destroying act that
saved the Romans, Scaevola, the condemned criminal, becomes a
legendary hero; so also the author, pen in hand, surrendering himself through inscription to the collective mind hidden within the
structures of language is both annihilated and redeemed. As that
other form of consciousness in which the private self is overwhelmed or destroyed, yet saved, the text is the ultimate alter ego.
On that waxed tablet both incised and cancelled by the stylus, the
Paterian interplay between the writing point and the cancelling
finial parallels the relation between Borges and the textual
"Borges." Thus Borges creates "Borges"; and this "Borges"
nourishes, let us say, John Barth, who in turn recreates "Borges"
in the guise of "Barth" (as, for example, in the Borgesian "Life-
Story" from his *Lost in the Funhouse*). For this reason, Borges can
say that he recognizes himself less in "Borges" than in the books of
"many others." Anticipating much the same attitude or stance as
Borges, Pater insists that all invention is but echoing, that to trans-

late, to "re-echo" (*Renaissance*, 118; *Miscellaneous Studies*, 84), is itself an art of literary creation—the only sort of creation possible for the artist. Thus Pater claims that Giorgione exists in work he did not execute: "over and above the real Giorgione and his authentic extant works, there remains the *Giorgionesque* also—an influence, a spirit or type in art" (*Renaissance*, 148). And Leonardo da Vinci, the number of whose "authentic works is very small indeed," also is present like Giorgione in "a multitude of other men's pictures" (117).

My perception that Pater's work bridges the gap between romanticism and post-modernism (between, ultimately, such autobiographical monuments as Wordsworth's *Prelude* and what might be called the contemporary autobiography of the margin) evolved only gradually, however. I believe it was Fichte who rather contemptuously referred to Schelling's "carrying on his education in public" when that philosopher published his fourth or fifth still-more-inclusive system of thought. I have written only three books on Pater (so far), but I suppose I stand convicted of Fichte's charge. Just how this rage for reordering evolved becomes for me enmeshed in any discussion of Pater's currency, since the textual reflexivity described in this essay is also a mirror image of Pater's textually specular relation to *my* own work. In the writing of any essay I inevitably insert myself on the critical level as the decentered object of its discussion—exactly as Pater had done by completing Marie-Marguerite's portrait—thus raising criticism to the level of creation and, more shockingly, aligning myself with my avowed subject. In short, who's the *pater* here? Gerald who now fathers Walter's texts anew, reordered as *his* criticism? Or Walter who supplies Gerald with texts to decipher? Lanin Gyurko observes that

Alaistar Reid, in a letter to a fellow translator of Borges, Anthony Kerrigan, discusses the great impact that the Argentine author has exerted on his own identity. Reid first thinks that Kerrigan and he have created Borges, in that they have made him exist in English. But then he realizes that just the opposite may have happened—that Borges may have usurped both of their identities and now may be existing [as] them. As Reid states to Kerrigan: . . . 'Borges has involved me so utterly in his unbeing that I have translated some of myself out of existence.' . . . The two translators who have thought themselves to be the doublers of Borges into English find that they have become converted into the doubles of their own re-creation—to the extent that Reid feels that he must now translate some poems that Borges had originally written in English back into Spanish in order to recover some of his own lost identity.

Since I cannot so literally recode Pater, I escape the burden of belatedness only by subtly using my criticism as a covert mode of self-exploration or self-portraiture. But the occasion of this essay allows me to give yet one more mischievous turn to the screw, transforming my discussion of Borges's affinity with Pater into an autobiographical account of how I as critic came to formulate that connection and to figure in it myself. Extravagating (we still need that word) beyond the strict diocese of criticism, I shall try to give Austin Warren an answer to the rhetorical question in his review of my latest study: "What, finally, does Monsman think of Pater? Does he like him? or admire him? identify with him? I can't say."

My discovery of Walter Pater occurred as an undergraduate at The Hopkins. A. O. Lovejoy (with whom in the first weeks of my life I'd formed an acquaintance, though necessarily "rather unilateral at first," and for whom, in his blindness, I read three afternoons a week) mentioned, perhaps not quite endorsing, Pater's *Plato and Platonism.* This was in connection with a paper on classical antecedents in the political thought of Marsiglio of Padua and Machiavelli that I had begun to prepare for Charles Singleton's class in Italian renaissance literature. Since Singleton had opened his course with a reference to Burckhardt's and Pater's renaissance studies, I afterward also read those books. For me, Pater was not the revelation that he had been for Berenson, Santayana, and younger contemporaries at Harvard (in the 90s Wallace Stevens and, as a graduate student but no disciple of aestheticism, Lovejoy himself); indeed, I reported later to Lovejoy that I found Pater (may his shade forgive me) "too simple-minded." Lovejoy maintained that ideas have a history—a very precise history. Pater believed much the same thing about ideas having a history, but he was less interested in the precise fortunes of the unit-idea *per se* than in using history as a mask for his own psychology. Pater's aestheticism seemed always flirting with decadence. Why should this Oxford don who vaguely dreamed of burning with a gemlike flame and who died before his best-known disciple, Oscar Wilde, went to jail for confusing that hard, gemlike flame with his flaming gem-like . . . something else—why should he be taken seriously? What sort of scholarship was that?

Several years later having by then encountered in Hillis Miller's lectures structural and phenomenological ways of reading literary texts, I spontaneously returned to Pater—now, suddenly, a "viable" author. I defined my basic aim in *Pater's Portraits* (1965, 1967) as the treatment of Pater's central preoccupations at length and from a non-traditional point of view. Bypassing the methodology of the literary history with its study of sources, influences, and biograph-ical data, I focused instead on an analysis of the component struc-tural patterns and their inner relationships: those multi-level dualisms in the texts. My sense at that moment (mid-1960s) was that the most relevant experience in confronting the "essential Pater" did not lie in tracing those centrifugal-centripetal patterns either outward to Schelling and others or inward to the depths of Pater's psyche. The advantage of my approach, which was primar-ily explicative-expository and only secondarily evaluative, was pin-pointed by a friendly (thus intelligent and sensitive) reviewer: "Vir-tually for the first time Pater's text is given the serious closeness of attention that is normally devoted to verse." But my elaboration of the play of patterns to which Pater's work gave access conspired against discussion of his intellectual development and literary rela-tionships; I could at best merely suggest Pater's evolution through personal crises and only roughly scale him against his contempo-raries.

My second study, *Walter Pater* (1977), represented a gathering of my graduate lectures and attempted, centering on the image of the aesthetic hero, to fit Pater into the intellectual context of his time. But what became increasingly evident to me during the elephantine parturition of this study in the hands of my publisher (1972–1977) was that Pater's work really led one out of the nineteenth century and into the twentieth via its covertly autobiographical mode of ar-tistic self-consciousness. Yet, ironically, my lectures were so intent upon establishing the thematic unity of works often dismissed as dilettantish and incoherent, that ever since the late 1960s I had criti-cized the notions of Edwin Burgum, Germain d'Hangest, and others of the self-expressiveness implicit in Pater's art criticism (the essays on Leonardo, Botticelli) and fiction (*Marius*). I stressed

236

Pater's prescriptive meanings and intellectual associations. But responding to the growth of deconstructive criticism, I eventually returned to a Continental methodology, focusing on the reflexivity of the text and on Pater's anxious relation to his textual predecessors. Because the subject of reflexivity involved such a close relation between the structure of Pater's fiction and his private psychological states, it became necessary to pull together those hints and surmises Paterians always exchanged when they met face to face to limn the sort of psychic profile that lay behind the masks. But what kind of identification could I as critic form with Pater's psychology? The birth of my first child in 1977, coinciding to the month with the belated publication of my second book, crystallized my understanding of Pater's evident impotence in life, underscoring for me its potential significance for all of his artistic production. Pater's psychology now fascinated me precisely because I could bring to it the very thing Pater himself lacked: literal paternity. Instead of ignoring or decrying Pater's difficult psyche, I transposed my doubling of Pater from the textual sphere to the arena of life itself, folding back upon Pater's impotence and upon my own critical belatedness (a form of imaginative impotence) a life event from the next frame out in which I had established my originality or priority (paternal potency). The opposed terms of author and critic, original and repetition, art and life, were not forced into some grotesque synthesis, but instead engaged in a decentered interplay authorized by a pun on Pater's name that he himself recognized. Once I had become a father, and so out-patered Pater, the text that eventually was published as *Walter Pater's Art of Autobiography* (1980) became the mirroring original in which Pater's troubled image could be, like culture itself, "drawn back to its sources to be clarified and corrected" (*Renaissance*, 199).

This claim is not meant to be smug or reductive of Pater's richer achievement; I am simply allowing my own critical activity to enact a deconstructive-reconstructive role that both Borges and Pater themselves had modeled, recognizing that the act of inscription is always (perhaps with loss of force or incisiveness) a re-creation of oneself within the work of others. As Harold Bloom says in *The Anxiety of Influence*, "Conceptually the central problem for the latecomer necessarily is repetition, for repetition dialectically raised to re-creation is the ephebe's road of excess, leading away from the horror of finding himself to be only a copy or a replica." Because in the final analysis origin and repetition, fact and fantasy, father and son are all decentered, all grounded only in the play of differences within the text, " 'there can be no plagiarism' " (*Appreciations*, 75) quotes (but also says in his own right) Pater in his essay on Coleridge. Creation *ex nihilo* may indeed be an attribute only of the Deity, but even He achieved his full splendor through an act of repetition or imitation. Pater quotes with approval (thus recreates) Sir Thomas Browne: " 'At the blast of His mouth were the . . . creatures made, and at His bare word they started out of nothing . . . : but having raised the walls of man, He was driven to a second and harder creation—a substance like Himself, an incorruptible and immortal soul' " (126). So also Pater establishes a reflection of himself within a tradition that, in effect, comes to be of his own making; for neither past nor present has any ground of being apart from its interplay with the other. In the realm of the text, Pater, the son who early lost his father, is reborn, no longer as the plagiaristic repetition of his intellectual predecessors, a mere son, but, by inscribing his life autobiographically on the palimpsestic tablet, as the father. Perhaps it was an intuitive sense of all this that led W. B. Yeats to hail *Marius* as "the only great prose in modern English." And might, perhaps, George Moore indeed be right after all, that to read Pater is the greatest thing that can happen "in any life worth talking about"?

NOTES

Parenthetical citations made within the text are to the Library Edition of *The Works of Walter Pater*, 10 vols. (London: Macmillan, 1910); these citations are shortened to only the page number if they follow a previous reference to the identical work. In the spirit of this collection of essays, I have not footnoted other quotations, which for the most part are reasonably easy to track down. I should mention, however, that I found useable for my purposes several references to works of modern art in R. C. Schweik's 1979 MLA paper, "Hardy and Modern Art: A Revaluation"; that Billie Andrew Inman connected Fichtean solipsism with Pater's "Conclusion" in a paper entitled "The Evolution of Pater's 'Conclusion' to *The Renaissance*: a Study of Sources" read to the conference on Pater at Brasenose College, Oxford, in July, 1980; and that the etymological meaning of "style" as an antique writing instrument was first noted by Harold Bloom in the "Introduction" to *Selected Writings of Walter Pater* (New York, 1974), p. xxiv. I also wish to thank here both J. C. Medley for permission to quote from the unpublished letters of George Moore to Edmund Gosse (December 10, 1918, and August 13, 1914) with which I open my essay; and Sharon Bassett for permission to quote from Pater's unpublished essay, "Moral Philosophy," and from an unpublished portion of *Gaston de Latour.*

J